California's National Parks

A DAY HIKER'S GUIDE

John McKinney

WILDERNESS PRESS · BERKELEY, CA

California's National Parks: A Day Hiker's Guide

1st EDITION August 2005
2nd printing April 2006

Copyright © 2005 by The Trailmaster, Inc.

Front cover photos copyright © 2005 by Ed Cooper
Maps designed by: Hélène Webb
Cover design: Larry B. Van Dyke
Book design: Emily Douglas
Book production: Lisa Pletka
Book editor: Cheri Rae

ISBN 0-89997-387-6
UPC 7-19609-97387-4

Manufactured in the United States of America

Published by: **Wilderness Press**
1200 5th Street
Berkeley, CA 94710
(800) 443-7227; FAX (510) 558-1696
info@wildernesspress.com
www.wildernesspress.com

Visit our website for a complete listing of our books and for ordering information.

Previously published as *Day Hiker's Guide to California's National Parks* by Olympus Press.
Portions of this book have appeared in the author's hiking column in the *Los Angeles Times*,
as well as in *Sunset* and *Westways* magazines.

Cover photos: Yosemite Valley; El Capitan on left, Half Dome in center;
Yosemite National Park *(top left)*
Sand dunes and the Funeral Mountains in background;
Death Valley National Park *(top right)*
Giant Sequoias; Sequoia National Park *(bottom right)*
San Francisco, Golden Gate Bridge, and California poppies;
Golden Gate National Recreation Area *(bottom left)*

SAFETY NOTICE: Although Wilderness Press and the author have made every attempt to ensure that the information in this book is accurate at press time, they are not responsible for any loss, damage, injury, or inconvenience that may occur to anyone while using this book. You are responsible for your own safety and health. The fact that a trail is described in this book does not mean that it will be safe for you. Be aware that trail conditions can change from day to day. Always check local conditions and know your own limitations.

ACKNOWLEDGMENTS

I would like to express my sincere appreciation for the enthusiasm and guidance offered during the preparation of this guide by the National Park Service. A special thanks goes to all rangers, superintendents, and the many park employees who were unfailingly courteous and helpful to me during my many visits to California's national parks. Another thank you goes to the national park rangers and superintendents, as well as Park Service staff who field- and fact-checked the information in this guide.

PHOTO CREDITS

Roslyn Bullas/Michael McKay 10, 138, 240, 246 (bottom), 248, 252; California Coastal Commission 109, 119; Joseph Smeaton Chase 179, 333; Peg Henderson 326, 329; F.G. Hochberg 298; Bob Howells 230, 308; Laura Keresty 96, 106, 112; Jessica Lage 76, 79, 82; Mammoth Lakes Visitors Bureau 192; National Park Service xiv, 2, 6, 36, 52, 53, 55, 57, 63, 91, 92, 130, 131, 134, 140, 145, 149, 157, 159, 168, 199, 218, 238, 242, 246 (top), 260, 331; Redding Convention and Visitors Bureau 42, 45; Larry Van Dyke 34, 48; David Werk 290; all other photos by John McKinney.

Thanks to Jessica Lage for permission to use her Point Reyes images from her book, *Point Reyes: A Complete Guide.*

ABOUT THE AUTHOR

John McKinney is the author of a dozen books about walking, hiking, and nature, including *The Joy of Hiking: Hiking the Trailmaster Way.* The Trailmaster writes articles and commentaries about walking for national publications, promotes hiking and conservation on radio and television, and serves as a consultant to a hiking vacation company. Contact him at: www.thetrailmaster.com.

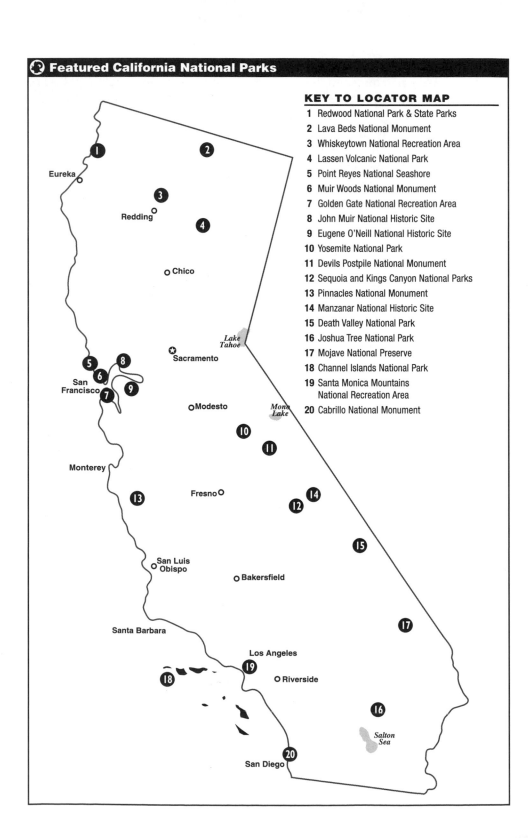

Featured California National Parks

KEY TO LOCATOR MAP

1 Redwood National Park & State Parks
2 Lava Beds National Monument
3 Whiskeytown National Recreation Area
4 Lassen Volcanic National Park
5 Point Reyes National Seashore
6 Muir Woods National Monument
7 Golden Gate National Recreation Area
8 John Muir National Historic Site
9 Eugene O'Neill National Historic Site
10 Yosemite National Park
11 Devils Postpile National Monument
12 Sequoia and Kings Canyon National Parks
13 Pinnacles National Monument
14 Manzanar National Historic Site
15 Death Valley National Park
16 Joshua Tree National Park
17 Mojave National Preserve
18 Channel Islands National Park
19 Santa Monica Mountains
   National Recreation Area
20 Cabrillo National Monument

Eureka
Redding
Chico
Sacramento
Lake Tahoe
San Francisco
Modesto
Mono Lake
Monterey
Fresno
San Luis Obispo
Bakersfield
Santa Barbara
Los Angeles
Riverside
Salton Sea
San Diego

CONTENTS AT A GLANCE

CONTENTS

NORTHERN CALIFORNIA

CENTRAL CALIFORNIA & HIGH SIERRA

DEVILS POSTPILE NATIONAL MONUMENT · 191

12 SEQUOIA AND KINGS CANYON NATIONAL PARKS 197

13 PINNACLES NATIONAL MONUMENT   225

CALIFORNIA DESERT

The Three Brothers, distinctive granite peaks that
define the grandeur of Yosemite National Park

INTRODUCTION

CALIFORNIA'S NATIONAL PARKS

From Zabriskie Point, high above Death Valley, early-rising hikers watch the desert sun illuminate perfectly named Golden Canyon. In Point Reyes National Seashore, a family follows Earthquake Trail through Bear Valley and learns about that mover and shaker of continents—the San Andreas Fault. Just-retired seniors meander through Giant Forest in Sequoia National Park and are so moved by the experience that they resolve to tour all of the Golden State's federally protected wonders.

From the foggy shores of San Francisco to the icy summits of the Sierra Nevada, and from the Santa Monica Mountains, which bisect metropolitan Los Angeles, to the towering redwoods of the north coast, California, in all its beauty and environmental diversity, is preserved in national parks.

Other states have national parks with tall trees, high peaks, deep canyons, long seashores and vast deserts, but only California can claim all these grand landscapes within its boundaries.

This book collects and presents 150 of my favorite day hikes on trails in all 20 of California's national parklands. The selected hikes range from an easy nature walk among the redwoods to a challenging all-day climb of Yosemite's Half Dome.

California boasts eight national parks, the most in the nation, an honor shared only with the state of Alaska. In addition, the state's national parklands include national recreation areas, national monuments, a national seashore and a national preserve.

The state features one of America's oldest national parks—Yosemite, set aside in 1890—and one of its newest—Mojave National Preserve, established in 1994.

Mere acreage does not a national park make, but California's national parks include the largest park in the continental U.S.—3.3-million-acre Death Valley National Park—and the third largest—1.6-million acre Mojave National Preserve. Yosemite (748,542 acres) and Joshua Tree (794,000 acres) are also huge by any park standards. Even smaller parklands like Redwood National Park and Point Reyes National Seashore are by no means small.

The parks around San Francisco and Los Angeles—Golden Gate National Recreation Area and Santa Monica Mountains National Recreation Area—each include a dozen sites scattered around their respective metropolitan areas.

This guide is your invitation to discover:

MOUNTAINS Climb Sequoia National Park's 14,495-foot Mt. Whitney, California's highest peak (and tallest summit in the U.S. outside Alaska). Explore

Classic view of Death Valley—it stretches for miles and includes mountains, sand dunes and tenacious desert scrub.

the alpine peaks towering above Mineral King Valley in Sequoia National Park, as well as the vast backcountry of Yosemite National Park. Experience the greatest vertical rise in the lower 48 states by ascending Death Valley National Park's highest summit, 11,044-foot Telescope Peak, and gazing down at Badwater (282 feet below sea level), the lowest point in North America.

In Lassen Volcanic National Park, hike to the top of Lassen Peak, one of the world's largest plug dome volcanoes. California's national parks hold some smaller volcanoes, too, such as Whitney Butte in Lava Beds National Monument.

Along with mountains sculpted by fire and ice, California's national parklands include mountains of sand—the Kelso Dunes in Mojave National Preserve, Eureka Dunes in Death Valley National Park, and the Pinto Dunes in Joshua Tree National Park.

LAKES The five lakes perched above the rugged coast of Point Reyes National Seashore—Bass, Pelican, Crystal, Ocean and Wildcat—are grouped together in a way that remind some hikers of England's Lakes District. Lassen Volcanic National Park boasts many beautiful backcountry lakes—Echo, Summit, Horseshoe and more; Lassen's gentle lake country is a marked contrast to the rugged lava-land that makes up the rest of the park.

Hikers will enjoy tramping the hillsides and shoreline around Whiskeytown Lake in Whiskeytown Shasta-Trinity National Recreation Area. In Yosemite, hike to Lukens, Dog, and May lakes, plus many more lakes, ponds and tarns. Trails lead to Mosquito Lakes, Eagle Lake and several more jewels in the Mineral King area of Sequoia National Park.

WATERFALLS   Yosemite National Park's world-famous cascades include Yosemite (North America's highest), Vernal, and Nevada falls. Rainbow Falls in Devils Postpile National Monument is surely one of California's most photogenic; when the light is right, the waterfall's characteristic rainbows are projected above it. A favorite Kings Canyon cascade is Mist Falls, sometimes all but lost in a mist of its own making.

TREES   Redwood, Sequoia and Joshua Tree national parks were preserved primarily for their namesake trees. Hike the Tall Trees Loop Trail to a 365.5-foot redwood, the world's tallest tree. Walk to the world's largest living thing, the General Sherman Tree in Sequoia National Park's Giant Forest. Joshua Tree National Park hosts not only thousands of specimens of its namesake tree, but also groves of the native California fan palms that congregate in remote oases. Mojave National Preserve, too, features a vast Joshua tree forest, with Joshuas of a slightly different species than those in Joshua Tree National Park. Antiquarian oaks and one of the state's finest sycamore savannas are highlights of Santa Monica Mountains National Recreation Area.

COAST   From Prisoners Harbor out on Santa Cruz Island to Lands End in San Francisco, national parks preserve notable segments of the state's shoreline. Visit the historic Point Loma Lighthouse overlooking San Diego Bay at Cabrillo National Monument. Hike all five islands of Channel Islands National Park, "America's Galapagos," where plants and animals have evolved in ways different from those of their mainland relatives. Walk over the Golden Gate Bridge to a Park Service Vista Point and behold dramatic panoramas of San Francisco Bay. Some of the finest examples of the state's northern coast are well protected by Golden Gate National Recreation Area, Point Reyes National Seashore and Redwood National Park.

California History

California's national parks preserve not only stunning landforms but the state's diverse cultural history as well. Satwiwa Native American Natural Area in the Santa Monica Mountains offers a chance to explore a place where Chumash walked for thousands of years before Europeans arrived on the scene. The islands comprising Channel Island's National Park were also once the domain of the Chumash, equally adept at land and sea.

Visitors can learn more about the ancient ways of the Paiute in Mojave National Preserve, the Coastanoan in Pinnacles National Monument, the Miwok in Golden Gate National Recreation Area, the Modoc in Lava Beds National Monument, and the Yurok in Redwood National Park.

California's national parks highlight the European discovery and settlement of California. Cabrillo National Monument honors Juan Rodríguez Cabrillo, who claimed San Diego Bay for Spain way back in 1542. Hikers can climb to the San Francisco Bay Discovery Site in Golden Gate National Recreation Area to view the panorama that greeted explorer Gaspar de Portolá in 1769.

Beginning with the Forty-niners, prospectors swarmed over the High Sierra, then out into the Mojave Desert. While retracing an old prospector's trail or trekking to a remote mine, today's hiker may be astonished by the lengths to which miners went in order to discover, then dig for, gold, silver and other riches from the earth. In Yosemite's Gaylor Lakes Basin, 2 miles high in the High Sierra, miners of the 1880s dug for three years in a fruitless attempt to find silver. As you traverse the Mojave Desert parks, you'll discover colorful stories of the Lost Horse and Desert Queen mines in Joshua Tree National Park and enjoy tales of the twenty-mule teams that hauled cargo from the Harmony Borax Works in Death Valley.

California's national parks not only display and interpret how the land was formerly used—mining, logging, ranching, homesteading, railroading and more—but also illustrate how the land was preserved. Hikers can trace California's early conservation history by visiting the home and haunts of naturalist John Muir. Tour Muir's home and "scribble den" at John Muir National Historic Site, then roam the surrounding hills where the author loved to walk with his two daughters. Muir Woods National Monument honors the great conservationist with grand redwood groves that attract visitors from around the world. Muir's praises of Yosemite's beauty and pleas for its protection have inspired generations of environmental activists, and continue to uplift and inspire us today.

To hike California's national parks is to witness great environmental battles won—Mineral King preserved from ski-resort development and placed under the protection of Sequoia National Park—as well as environmental battles lost—Hetch-Hetchy Valley (equal in beauty to Yosemite Valley, John Muir believed), dammed and flooded by the city of San Francisco to create a reservoir.

More recent conservation activity is evident in the parks around California's big cities. Golden Gate National Recreation Area faces an enormous challenge in managing the newly acquired Presidio in the heart of San Francisco. The Santa Monica Mountains National Recreation Area expands acre by acre as conservationists struggle to purchase the tremendously expensive land on the west side of Los Angeles.

The National Park System

The National Park Service is headquartered in Washington, D.C. It's an agency under the broader administration of the U.S. Department of the Interior. California's national parks are overseen by the Pacific Field Area office in San Francisco. Each park has a superintendent and a staff who manage the park's resources and recreational sites.

Besides parks per se, the National Park Service oversees more than twenty other segments of the great outdoors, including national lakeshores and national seashores, national battlefields and national military parks, national recreation areas, national rivers, national trails and more.

I'm indebted to the National Park Service for explaining to me (more than once) the difference between the various kinds of parks.

A National Park:
• generally contains a variety of natural resources and is large enough to adequately protect these resources.
• can be created only by an act of Congress.
• has boundaries that can be altered only by Congress.
• with few exceptions does not allow consumptive uses such as grazing, hunting, mining, logging, oil drilling or dam building.

A National Monument:
• can be created by either Presidential Proclamation or an act of Congress.
• preserves at least one significant resource and is usually smaller than a national park.
• has boundaries that can be altered either by Congress or by Presidential proclamation.
• is protected much the same as a National Park but may be affected by one or more consumptive uses.

A National Recreation Area:
• emphasizes the recreation in its name.
• often is centered around a place-to-play such as a lake or waterway, or is located in fairly close proximity to a city.

Four of California's national parks were originally designated national monuments: Lassen Volcanic, Channel Islands, Joshua Tree and Death Valley. National monuments often push for a gradual phase-out of commercial activity. In the case of Death Valley, designated a national monument by President Hoover in 1933, the phase-out took 61 years; Death Valley was not "upgraded" to national park status until 1994, by which time some 50,000 mining claims had dwindled to but one active mine.

The state's first national preserve was established when Congress approved the California Desert Protection Act of 1994 and created Mojave National Preserve from East Mojave desert lands previously administered by the U.S. Bureau of Land Management. The preserve allows limited amounts of grazing and some mining.

America's earliest Park Service staff: Horace Albright (left) and Director Stephen T. Mather (with an early vanity license plate!).

California and The National Park Idea

From the time John Muir walked through Mariposa Grove and into Yosemite Valley, preserving California's national parks has been one huge conservation battle after another. Logging, mining, grazing and ski-resort development are a few of the many consumptive uses of national parks that conservationists have fought. Such struggles have continued in California for more than a century now.

As John Muir put it in 1898: "Thousands of nerve-shaken, overcivilized people are beginning to find out that going to the mountains is going home; that wilderness is a necessity; and that mountain parks and reservations are useful not only as fountains of timber and irrigating rivers, but as fountains of life."

The National Park Service, founded in 1916, was initially guided by borax tycoon-turned-park-champion Stephen T. Mather and his young assistant, California attorney Horace Albright. The Park Service's mission was the preservation of "the scenery and the natural and historic objects and the wild life," and the provision "for the enjoyment of the same in such manner and by such means as will leave them unimpaired for the enjoyment of future generations."

The invention of the automobile completely revolutionized national park visitation, particularly in car-conscious California. John Muir called them "blunt-nosed mechanical beetles," yet as one California senator pointed out, "If

Jesus Christ had an automobile he wouldn't have ridden a jackass into Jerusalem."

With cars came trailers, and with trailer camps came concessionaires. National parks filled with mobile cities of canvas and aluminum, and by visitors anxious to see California's natural wonders. During the 1920s and '30s, the Park Service constructed signs identifying scenic features and rangers assumed the role of interpreting nature for visitors.

By 1930 California had four national parks: Yosemite, Lassen, Sequoia and General Grant (Kings Canyon.) In the 1930s, two big desert areas—Joshua Tree and Death Valley—became national monuments.

With the 1960s came the hotly contested, and eventually successful battle for Redwood National Park. During the 1970s Congress established parks near the state's big cities—Golden Gate National Recreation Area on the San Francisco waterfront and the Marin headlands and Santa Monica Mountains National Recreation Area, a Mediterranean ecosystem near Los Angeles. Also during that decade, Mineral King Valley was saved from a mega-ski-resort development and added to Sequoia National Park. Channel Islands National Park, an archipelago offshore from Santa Barbara, was established in 1980.

The most recent major conservation battle took place in the desert. After more than two decades of wrangling, Joshua Tree and Death Valley national monuments were greatly expanded and given national park status, and the 1.6-million acre Mojave National Preserve was established under provisions of the 1994 California Desert Conservation Act.

As the 21st century unfolds, the National Park Service faces some difficult issues: How best to regulate concessionaires? Should motor vehicles be banned from Yosemite Valley? How can aging park facilities cope with many years of deferred maintenance?

While the parks don't lack for fame, or even friends, they do lack for funds. By all accounts they are under-funded and under-staffed. Experts estimate a backlog of infrastructure repairs, new construction and critical resource protection projects ranging from 4 to 6 billion dollars. Deferred maintenance adds up into the hundreds of millions in California alone.

Perhaps the root struggle is with an ever-increasing number of visitors. California's Division of Tourism charts visitation to national parks along with airports, hotel occupancy and other attractions such as Disneyland and Universal Studios. Yosemite is California's most-visited park, with four million visitors a year, and many other parks count millions of visitors or "visitor days," per year.

What may be the saving grace of national parks is the deep-seated, multi-generational pride Americans have for their national parklands. We not only love national parks, we love the very idea of national parks. Even in an era of public mistrust toward government, national parks remain one of the most beloved institutions of American life.

In no way are national parks frozen in time. Several parks, including those as diverse as remote Mojave National Preserve and the close-to-the-metropolis

Santa Monica Mountains National Recreation Area have recently added small parcels of land. Several parks intend to purchase privately held "inholdings" or to preserve critical habitat now outside park boundaries.

Undoubtedly new parks will be added this century. Some desert conservationists advocate the creation of additional parklands in the Mojave and Colorado deserts from lands set aside by Congress as wilderness areas. Some park proposals face stiff opposition from industry and private property rights advocates. Anti-parks groups have fought coastal conservationists promoting a "Gaviota National Seashore," which would make a national parkland of the mountains and coast near Santa Barbara.

The National Parks Rivers and Trails Conservation Agency works on projects near home in California. For a review of this agency's fine work, see Chapter 21 in this book.

The Trails

In my judgment, the state of the state's national park trail system is quite good. Trailhead parking, interpretive panels and displays, as well as signage are generally excellent. Backcountry junctions are usually signed, and trail conditions generally range from good to excellent.

Of course parks are not static ecosystems and are subject to natural and not-so-natural disasters that may affect trails. During the 1990s, wildfires scorched the Santa Monica Mountains, floods inundated Yosemite Valley, and record snowfalls buried Lassen. Such natural phenomena inevitably damage trails.

The various trail systems evolved on a park-by-park basis and it's difficult to speak in generalities about their respective origins. A good deal of Yosemite's trail system was in place before the early horseless carriages chugged into the park. Newer parks, such as the Santa Monica Mountains National Recreation Area, will be building trails well into the 21st century.

Several national parks were aided greatly by the Depression-era Civilian Conservation Corps. Pinnacles National Monument, for example, has some hand-built trails that are true gems, highlighted by stonework and bridges that would no doubt be prohibitively expensive to construct today.

Scout troops, the hard-working young men and women of the California Conservation Corps and many volunteer groups are among the organizations that help park staff build and maintain trails.

The trail system in California's national parklands shares many characteristics in common with pathways overseen by other governmental bodies. A hiker will notice no profound differences in pathways when, for example, traveling from the Santa Monica Mountains National Recreation Area into Malibu Creek State Park or from Yosemite National Park into the U.S. Forest Service-administered Ansel Adams Wilderness.

While sharing similarities with trails in other jurisdictions, national parkland trails nevertheless have unique qualities, too, that distinguish them from pathways elsewhere. One major difference between national parks and, for example,

A new park at rainbow's end? Conservationists hope to preserve the Gaviota coast near Santa Barbara as a national seashore.

California's state parks, is the amount of land preserved as wilderness: A majority of Yosemite, Sequoia, Death Valley, Joshua Tree and several more parks are official federally designated wilderness. Wilderness comprises some 94 percent of Yosemite National Park.

On national park maps you'll find such wilderness areas delineated as simply "Wilderness." Unlike the Forest Service, the Bureau of Land Management and other wilderness stewards, the National Park Service does not name its wilderness areas.

Wilderness designation is more than a name for a wild or pristine area. By law, a wilderness is restricted to non-motorized entry—that is to say, equestrian and foot travel. Hikers do not have to share the trails with snowmobiles or mountain bikes in national park wilderness.

Other National Park Service wilderness regulations are designed to protect resources and ensure visitor safety. Review these wilderness regulations before hitting the trail.

The hikers you meet on a national park trail may be different from the company you keep on trails near home. California's national parks attract visitors from across the nation and around the world. While all national parks are something of an international draw, none are more so than the ones in California. I've walked with Japanese visitors across Death Valley's sand dunes, with New Zealanders through the redwoods, with a French couple to the top of Lassen Peak, with Germans on Yosemite's Panorama Trail, with Brazilians in the Santa Monica Mountains.

Once I counted ten different languages on a popular nature trail in Muir Woods National Monument. Not surprisingly, the Park Service has printed selected brochures in French, German, Spanish, Japanese and Chinese.

Yosemite's Tuolumne Grove giant sequoias dwarf the happy hikers.

Because of the park's attraction to visitors worldwide, the Park Service uses lots of international symbols on its signage, and the metric system as well. This international orientation explains why the National Park Service seems to be about the only American institution—outside of scientific and medical circles of course—still promoting the metric system.

Long-Distance Trails in California's National Parks

California's national parkland trails include portions of the nation's best-known long-distance pathways.

Pacific Crest Trail, the West's premiere long-distance trail, extends some 2,650 miles from Mexico to Canada. Some of the most stunning sections of the trail cross the High Sierra backcountry of Sequoia–Kings Canyon and Yosemite national parks. Much of the splendid 225-mile long John Muir Trail traverses the Sierra in tandem with the PCT. Another sterling section of the PCT traverses Lassen Volcanic National Park.

California Coastal Trail When completed, this 1,600-mile system of interconnecting beach and coastal-range trails will guide ambitious hikers from Mexico to Oregon. Some of the most magnificent lengths of CCT extend across three of California's national parklands—Golden Gate National Recreation Area, Point Reyes National Seashore, and Redwood National Park.

Backbone Trail This 65-mile-long pathway (nearly complete) extends across the spine of the Santa Monica Mountains and both literally and symbolically links the scattered beauties of the Santa Monica Mountains National Recreation Area. The Backbone Trail network is a rich blend of footpaths, fire roads and horse trails, leading through diverse environments: meadows, savannas, yucca-covered slopes, handsome sandstone formations and seasonal and all-year creeks.

Bay Trail extends through parts of Golden Gate National Recreation Area. The new 400-mile-long trail (more than half completed) encircles San Francisco Bay and links wildlife refuges, city parks, historic sites, urban and residential

areas, as well as a diversity of waterfronts ranging from the trendy and bou-
tiqued to the commercial and industrial.

Bay Area Ridge Trail, a 500-mile-long trail-in-the-making around San
Francisco Bay, also extends through parts of Golden Gate National Recreation
Area. The path follows the main ridgelines closest to the bay, and offers many
glorious bay views.

Juan Bautista de Anza National Historical Trail was the route of the Juan
Bautista de Anza Expedition of 1775-76, which brought 200 colonists from
Mexico across the Colorado Desert and up the coast to locate San Francisco
Bay. In 1990, Congress established the Juan Bautista de Anza National Historic
Trail and assigned the National Park Service to preserve, develop and sign the
path.

Using this Guide

Hiking opportunities are detailed in the 20 national parklands mentioned in
this book. The parks are grouped by park into chapters, then further organized
in rough north-to-south order.

Distance, expressed in round trip mileage figures, follows each hiking destination. The hikes in this guide range from 1 to 16 miles, with the majority in
the easy (under 5 miles) range and moderate (5 to 8 mile) category. Gain or loss
in elevation follows the mileage.

In matching a hike to your ability, you'll want to consider both mileage and
elevation as well as condition of the trail, terrain, and season. Hot, exposed
chaparral or high altitude ascents can make a short hike seem long.

Hikers vary a great deal in relative physical condition, but you may want to
consider the following: An easy walk suitable for beginners and children would
be less than 5 miles with an elevation gain of less than 700 to 800 feet. A moderate walk is considered a walk in the 5- to 10-mile range, with under 2,000 feet
of elevation gain. You should be reasonably fit for these. Preteens sometimes
find the going difficult. Hikes of more than 10 miles and those with more than
a 2,000-foot gain are for experienced hikers in top form.

Season is the next item to consider. California is one of the few places in the
country that offers four-season hiking. You can hike some of the trails in this
guide all of the time, all of the trails some of the time, but not all of the trails
all of the time.

An introduction to each hike describes the attractions of this particular
national park trail and what you'll observe along the way: plants, animals,
panoramic views. You'll also learn about the geologic and human history of the
region.

Directions to trailhead take you from the nearest major highway to trailhead
parking. For trails having two desirable trailheads, directions to each are given.
A few trails can be walked one way, with the possibility of a car shuttle. Suggested car shuttle points are noted.

After the directions to the trailhead, you'll read a description of the hike. Important junctions and major sights are pointed out, but I've left you to discover the multitude of little things that make a hike an adventure.

About the Maps

The maps in this book support the author's mission, which is to provide an introduction for the day hiker to the state's best state, national, coastal and desert parklands.

Many of the Golden State's parklands are regarded by rangers, administrators—and most importantly by hikers—as true "hiker's parks." These footpath-friendly parks offer miles and miles of maintained trails, with plenty of options for great day hikes. For these adventures, in contrast with, say, easy "walks in the park," route descriptions are described in more detail and accompanying maps highlight more trails and park features.

It's a delight for me to share some of my favorite, often carefully selected, shorter California trails, too. Among these short but scenic paths are nature trails and history interpretation trails, as well as beach trails and informal footpaths along a river. These short hikes have correspondingly short route descriptions, and the accompanying maps chart a minimal number of features. A handful of the selected hikes are so short, and the on-the-ground orientation for the hiker so obvious, that mapping them would not add anything to the visitor's experience and, in a few instances, would be downright silly.

Fellow hikers, do give us a heads-up about any trail changes you notice or any discrepancies you observe between the map and territory.

For reasons I can't explain, during the 20-plus years that I've been chronicling hiking trails, you hikers have been lots more vigilant about pouncing on errant or out-of-date prose and telling me about it than you have been about pointing out the need for any trail map updates. (Jeez, I can't even misidentify a rare plant or obscure bird without hearing about it from so many of you...) Anyway, your cartographic input is always welcome.

CHAPTER ONE

REDWOOD NATIONAL PARK
& STATE PARKS

Something in our collective national character is drawn to the superlative—the highest, deepest, widest, oldest—and our national parks collect and reflect what is extraordinary in the American landscape.

Not surprisingly, it was the discovery of "the world's tallest tree" by a 1963 National Geographic expedition that provided the impetus for a national park. The 367-foot-high redwood and the ancient giants around it served as the rallying point for conservationists who for decades desired a redwood national park.

Amidst much controversy, Congress approved park legislation in 1968 and President Lyndon Johnson signed into law the bill creating 58,000-acre Redwood National Park. While conservationists were pleased that the redwoods

The sword fern co-exists quite happily with the rugged redwoods.

had finally gained national recognition, the new national park—a collection of cutover land, Tall Trees Grove and a trio of existing state parks—was hardly the dynamic ecosystem envisioned. Redwood Creek, where the tall trees thrived, was a gerrymandered island on the land, endangered by ruthless logging practices. Slopes were clearcut right up to the park boundary, and subsequent erosion threatened "the worm," as the narrow corridor of tall trees along Redwood Creek was known.

In 1977, Bay Area Congressman Phillip Burton introduced a bill to expand the park. Timber company resistance was fierce. A logging truck convoy, with a mammoth redwood peanut in tow, converged on Washington but failed to stop Congress and President Jimmy Carter from approving a 48,000-acre park expansion act.

Today the park includes several tall tree sanctuaries and a lot of logged land undergoing rehabilitation. Miles of tractor trails and logging roads, which turn into stream channels and cause terrible erosion during winter rains, must be removed, the land recontoured, the hillsides replanted. Restoring the ancient forest takes a very, very long time.

The namesake redwoods are obviously what draw Americans to this (rather lightly visited) national park, but often it is the region's spectacular coast that prompts a return visit. Dramatic bluffs, hidden coves, tidepools and wilderness beaches are linked by a 40-mile length of the California Coastal Trail. The trail, one of the most scenic stretches of pathway on the West Coast, offers splendid day hiking and backpacking opportunities.

One of my favorite times to visit the redwoods is in late spring, when the rains (usually) stop. June, in the form of rhododendrons, is busting out all over, pink and conspicuous beneath the tall trees.

I come to the redwoods to hike not only to contemplate the tall trees, but to notice all the little things as well. The most overwhelming little thing I notice from my 2.5-mile an hour pace is the shade-loving undergrowth of the redwood forest. Poison oak climbs 150 feet up some of the tall giants. California huckleberry, azalea, mosses, lichen and five-fingered ferns are everywhere— springing out of logs and stumps in a wild and dazzling profusion that I had previously associated only with the Amazon.

There's little light on the trail; it could be any time of the day or night. Minutes, hours and days have little meaning amidst 2,000-year-old trees and a 20-million-year-old forest.

It occurred to me, as I followed a trail past solemn colonnades of redwoods named for conservationists and long-departed industrialists, that in the redwoods the only meaningful time distinctions are Now and Forever. Now, in the form of shopping centers, drive-through trees and clear-cut lands is sometimes disheartening. Forever, however, are the redwoods, whose species name sempervirens means "everlasting." Although nothing in nature lasts forever, the redwood is about as close to everlasting as any living thing can get.

Some 160 million years ago or so, great forests of the tall trees grew in Europe, Asia and North America. Redwoods towered over the tallest dinosaur. A million or two years ago, with the coming of the Ice Age, the redwoods retreated and made a last stand along the northern California coast and the southwestern tip of Oregon. Ninety-six percent of the ancient coast redwood forests have been chopped down; of the four percent remaining, most now are under public protection, hopefully forever.

■ ENDERTS BEACH
Last Chance Trail (California Coastal Trail)
To Enderts Beach is 2 miles round trip; to Highway 101 is 7 miles one way; shorter options possible

Sometimes we hikers become so enamored by the majestic coast redwoods in Redwood National Park, we overlook the park's magnificent coast. The national park, and adjoining state parks, are linked by a series of coastal trails that present panoramas of both a spectacular shoreline and some of the world's tallest trees.

Like Redwood National Park, Del Norte Coast Redwoods State Park delivers the scenery in its name: an impressive coastline, as well as magnificent old-growth redwoods. The combination of redwoods—as well as a mixed forest of Sitka spruce, Douglas fir and red alder—with the coast, adds up to a hike to remember.

What is now a splendid hiking trail used to be the Redwood Highway (101). The old highway was abandoned in 1935 for its present route. Part of the old road is on the National Register of Historic Places.

The Last Chance Trail is the northernmost stretch of the California Coastal Trail; this is the "last chance" to walk part of the California Coastal Trail (part hiker's dream, part reality) before joining the Oregon Coast Trail.

Damnation Creek Trail, a historic Yurok Indian path, descends steeply 2.5 miles through dense redwood forest to a hidden beach; it connects with Last Chance Trail.

DIRECTIONS TO TRAILHEAD From Highway 101, about 2 miles south of Crescent City, turn south on Enderts Beach Road

A lovely hidden beach is your reward for venturing beyond the redwoods and on to the coast.

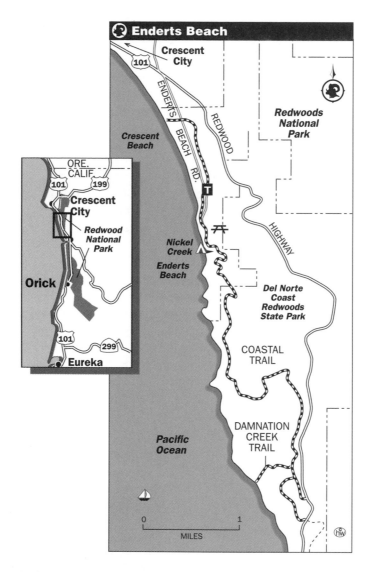

and wind 2.5 miles to road's end at Crescent Beach Overlook and the beginning of Last Chance Trail.

THE HIKE As you hike south on the old coast highway, you'll get grand views behind you of the Crescent City coastline. A 0.6-mile descent brings you to a three-way junction: a 0.25-mile path leads left along lush, fern-filled Nickel Creek; straight ahead is the southbound Coastal Trail; the right fork continues to Nickel Creek Campground and on to Enderts Beach. The beach is an attractive mixture of both a wilderness-looking-boulder-and-driftwood-strewn shore and a long sand strand.

Back on Last Chance Trail, you'll begin a very steep climb of a bit more than a mile, ascending through old-growth redwoods. Two miles along, you top out and begin a descent, entering Del Norte Coast Redwoods State Park.

Three miles along are the magnificent redwoods thriving in the headwaters of Damnation Creek. Another mile of travel and a short descent bring you to a ford of Damnation Creek. (This is a good turnaround point; it's an 8-mile round-trip hike by the time you get back to the trailhead.)

Those hikers continuing with Last Chance Trail will cross (use caution, the log "bridges" are slippery) Damnation Creek and travel another mile through the forest. The path nears Highway 101 at mile 5, junctions with Damnation Creek Trail at the 6-mile mark, leads through some more redwood forest primeval and reaches Highway 101, 7 miles from the trailhead.

■ LAGOON CREEK AND HIDDEN BEACH
Coastal Trail
From Lagoon Creek to Hidden Beach is 2 miles round trip; to Requa Overlook is 8 miles round trip with 200-foot elevation gain

Coastal Trail is a 40-mile pathway that connects redwood state and national parklands. One of the more spectacular sections of the trail is the 4 miles between Lagoon Creek and the mouth of the Klamath River.

Lagoon Creek empties into a pond, formed in 1940 when the lumber mill dammed the creek to form a log pond. The creek and pond became part of Redwood National Park in 1972. Heart-shaped yellow pond lilies float in the tranquil pond, which is habitat for ducks, egrets, herons and red-winged blackbirds.

Adding to the pleasure of a walk in this area is the Yurok Loop Nature Trail, which explores the lagoon area. The walker may use one-half the loop on departure and the second half on the return. Interpretive brochures are (sometimes) available at the parking area or at park information centers.

DIRECTIONS TO TRAILHEAD
Lagoon Creek Fishing Access is located west of Highway 101, 5 miles north of the town of Klamath.

Lagoon Creek & Hidden Beach

False Klamath Cove

YUROK LOOP TRAIL

Redwood National Park

Lagoon Creek Fishing Access

101

Klamath Overlook

Requa

Klamath River

Pacific Ocean

0   2.5

MILES

Enjoy an easy meander along the lagoon, or a more strenuous walk to Requa Overlook.

THE HIKE Head south along the Yurok Loop Nature Trail, which travels through a dense canopy of oak, alder and willow. From the blufftop are occasional views of the beaches below.

Coastal Trail veers right from the nature trail and follows a fern-lined path to a grove of red alder. During spring and summer, hikers may observe hummingbirds extracting nectar from pink-flowered salmonberry bushes.

About a mile from the trailhead is the turn-off to Hidden Beach, a driftwood-piled sandy beach that's ideal for a picnic.

From the Hidden Beach turn-off, the trail ascends into Sitka spruce forest. Halfway to Requa Overlook, Coastal Trail crests a divide and continues on through thick forest. A few overlooks allow the walker glimpses of the bold headlands north and south, and of the wave-cut terraces below. Sea lions and seals may haul out on offshore rocks.

Coastal Trail bears southeast to Requa Overlook, which offers picnic sites and striking views of the mouth of the Klamath River. The overlook is also a good place to watch for migrating California gray whales.

See Map on Page 21

■ GOLD BLUFFS BEACH
Coastal Trail

From Fern Canyon to Gold Dust Falls is 2 miles round trip; to Butler Creek Backpack Camp is 4.5 miles round trip; to Ossagon Rocks is 6 miles round trip; return via West Ridge, Friendship Ridge and James Irvine trails is 7.5 miles round trip

Wildlife-watching, waterfalls, and a wilderness beach are just a few of the highlights of a hike along the northern reaches of Gold Bluffs Beach. While even one of these en route attractions makes for a compelling hike, the mere prospect of so many engaging environments can put a hiker into sensory overload before reaching the trailhead.

Gold Bluffs Beach (both bluffs and beach) is prime Roosevelt elk territory. Roosevelt elk are enchanted-looking creatures with chocolate-brown faces and necks, tan bodies and dark legs. And they're big: a bull can tip the scales at one thousand pounds.

While nearby elk-viewing opportunities abound—particularly along more southerly stretches of Gold Bluffs Beach and on namesake Elk Prairie up by Highway 101 and the Prairie Creek Visitor Center—the Roosevelts seem all the more majestic in a wilderness setting.

Waterfalls near the coast are a rarity, so the presence of three of them in close proximity to Coastal Trail is a special treat indeed. Gold Dust Falls, a long, slender tumbler, spills some 80 feet to the forest floor. An unnamed waterfall is just south of Gold Dust; another is just north.

While in this hike, the journey overshadows the destination, the odd Ossagon Rocks are intriguing in their own way. The rocks resemble sea stacks, though they're positioned right at land's end, not in their usual offshore location.

Truly this is a trail worth repeating, so you won't mind retracing your steps back to the trailhead. However, if you want to extend the adventure, you can loop back from Butler Creek Camp onto the state park's bluffs and return via West Ridge, Friendship Ridge and James Irvine trails.

Three delicate falls cascade just steps from the coastal trail.

DIRECTIONS TO TRAILHEAD From Highway 101 in Orick, drive 2 miles north to signed Davison Road. Turn left (west) and proceed 7 miles to road's end at the Prairie Creek Redwoods State Park Fern Canyon trailhead.

THE HIKE Coastal Trail begins on the other side of Home Creek, which is an easy ford in summer but may present a challenge during the rainy season. Usually a signpost on the north side of the creek shows the way to the start of Coastal Trail.

Join the path for a brief meander through the forest, then out across the grass-topped dunes. Coastal Trail is bordered by high bluffs on its inland side and by the mighty Pacific on the coastal side. The hiker is often out of sight of

The Ossagon Rocks, oddly shaped and oddly placed, are an unusual destination for this journey.

the surf, but never altogether removed from its thunderous roll, even when the trail strays 0.1 mile inland.

A mile out, the sound of falling water and an unsigned path forking right into the forest calls you to Coastal Trail's first cascade, a long, wispy waterfall framed by ferns.

Another 0.25 mile along the main path brings you to the short connector trail leading to Gold Dust Falls. A well-placed bench offers repose and a place to contemplate the inspiring cataract.

A minute or so more down the main trail brings you to another brief spur trail and the third of Coastal Trail's cascades.

Coastal Trail edges from prairie to forest and reaches Butler Creek Camp, a hike-in retreat at 2.25 miles. The small camp is located at a convergence of environments—creekside alder woodland, a prairie matted with head-high native grasses, the creek mouth and the beach beyond.

Cross Butler Creek and travel the grassy, sand-verbena-topped prairie for a final 0.5 mile to cross Ossagon Creek and junction with Ossagon Trail. Continue on Coastal Trail a bit farther north, then bid adieu to the path and head oceanward to Ossagon Rocks.

■ FERN CANYON
James Irvine, Clintonia, Miners Ridge Trails
Loop through Fern Canyon 1 mile round trip; via Gold Bluffs, Gold Bluffs Beach is 6.5 miles round trip with 500-foot elevation gain

Dim and quiet, wrapped in mist and silence, the redwoods roof a moist and mysterious world. Park trails meander over lush ground and the walker is treated to the cool feeling and fragrance of wood and water.

A couple beautiful "fern canyons" are found along the North Coast, but the Fern Canyon in Prairie Creek Redwoods State Park is undoubtedly the most awe-inspiring. Five-finger, deer, lady, sword, and chain ferns smother the precipitous walls of the canyon. Bright yellow monkeyflowers abound, as well as fairy lanterns, those creamy white, or greenish, bell-shaped flowers that hang in clusters. Ferns are descendants of an ancient group of plants which were much more numerous 200 million years ago. Ferns have roots and stems similar to flowering plants, but are considered to be a primitive form of plant life because they reproduce by spores, not seeds.

Gold Bluffs was named in 1850 when prospectors found some gold flakes in the beach sand. The discovery caused a minor gold rush. A tent city sprang up on the beach but little gold was extracted.

Gold Bluffs Beach is a beauty—11 miles of wild, driftwood-littered shore, backed by extensive dunes. Sand verbena, bush lupine, and wild strawberry splash color on the sand.

This walk explores some of the highlights of Prairie Creek Redwoods State Park—Fern Canyon, magnificent redwood groves, and Gold Bluffs Beach.

DIRECTIONS TO TRAILHEAD From Highway 101, 3 miles north of Orick, turn west on Davison Road. The dirt, washboard road (suitable only for vehicles under 24 feet in length) descends logged slopes and through second-growth redwoods to the beach. The road heads north along Gold Bluffs Beach. About 1.5 miles past the campground, the road dead-ends at the Fern Canyon Trailhead.

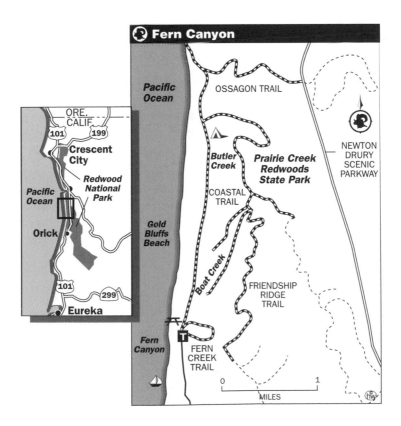

THE HIKE   The path leads along the pebbled floor of Fern Canyon. In the wettest places, the route follows wooden planks across Home Creek. With sword and five-finger ferns pointing the way, you pass through marshy areas covered with wetlands grass and dotted with a bit of skunk cabbage. Lurking about are Pacific giant salamanders.

A half-mile from the trailhead, the path climbs out of the canyon to intersect James Irvine Trail, named for a man who contributed much to the formation of redwood parks.

The James Irvine Trail crosses to the south side of the canyon and proceeds southeast with Home Creek. The trail reaches the upper neck of Fern Canyon and junctions with Clintonia Trail. (James Irvine Trail continues ascending through dense redwood forest to a trailhead near the park visitors center.) Clintonia Trail leads a mile through virgin redwood groves to a junction with Miners Ridge Trail. Bear right.

Part of Miners Ridge Trail is an old logging road, once used by mule-drawn wagons. The trail was also a pack train route for the Gold Bluffs miners. You'll descend with Squashan Creek to the ocean. It's a 1.5-mile beach walk along Gold Bluffs Beach back to the trailhead.

Lucky walkers might catch a glimpse of the herd of Roosevelt elk that roam the park. These graceful animals look like a cross between a deer and a South American llama; they easily convince walkers that they have indeed entered an enchanted land.

■ SKUNK CABBAGE CREEK
Skunk Cabbage (Coastal) Trail
To Gold Bluffs Beach (Mussel Point) is 6 miles round trip with 500-foot elevation loss; to Gold Bluffs Beach (Davison Road) is 10 miles round trip

Moss-draped Sitka spruce and a multitude of skunk cabbage massed on the muddy flats by Skunk Cabbage Creek make this a rainforest ramble to remember. After Skunk Cabbage Trail tours this lush jungle, it delivers the surprised hiker to Gold Bluffs Beach, where miles of dark, driftwood-strewn sand offer a second coastal adventure.

Many hikers would opine that the Skunk Cabbage section is the most enchanting length of the National Park's coastal trail.

The skunk cabbage appears to be a pituitary freak of the plant world: some specimens measure more than four feet across, with foot-long leaves. In the tall tree-filtered light, the cabbages glow an otherworldly green.

The skunk cabbage is not a science experiment gone awry, but a botanic cousin to the corn lily. Some skunk cabbages grow along their namesake trail; many more crowd the banks of their namesake creek.

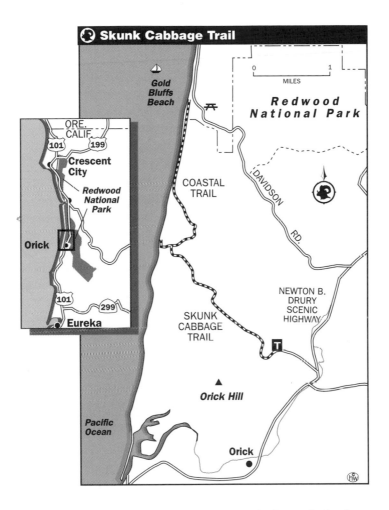

Enjoy this trail in two ways: (1) Follow the path through the forest to a junction at the edge of the bluffs, then descend to the beach via a short connector trail. This trail is overgrown, a bit precipitous, and closed by the National Park Service. (2) Upon reaching the blufftop junction, stay on the main trail for another 2 miles north, then descend to Gold Bluffs Beach. You could then walk up-coast to meet Davison Road as it descends to Gold Bluffs Beach. With a car shuttle, the latter option offers one-way hiking possibilities.

DIRECTIONS TO TRAILHEAD From Highway 101, about 2 miles north of Orick (and just north of the turn-off on the right for Bald Hills Road), turn left (west) on the signed park road for Skunk Cabbage/Coastal Trail and drive 0.75 mile to road's end at the parking area and trailhead.

THE HIKE The alder-lined, mostly level trail probes a very green world. About 0.5 mile out, where the path closely parallels the creek, you'll spot masses of

At the end of Skunk Cabbage Trail, remarkable drift-wood formations are strewn about beautiful Gold Bluffs Beach.

skunk cabbages, sprouting head to head from the boggy ground.

The trail repeatedly crosses and re-crosses Skunk Cabbage Creek, traveling amongst Sitka spruce and occasional old red-woods that somehow escaped the logger's ax. Ferns floor the forest primeval.

After 2 miles, the trail sud-denly climbs 0.75 mile out of the canyon and up a forested ridge. Even more suddenly, the forest fades, you reach a trail junction, and there's Gold Bluffs Beach at your feet.

Well, almost at your feet. A spur trail (sometimes closed to travel) switchbacks 0.25 mile down the bluffs to the beach.

The main Skunk Cabbage Trail climbs a bit more before descending and then dipping in and out of two fern-filled canyons. Finally the path emerges from the lush vegeta-tion to meet Gold Bluffs Beach.

If you're expecting a ride back, walk up the beach and then over the dunes to the Prairie Creek Redwoods State Park entry station. Otherwise, return the same way.

See Map on Page 26

■ LOST MAN CREEK TRAIL
Lost Man Creek Trail
2 miles round trip

A lovely tumbling creek, rocky pools and a lush forest are highlights of Lost Man Creek, one of the less discovered gems of Redwood National Park. You'll keep company with some impressive redwoods as you hike this creekside trail.

In 1982, when Redwood National Park was designated a World Heritage Site by UNESCO (United Nations Educational, Scientific and Cultural Orga-nization) the ceremony was held at Lost Man Creek. Such a designation is extended to natural and cultural sites around the world that are adjudged to have international significance.

As the story goes, the "Lost Man" was a timber locator who never returned; he was scouting for tall trees in the remote forested canyon of upper Lost Man Creek when he became permanently lost.

Obviously other timber locators were more successful with their missions. The slopes in the upper canyon of Lost Man Creek, as well as surrounding slopes, were heavily logged.

Lost Man Creek Trail is, in fact, an old logging road. It continues for considerable distance past the old-growth redwoods through logged land all the way to Bald Hills Road. I can't think of any reason why any sane hiker would choose to take this 18-mile round trip trek over sadly denuded land. Opt instead for this short sojourn through a still-standing forest.

DIRECTIONS TO TRAILHEAD From Highway 101, some 4 miles north of the town of Orick, turn east and follow a gravel road 2 miles to Lost Man Creek Picnic Area.

THE HIKE Slip past a hiker stile, pass the picnic ground, and begin a gentle climb through the forest. A quarter-mile out, the path crosses an old bridge over Lost Man Creek. Admire the view up-creek of the handsome watercourse.

You'll ascend through a mixed forest of redwoods and Douglas fir until the road begins to climb uphill toward a logged area. This is trail's end for the pretty part of the path and the usual turnaround point.

■ LADY BIRD JOHNSON GROVE
Lady Bird Johnson Grove Loop Trail
1.3 miles round trip

During her 1960's stint as First Lady, Lady Bird Johnson promoted many beautification and conservation projects, and was a staunch advocate for the creation of Redwood National Park. With her help, conservationists prevailed upon a recalcitrant Congress to acquire land for the new park.

In 1968, the First Lady attended the park dedication ceremony in what today is named Lady Bird Johnson Grove. Somewhat ironically, it was Lyndon Johnson's longtime political foe, President Richard Nixon, who dedicated the grove to Lady Bird Johnson the following year.

An easy, self-guiding nature trail (pamphlet available at the trailhead) loops through the redwoods that crown Bald Hills Ridge. Numerous benches en route offer a chance to rest and to contemplate the park below. While hiking the trail you emerge from the redwoods to gaze out past an ugly clear-cut to the coast. Much of the vista is now protected state and national park domain; it

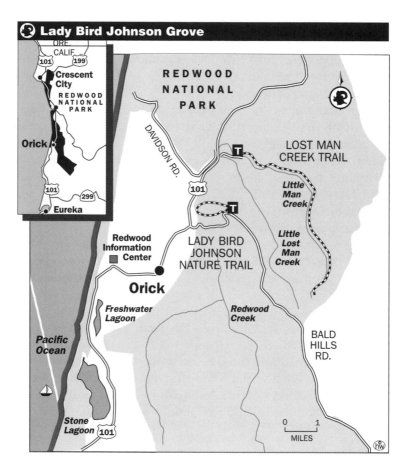

Lady Bird Johnson Grove

would no doubt all be stump-land had conservationists of the 1960s and after failed in their efforts.

DIRECTIONS TO TRAILHEAD From Redwood Information Center, travel 3 miles north on Highway 101 to Bald Hills Road. Turn right and drive 2.7 miles to the Lady Bird Johnson Grove parking area on the right side of the road.

THE HIKE Cross Bald Hills Road on a handsome wooden pedestrian bridge. The path leads through a forest of redwood, Douglas fir and western hemlock. A quarter-mile out, the trail forks; bear left to begin a clockwise loop of the grove, treading past a lush undergrowth of sword ferns, salal, salmonberry, redwood sorrel and (some particularly large) rhododendrons.

At about the halfway point, the trail makes a hairpin turn and returns along the forested north side of Bald Hills Ridge.

■ REDWOOD CREEK
Redwood Creek Trail
To Tall Trees Grove is 8.2 miles one way
with 500-foot elevation gain

Redwood Creek Trail travels through the heart of Redwood National Park to Tall Trees Grove, site of the world's tallest measured tree. After one of the classic conservation battles of the 1960s, a narrow corridor of land along Redwood Creek was acquired to protect the world's tallest tree, a coast redwood measuring 365.5 feet. This giant was discovered in 1963 by a National Geographic expedition.

The nine-mile stretch along Redwood Creek known as "the worm" was downslope from private timberlands, where there was extensive and insensitive clear-cut logging. Resulting slope erosion and stream sediments threatened the big trees, so to protect this watershed, the National Park Service purchased an additional 48,000 acres, mostly in Redwood Creek basin. For more than a decade, the Park Service has been rehabilitating scarred slopes.

Redwood Creek Trail follows an abandoned logging road on a gentle ascent from the outskirts of Orick to Tall Trees Grove. From the Tall Trees, hikers may follow Redwood Creek Trail back to their vehicles.

One word of caution: The three bridges that cross Redwood Creek are in place only during the summer. Use your best judgment and inquire at the Visitor Center before attempting this hike during the wetter seasons.

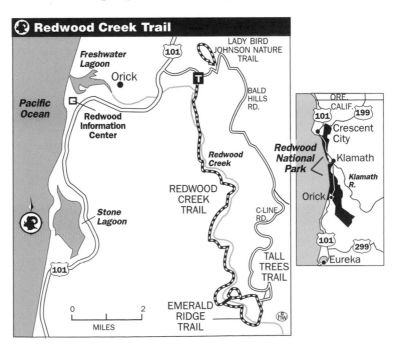

DIRECTIONS TO TRAIL-HEAD From Highway 101, about 3 miles north of Redwood Information Center and 2 miles from the town of Orick, turn east on Bald Hills Road. Take the first right to the Redwood Creek trailhead. A free permit is necessary for overnight camping along this trail and can be obtained at Redwood Information Center.

THE HIKE The first 1.5 miles of trail, from the trailhead to the first bridge crossing of Redwood Creek, passes through regenerating forest as well as old-growth Sitka spruce and redwood. The trail also passes a meadowland that flanks the river.

Occasional clearings and the bridge crossings allow the walker to get the "big picture" of Redwood Creek. Three distinct

No matter what your politics, thank the one-time First Lady, Lady Bird Johnson, for saving some very big trees.

communities of flora can be discerned: Extensive grass prairie—emerald green during the wet season and golden brown during the drier months—dominates the eastern slopes above Redwood Creek. Downslope of the grassland are vast clearcuts, slowly recovering as new-growth red alder forest. Near the creek are the groves of old-growth redwoods and a lush understory of salmonberry, oxalis and sword fern.

During the summer months, the walker may descend to Redwood Creek and travel the creek's gravel bars nearly to Tall Trees Grove. The river bars are fine pathways and also serve as campsites for backpackers.

Continue through the forest primeval. The redwoods congregate in especially large families on the alluvial flats along the creek.

Enjoy the loop trail through the Tall Trees Grove before returning back the way you came or, if you have a vehicle waiting, take the Tall Trees Trail up to C-Line Road.

See Map
on Page
27

■ TALL TREES GROVE
Tall Trees Loop Trail
3.4 miles round trip with 500-foot elevation gain

A visit to the majestic colonnades of redwoods that form the heart of the national park is apt to be a humbling experience. Voices hush, children shush, eyes look skyward in reverence. It's little wonder that some hikers feel they've entered a natural cathedral and regard their time with the tall trees as a kind of spiritual experience.

Oh, and we hikers come to gawk, too; here is the "World's Tallest Tree," a 365.5-foot redwood. At least the ancient giant has been considered the world's tallest since its discovery by a National Geographic expedition in 1963. Some experts believe as yet undiscovered taller trees may grow in the park.

This trail is the most-traveled route to the tall trees. (See the Redwood Creek hike for a longer approach.) Trailside markers are keyed to a Park Service interpretive brochure.

DIRECTIONS TO TRAILHEAD A (free) permit is required to drive to the trailhead. Obtain one of the limited number of permits as well as the combination to the locked gate from the Redwood Information Center. Motorhome travel is not advised on Bald Hills Road, the approach to the trailhead.

From the Redwood Information Center, travel 3 miles north on Highway 101 to Bald Hills Road. Turn right on Bald Hills Road and follow the signs 14 miles to Tall Trees Trailhead.

THE HIKE From the parking area, the trail descends, soon passing a junction with Emerald Ridge Trail. Showy rhododendrons color the dark forest.

About 1.25 miles from the trailhead, the path meets the loop trail. As described in the Park Service pamphlet, the nature trail circles clockwise, soon passing a side trail on the left that leads to Redwood Creek.

The highlight of the loop is, of course, the tallest measured redwood. En route are the third-largest and sixth-largest sempervirens as well. After completing the loop, retrace your steps to the trailhead.

■ DOLASON PRAIRIE
Dolason Prairie, Emerald Ridge Trails
To Dolason Barn is 2.5 miles round trip; to Tall Trees Grove is 6 miles one way with a 2,100-foot elevation loss

R edwood National Park visitors usually choose one of two options in order to visit Tall Trees Grove, a grand stand of redwoods that includes the world's tallest living thing. A few visitors trek 8 miles up Redwood Creek to pay homage to the giants; most others drive to the grove.

Happily, there's a third way to go to the Tall Trees—the captivating, near-secret Dolason Prairie Trail, which descends from the Bald Hills to the redwoods.

While the goal of reaching the tallest tree in the world is reason enough to take this path, Dolason Trail offers a journey that's nearly as engaging as its destination. The trail tours ancient redwoods and towering Douglas fir, as well as oak woodland, wildflower-splashed meadows and a cascading creek. All this and an ocean view, too!

Dolason Prairie, a spread of waist-high perennial grasses, was once a sheep pasture. As the story goes, 19th-century rancher James Donaldson was the first to settle here; subsequent sheep ranchers slaughtered the spelling of his name. The still-standing Dolason Barn was constructed as a sheep shed to shelter flocks during the rainy winters.

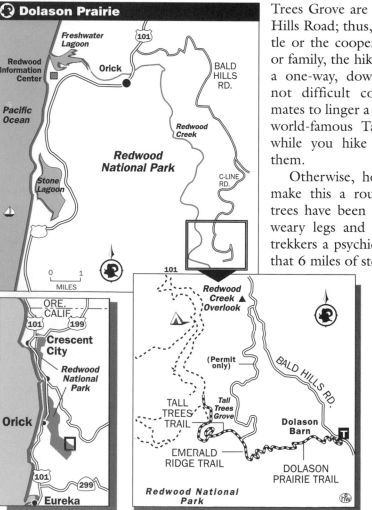

Both Dolason Prairie and Tall Trees Grove are located off Bald Hills Road; thus, with a car shuttle or the cooperation of friends or family, the hiker can make this a one-way, downhill jaunt. It's not difficult convincing helpmates to linger a few hours at the world-famous Tall Trees Grove while you hike down to meet them.

Otherwise, heroic hikers can make this a roundtrip; the tall trees have been known to uplift weary legs and spirits and give trekkers a psychic boost back up that 6 miles of steep trail.

DIRECTIONS TO TRAILHEAD Check in at the Redwood Information Center, located off Highway 101 2 miles south of the town of Orick, and get a free permit to visit Tall Trees Grove and the gate combination for the access road.

From Highway 101 in Orick, turn east on Bald Hills Road and drive 11 miles to the signed turn-off for Dolason Prairie Trail.

To reach the Tall Trees Grove trailhead: From Highway 101 in Orick, turn east on Bald Hills Road and drive 7 miles to the Tall Trees access road (C-Line Road on some maps). Turn right, open the gate with the combination and drive 6 miles to the parking lot.

THE HIKE The path immediately begins its descent, passing over a Douglas fir-cloaked slope. At 0.5 mile, the path joins an old gravel logging road for 0.25 mile, then resumes as a footpath and continues through a mixed woodland to Dolason Prairie and the picturesque Dolason Barn.

If it's clear down at the coast, the prairie's the place to partake of vistas of the canyon cut by Redwood Creek and the Pacific. Much less inspiring is the view of clear-cut ridgetops (they're not called the Bald Hills for nothing), shorn of their redwoods prior to the creation of Redwood National Park.

As the path departs the prairie, oak-lovers will note the stand of Oregon white oak, which look a bit like smaller cousins of the valley oak.

For a mile or so, the path alternates between Douglas fir forest and grassland. The trail then descends into dense forest where tanoak and madrone keep company with ancient redwoods and tall firs.

At about 4.75 miles from the trailhead, the path crosses the sparkling waters of Emerald Creek on a wooden footbridge. Bordering the creek's dancing waters and quiet pools are dogwood and an assortment of ferns. Dolason Prairie Trail climbs briefly to meet Tall Trees Trail. The last mile or so is a grand excursion through the redwood forest primeval to the Tall Trees Grove trailhead.

Tall trees, historic Dolason Barn and a lovely oak woodland are just a few highlights of this special hike.

A climb to the top of Schonchin Butte is one highlight of a visit of Lava Beds National Monument.

CHAPTER TWO

LAVA BEDS NATIONAL MONUMENT

Millions of years of volcanic activity have left a landscape of lava tubes, spatter cones and cinder cones in remote northeastern California. Something about the fiery origins of this land, and the resultant caves and chasms attracts visitors to Lava Beds National Monument.

John Muir explained his fascination with the lava landscape in Modoc Memories: "The Modoc lava beds have an uncanny look, that only an eager desire to learn their geology could overcome."

The lava beds, along with surrounding lakes, mountains and forest are the ancestral home of the native Modoc. It was to this natural fortress created by the lava beds that the Modoc retreated during the Modoc War of 1872-73. A Modoc group escaped an Oregon reservation where they had been confined and fled back to their homeland with the U.S. Army in pursuit. Modoc leader Captain Jack and his greatly outnumbered warriors holed up in the rugged terrain and held off the Army for more than five months before surrendering.

For a majority of visitors, Lava Beds' leading attraction is its many caves. These caves are not your basic, drippy, stalactite-hung limestone caverns, but caves fashioned by lava that erupted from Mammoth Crater some 30,000 years ago.

When hot lava (1,800°F.) flows from a volcano, the surface and edges cool quickly: the molten lava beneath, however, continues to flow—like a river that's frozen on top but continues to run. When the lava flow finally stops, a hollow tube known as a lava tube is left inside a hardened crust.

Catacombs, Hopkins Chocolate, Hercules Leg and Mushpot are among the colorfully named caves accessible from turnouts off Cave Loop Road. Hardhats and flashlights are available from the visitors center for adventurers wishing to check out the clinker aa and pahoehoe lavas in the network of underground passages. More elaborate caves, two with labyrinths a mile long, are open only to experienced spelunkers.

Cave enthusiasts, joined by nature lovers, historians and the local populace pushed for preservation of the lava beds. President Calvin Coolidge proclaimed Lava Beds National Monument in 1925.

In its early years, the national monument was managed by the U.S. Forest Service, but it was transferred to the National Park Service in 1933. During the 1930s, the Civilian Conservation Corps labored mightily to make the national monument more "visitor friendly." Workers built roads, constructed picnic grounds and residences and improved access to the caves.

The national monument has many above-ground attractions, too. Hikers can ascend several large cinder cones such as Schonchin Butte, which has a look-out on the summit. Another butte to climb is Whitney, which affords panoramic views of the volcanic landscape, including mighty Mt. Shasta.

Lava Beds National Monument is open all year. Summer is a popular time to tour the volcanic terrain, but many visitors prefer a spring or fall outing in order to see millions of migratory birds touch down at adjacent Tule Lake National Wildlife Refuge.

View of the Devils Homestead Flow.

■ CAPTAIN JACK'S STRONGHOLD
Captain Jack's Trail
2 miles round trip with 100-foot elevation gain

It was a heartbreaking and all-too-familiar story in the saga of how the West was won: Native Americans forced off their ancestral land onto a reservation. In the case of the Modoc, they were displaced to Oregon and confined on a reservation with the Klamath, their longtime foes.

Desperately unhappy, their pleas ignored by governmental authorities, a band of Modoc escaped the reservation and returned to their homeland. In November 1872, the U.S. Army set out to round up the Modoc and bring them back to the reservation. For nearly six months, a small group of warriors held off some 700 (historic accounts provide varying numbers) soldiers.

The lava caves and trenches made a natural fortress for the Modoc under the leadership of Kientpoos, also known as Captain Jack. Eventually, the Modoc were forced to surrender. Captain Jack and three leaders were hanged, and the remaining Modoc were exiled to a reservation in Oklahoma.

As you walk the rocky stronghold, you'll note the obvious: it's an almost perfect natural fortress, with ideal sniper positions. The Modoc had excellent views of the approaching U.S. Army. Less obvious is the defensive value of the surrounding environs, which look relatively flat and easy-to-negotiate; actually

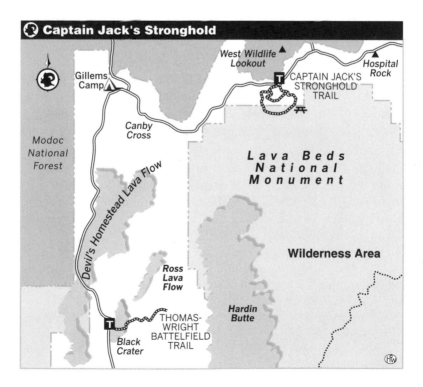

Kientpoos, also known as Captain Jack

this terrain contains deep fissures and sharp rocks, which took its toll on the advancing soldiers.

Along with some military history, a visit to the stronghold offers some insights into Modoc culture: the importance of the medicine flag believed to have magic powers and a ring called Curly Headed Doctor's Medicine Circle where the Modoc gave ritual expression to their feelings before battle.

DIRECTIONS TO TRAILHEAD From the Visitor Center, follow the main park road north 13 miles to the signed parking area for Captain Jack's Stronghold.

THE HIKE At the trailhead, pick up the Park Service interpretive pamphlet "Captain Jack's Stronghold," which sadly and succinctly sums up what took place here in 1872: "The cultural identity of an entire people was lost here . . . so settlers could graze a few cows."

A 1.5-mile loop trail and a 0.5-mile loop combine with the connector trail from the parking lot, and offer two options for exploration of the stronghold.

See Map on Page 35

■ THOMAS-WRIGHT BATTLEFIELD
Thomas-Wright Battlefield Trail
To Black Crater is 0.4-mile round trip; to Thomas-Wright Battlefield is 2.4 miles round trip with 100-foot elevation gain

Geology and history are two subjects painlessly absorbed by the hiker bound for Black Crater and Thomas-Wright Battlefield.

Geologists say Black Crater is actually a spatter cone, formed when masses of hot lava skyrocketed to the surface and launched into the air; the bursts of molten lava spattered one atop another, piling in a heap.

Thomas-Wright Battlefield was the scene of an early chapter in that sorry saga known as the Modoc War. Here in 1872, a 68-soldier patrol under the command of captains Thomas and Wright made an ill-fated lunch stop, just 4 miles from Army headquarters.

The Modocs caught the patrol completely by surprise and killed or wounded two-thirds of the soldiers. Things went from bad to worse for the soldiers—some of whom panicked and ran back to headquarters. It began to

Living History: Learn the sad saga of the Modoc War at Thomas-Wright Battlefield.

snow, and the rescue party got lost while somehow having forgotten to bring along food, water and the camp doctor.

DIRECTIONS TO TRAILHEAD From the national monument Visitor Center, drive 5 miles north to the signed parking area.

THE HIKE Follow the path amongst sagebrush and bunchgrass 0.1 mile to a junction and fork right for Black Crater. The crater is more than black; look for basalt rock in orange, red and dark purple hues.

After appreciating the 360-degree view from the crater's summit, return to the main trail, which descends along a lava flow. Your way to trail's end at the Thomas-Wright Battlefield is accompanied by interpretive signs.

■ WHITNEY BUTTE
Whitney Butte Trail
To Whitney Butte is 7 miles round trip
with 500-foot elevation gain

Whitney Butte is one of three trails in the wilderness area of the national monument. Though an official wilderness with a capital W, it's not a particularly remote area. Ranches and rural development are obviously visible in the near distance. Still, roads and vehicles don't penetrate this land, which offers hikers some memorable views, as well as the longest day hike in the national monument.

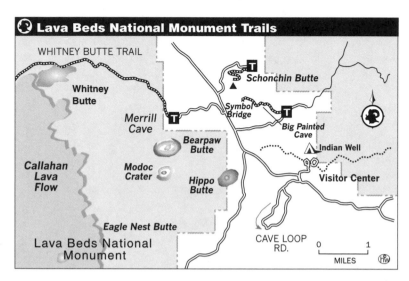

Whitney Butte Trail travels the wide-open spaces, tours a high desert environment of sagebrush, juniper and mountain mahogany, then approaches the massive Callahan Lava Flow. From atop Whitney Butte, a small 5,004-foot volcano, are great views of the national monument, nearby Modoc National Forest and Tule Lake National Wildlife Refuge, as well as that lord of all volcanoes— distant Mt. Shasta. Vistas compare well with those from atop Schonchin Butte, though Whitney Butte receives 99 percent less foot traffic.

Whitney Butte shares an access point with the Merrill Ice Cave. The ice cave, two lava tubes in a previous life, can be explored with the aid of stairs and a ladder. An always-iced-over pond refrigerates the cave. Wear warm clothing and bring multiple light sources.

DIRECTIONS TO TRAILHEAD From the park Visitor Center, drive 2 miles north to the signed turn-off for Merrill Cave. Turn left (west) and proceed a mile to the parking area and signed trailhead.

THE HIKE Hike past bunchgrass and black basaltic rock, sagebrush and juniper, as you gaze north toward Tule Lake. About 2 miles out you'll spot snow-capped Mt. Shasta.

Some 3.3 miles from the trailhead is the short connector route (actually a couple of different use trails) to the summit of Whitney Butte. Enjoy your view from atop the small volcano, then return to the main trail.

Heading west, Whitney Butte Trail ends at the massive Callahan Lava Flow, an intriguing but not-very-welcoming-to-hikers sheet of basalt.

■ SCHONCHIN BUTTE TRAIL
Schonchin Butte Trail
To summit of Schonchin Butte is 1.5 miles
round trip with 600-foot elevation gain

Sunrise and sunset are particularly good times to be on or around Schonchin Butte. The patterns of light and shadow on the cinder cone and surrounding lava fields can be dramatic.

The butte is named for Schonchin John, second in command to Captain Jack during the Modoc War. On the summit is a fire lookout tower, constructed by the Civilian Conservation Corps in 1939, that offers terrific vistas of the volcanic landscape—particularly the Schonchin Lava Flow to the northeast. Locator maps posted at the base of the tower interpret the near and far vistas. During the summer fire season, lookout staff (if not too busy) might invite you to enjoy the expansive view.

Because of its close proximity to the Visitor Center, the short but steep trail up the juniper-dotted slopes of Schonchin Butte is a popular one.

DIRECTIONS TO TRAILHEAD From the Visitor Center, follow the park road 2.5 miles north. Turn right at the signed turn off for Schonchin Butte and drive a mile on dirt road to the trailhead.

THE HIKE Long switchbacks lead up a juniper- and sagebrush-cloaked slope. Certainly there's no mystery where this trail is headed.

Strategically placed benches allow you to catch your breath while views of Mt. Shasta may take your breath away. Clear-day views from the mile-high summit are memorable, to say the least.

■ SYMBOL BRIDGE AND BIG PAINTED CAVE
Symbol Bridge Tube Trail
1.6 miles round trip with 100-foot elevation gain

A majority of the national monument's most compelling caves are easy to access from the main park road and require very little walking to reach them. Symbol Bridge and Big Painted Cave require a short hike to reach them. Reward for the modest effort to reach the pair of pictograph-filled caves may be a more intimate and more spiritual experience than that offered by the intriguing, but far more visited, caves near the Visitor Center.

Symbol Bridge, a collapsed lava tube "bridge," offers an open-ended presentation of its ancient drawings. Big Painted Cave is a more intact lava tube (more cave-like), but its pictographs are less distinct. Bring flashlights to illuminate the ancient artwork.

Observe all posted Park Service regulations. Keep your hands off the pictographs (skin oils can ruin them) and remember to approach with the respect expected of a pilgrim to a sacred or religious site.

DIRECTIONS TO TRAILHEAD From the Visitor Center, proceed 1.5 miles north on the monument road to the turn-off for Skull Cave. Turn right and drive 1 mile to the signed trailhead and parking area on the right for Symbol Bridge and Painted Cave.

THE HIKE Head out amidst the sagebrush and juniper. At 0.25 mile, the trail crosses a (collapsed) lava tube bridge and reaches a signed junction at 0.5 mile. Fork left very briefly to Big Painted Cave.

After your flashlight exploration of the cave, return to the main trail and continue to Symbol Bridge. What stories are illustrated on these rocks? Let your imagination wander in this very special place.

CHAPTER 3

WHISKEYTOWN NATIONAL RECREATION AREA

If the name Whiskeytown evokes images for you of grizzled miners, your imagination is right on track. Not long after that famous gold strike at Sutter's Mill, Forty-Niners swarmed into this part of the state and discovered gold in the waters of Clear Creek.

As the story goes, Whiskeytown and near-by Brandy Creek were named for the miners' most popular adult beverages. Another colorful Gold Rush tale tells of a mule slipping from the trail and spilling its eagerly anticipated cargo into what became known as Whiskey Creek.

More than a century later, Whiskeytown Dam was constructed and a great reservoir flooded Whiskeytown and adjacent canyon bottoms. President John F. Kennedy dedicated the dam in 1963.

The resultant lake, an important link in the Central Valley Water Project, is one of the more attractive recreation areas in the chain of reservoirs. Among the popular pasttimes are swimming, water-skiing, sailing, canoeing and fishing.

Whiskeytown's waters are considerably more trafficked than its shoreline and hillside trails, which receive light use from hikers and mountain bikers. Although it cannot be said to be a hiker's park, the national recreation area does have a sampling of nature trails, historic pathways and scenic dirt roads.

Sometimes nature, sometimes the U.S. Bureau of Reclamation and sometimes the two entities working together control the level of Whiskeytown Lake. After storms, the rain-swollen lake is said to have reached "full pool"; when this occurs, water exits the Glory Hole (spillway) near the dam. Water then heads into Clear Creek, and then into the Sacramento River, that huge supplier of water for Sacramento Valley agriculture.

Whiskeytown Lake, managed by the National Park Service, is one of three parts of the Whiskeytown-Shasta National Recreation Area; two other areas—

Snow-capped Shasta Bally is the dramatic backdrop for Whiskeytown Lake in this view from the Visitor Center.

Shasta Lake and Trinity Lake (Clair Engle Lake) are administered by the U.S. Forest Service.

Long before the arrival of miners and water project engineers, this area was the domain of the native Wintu, who lived in relative abundance for many centuries before being displaced and decimated by the miners and settlers. Some archeological evidence suggests a native presence in the area as long ago as four thousand years.

The land around the lake has felt the often heavy hand of humans. After the easy-to-pan gold played out, deep shafts were sunk into hillsides. Heavy stamp mills crushed tons and tons of rock, mercury was used to extract gold from the crushed ore, tailings were piled everywhere. Building a dam 272-feet above the creek bottom disturbed a lot of earth.

Time has softened Whiskeytown's wounds, however, and the lake today is an attractive destination. Get oriented at the Visitor Information Center located just off Highway 299 some 6 miles west of Redding. Another source of information, when the Visitor Center is closed, is park headquarters a half-mile from the center on John F. Kennedy Memorial Drive.

■ TOWER HOUSE
HISTORIC DISTRICT
Camden Water Ditch Trail, Mill Creek Trail
To El Dorado Mine is 1.4 miles round trip; to Mill Creek Road
is 5 miles round trip with 700-foot elevation gain

This part of the national recreation area delivers both history and one of the more attractive natural areas around the lake. Step back into the Gold Rush era with a walk through the Tower House Historic District and a visit to El Dorado Mine. Experience the wild side of the park with a hike along the lush canyon cut by Mill Creek.

Levi Tower and Charles Camden, two gold-seekers turned entrepreneurs, owned much of the land and many of the buildings in these parts. Tower built his Tower House Hotel along Camden's profitable toll road, used by area farmers and miners.

Camden's large house, constructed in 1852, still stands near the trailhead. (Tours are given during the summer, along with gold-panning programs.) It's an easy walk to the entrance of the old El Dorado Mine. An old ore car rusting on its rails and a stamp mill stand near the mine.

Hikers can continue past the mine on oak-, maple- and alder-lined Mill Creek Trail. Be warned, though—the path crosses Mill Creek 19 times. At low water levels, you can hop across on rocks; at high levels, you might get your feet wet.

DIRECTIONS TO TRAILHEAD Tower House Historic District is located off Highway 299, some 8 miles west of the Visitor Information Center. Park in the lot and walk over the Clear Creek footbridge into the historic district.

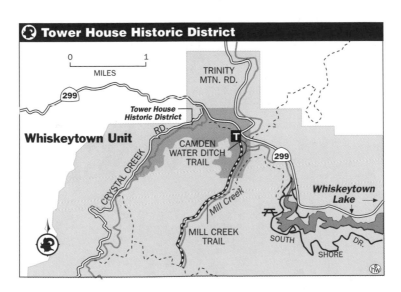

THE HIKE After crossing the Clear Creek footbridge, turn left, then cross the Willow Creek footbridge. (If you wish, visit the Levi Tower gravesite.) Join Camden Water Ditch Trail, then a dirt road leading a few hundred yards to the El Dorado Mine.

Past the mine, Mill Creek Trail passes through a lush creekside environment where a couple of inviting swimming holes beckon. Adding to the jungle-like feeling of the area are long grapevines trailing down from the trees. After crossing and re-crossing the creek many times, the path eventually ascends a steep ridge to meet Mill Creek Road.

The ambitious can extend this hike by turning left (east) on infrequently traveled Mill Creek Road and walking a mile to a junction with Boulder Creek Trail.

■ GREAT WATER DITCH
Great Water Ditch North Trail
4 miles round trip

Great Water Ditch is one of the few Whiskeytown trails that travel close to the lakeshore. The shady path is flat and family-friendly.

The trail passes through a woodland of gray pine, knobcone pine, oak and manzanita. Closer to the lake and along small creeks grow mosses, ferns and blackberries.

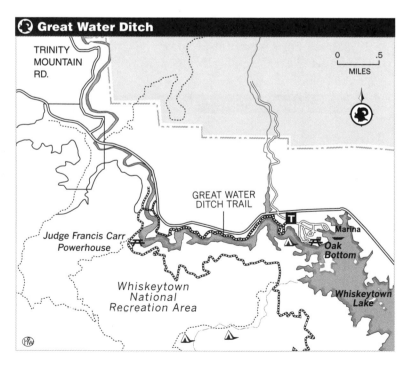

The path follows a segment of the 41-mile-long Great Water Ditch, which supplied water to mining operations of the 19th century.

Join the trail from either its west end at Carr Powerhouse Road or its eastern trailhead at Oak Bottom Campground and Marina. Most hikers prefer the latter trailhead, where a jogging trail complete with exercise stations offers campers a chance to work out.

DIRECTIONS TO TRAILHEAD From the Visitor Information Center, follow Highway 299 5 miles west to the turn-off for Oak Bottom Campground and Marina. Park in the wide area on the right side of the campground access road (across from the campground store).

THE HIKE Begin your outing from either of the two signed trailheads, "Jogging Trail" or "Access to Great Water Ditch." The jogging trail offers a scenic, more roundabout way to start the hike. The other route is more direct—a little too direct you might think, as the trail parallels noisy Highway 299 for a few hundred yards.

The trail soon returns to more rustic route closer to the lakeshore. Enjoy the mountain and lake views as you saunter along the mellow pathway. You can continue the entire 2 miles to trail's end at Carr Powerhouse Road (an old segment of Highway 299) or turn around whenever you're so inclined.

■ DAVIS GULCH AND BRANDY CREEK
Davis Gulch Trail
From JFK Memorial Dr. to Brandy Creek Picnic Area is 6.6 miles round trip with 100-foot elevation gain

Unlike most of the recreation area's trails, which began life as dirt roads or are accessible to many user groups, Davis Gulch Trail is specifically a hiking trail. Plaques along the first part of the path identify local lakeshore flora. Benches en route invite you to take it easy on this relatively flat trail. The leg-weary or families with small children may cut this trail a little short; the interpretive signs, as well as the best views and swim area are found within the first 2 miles of travel from John F. Kennedy Memorial Drive trailhead.

The path's second trailhead at Brandy Creek is a good place to begin

Birds'-eye view of Whiskeytown Lake from Davis Gulch Trail.

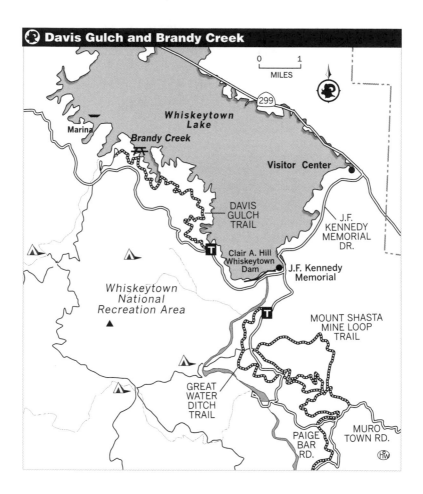

your walk if you're already picnicking with the family and desire a modest half-mile jaunt to escape the summer crowds near the main swim areas.

DIRECTIONS TO TRAILHEAD From the Visitor Information Center at the junction of Highway 299 and John F. Kennedy Memorial Drive, take the latter road to the dam, then another 0.7 mile to the signed trailhead on your right. To reach the trail's terminus, continue another 2 miles up the road to the turn-off for Brandy Creek Picnic Area.

THE HIKE The trail drops in and out of small ravines and over ponderosa-pine-clad slopes. Two miles out, the path drops to Whiskeytown's shoreline and to a perfect-for-a-swim cove. The trail then contours along the shore for 0.5 mile to another, smaller cove.

Davis Gulch Trail next climbs and contours around the hillsides above the lake before reaching the parking lot for Brandy Creek Picnic Area.

■ MT. SHASTA MINE
Mt. Shasta Mine Loop Trail
3.5-mile loop with 600-foot elevation gain

Mt. Shasta Mine was the region's most productive in its time—the turn of the 20th century. Piles of mine tailings, rock walls and a water ditch are other signs of the considerable mining activity that took place here a hundred years ago.

The long and deep mine shaft (fenced by the Park Service) is visited by a loop trail. You can follow the loop from either direction, but the preferred route is counter-clockwise.

DIRECTIONS TO TRAILHEAD From the Visitor Information Center at the junction of Highway 299 and John F. Kennedy Memorial Drive, follow the latter road 1.6 miles to Paige Bar Road. Turn left and drive 1.2 miles to the large dirt parking lot on the left.

THE HIKE The path heads southeast, paralleling Paige Bar Road and in 0.25 mile leading past the Whiskeytown Cemetery. Graves and headstones were relocated here from outskirts of old Whiskeytown just before the old mining town was covered by the lake.

A half-mile along, you'll pass an unsigned junction with Great Water Ditch Trail. As you might guess, the ditch carried water to the mines.

The path passes through a mixed oak and knobcone pine woodland before arriving at Mt. Shasta Mine, located a bit more than a mile from the trailhead.

After visiting the mine, continue on the main trail, which is cut in numerous spots by spur trails and mountain bike routes. The loop trail ascends alongside the banks of Orofino Creek, then climbs steeply from the creek channel up a ridge. From the ridgetop are views north to the lake and dam, as well as views westward of 6,209-foot Mt. Shasta Bally, highest summit in these parts.

The trail joins a dusty road and makes a 0.75-mile descent amongst knobcone pine back to the trailhead.

Bumpass Hell is Lassen's largest and most active thermal region. Discover it by taking an interpreted nature trail.

CHAPTER FOUR

4

LASSEN VOLCANIC NATIONAL PARK

L assen Peak is perhaps the least known of the major Cascade Range volcanoes. Mt. Rainier is one of our national park "crown jewels," majestic Mt. Shasta dominates northern California, and Mt. Saint Helens provided fireworks with its relatively recent (1980) eruption.

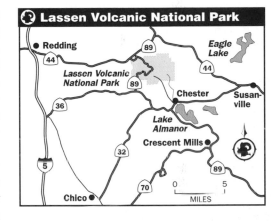

Lassen National Park's location, 250 miles north of San Francisco, in a remote, sparsely populated region of northeastern California, also contributes to its relatively obscure image.

Lassen's claim to volcanic fame rests on the diversity of its features. Scientists come from all over the world to examine the volcanic processes and steaming hydrothermal areas.

Lassen Peak was even less well-known before May of 1914 when the world's largest plug dome volcano began to erupt. By 1916 the area was set aside as a national park, though Lassen's eruptions, some 150 of them, continued until 1921.

Nineteenth-century trail guide and park namesake Peter Lassen is remembered as a not-so-dependable leader who sometimes led parties of emigrants astray. As the story goes, one group of pioneers became so irate at their lost leader they forced him at gunpoint to climb the 10,457-foot volcano that now bears his name in order to search for the correct trail.

The bizarre lavascape—a mini-Yellowstone of roaring fumaroles, bubbling mudpots and hissing vents—located in the southern part of the park is, for the most part, easy to reach by auto and short trails. Park service interpretive efforts in the thermal areas are excellent.

The park's eastern sector is enchanting in an altogether different way. A chain of lakes extends from Butte Lake in the north to Juniper Lake in the south. Forests of pine and fir and wildflower-sprinkled meadows beckon the backcountry adventurer.

With 150 miles of trail, Lassen is very much a hiker's park. The national park, located where the Cascade Range approaches the High Sierra, shares flora and wildlife common to both mountain ranges. Interpretive paths introduce strangers to a strange land of lava while forest trails, lake trails and a 17-mile length of Pacific Crest Trail explore surrounding wildlands.

■ BROKEOFF MOUNTAIN TRAIL
Brokeoff Mountain Trail
7.2 miles round trip with 2,500-foot elevation gain

Before it "broke off" it was a much bigger mountain, part of mighty high and wide (11,500 feet, 12 miles in diameter), ancient Mt. Tehama.

Numerous natural processes combined to shape Brokeoff Mountain and nearby Mt. Diller into the remnant hulks they are today: volcanic eruptions, sculpting by glaciers, slippage from the major fault underneath the area. (For more geological background, walk the nature trail through the Sulfur Works, located just 1.5 miles up Highway 89 from Brokeoff's trailhead.)

From Brokeoff's summit is a commanding view, nearly equal to that from famous Lassen Peak. North-by-northeast extends a prominent ridge capped by Mt. Diller, Eagle Peak, Lassen Peak, and beyond to Chaos Crags. Far to the northeast lie the little-known Warner Mountains. Dominating the northwest horizon is snowy Mt. Shasta. To the west lies the Sacramento Valley and, farther west, the Coast Range. The Sierra Nevada extends southward.

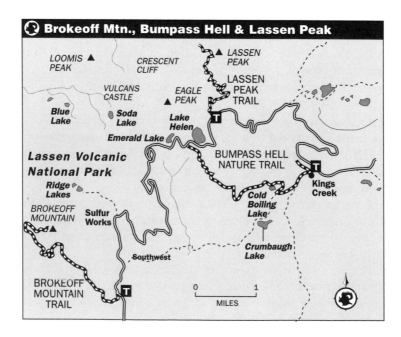

The trail to the top is, itself, attractive. Wildflower-strewn meadows, a mixed forest of pine, fir and hemlocks, and striking rock formations can be savored en route. Solitude-seekers will enjoy the very light foot traffic (compared to nearby Lassen Peak) on this trail.

DIRECTIONS TO TRAILHEAD The trail to Brokeoff Mountain is located off Highway 89 in the southwestern part of the park, just south of the information station. From the junction of Highways 36 and 89, it's 5 miles to the trailhead via the latter highway.

THE HIKE Begin near the creek that spills from Brokeoff's shoulder to eventually join Mill Creek. Somewhat confusingly, the trail trends south for a few hundred yards, away from the mountain, through wet and willow-vegetated terrain before curving west, then northwest and entering white pine forest. Your creekside route passes some intriguing lava landscapes and a pond. Nearly 1.25 miles out, you can leave the trail and follow the creek 0.1 mile to shallow little Forest Lake.

Better and better views are your reward for the ascent as the path breaks out into more open country near timberline. A final mile's climb through an alpine zone of rock and stunted trees brings you to the summit.

■ BUMPASS HELL
Bumpass Hell Nature Trail
To Bumpass Hell is 3 miles round trip; From Kings Creek Picnic Area to Bumpass Hell is 5 miles round trip with 1,200-foot elevation gain

Lassen's largest and most hyperactive hydrothermal region is Bumpass Hell, a 16-acre collection of steaming vents, mudpots and fumaroles. An interpreted nature trail leads to Bumpass Hell and back.

The path is a good introduction to the park. You'll learn about volcanism—hot rocks and cooling magma, cinder cones and shield volcanoes. Lassen's plant life is also on display: whitebark pine and mountain hemlock, accompanied by a ground cover of pinemat manzanita and mountain heather, Slopes are seasonally sprinkled with silver lupine.

Kendall V. Bumpass discovered the hellish landscape in 1864. A year later, while guiding a newspaper editor into the hot zone, he stepped through the crust over a mud pot. Bumpass lost a leg as a result of his plunge into the boiling water.

DIRECTIONS TO TRAILHEAD Well-signed Bumpass Hell Nature Trail begins from the south side of Lassen Park Road by Lake Helen, some 11 miles from the junction of Highways 36 and 89.

The churning, boiling waters of Bumpass Hell are an ever-present reminder of the area's volcanic past.

THE HIKE Bumpass Hell Nature Trail is the most popular pathway in the park. You can avoid the crowds by hiking to Bumpass Hell from King's Creek Picnic Area instead of the main trailhead by Lake Helen. This 5-mile round trip jaunt tours well-named Cold Boiling Lake, and offers excellent vistas of volcano country. (Keep the misadventure of Mr. Bumpass in mind when you explore his hell; stay on the wooden boardwalk for safety.)

See Map on Page **50**

■ LASSEN PEAK

Lassen Peak Trail
To Lassen Peak is 5 miles round trip
with 2,000-foot elevation gain

Lassen Peak, along with fellow volcano Mt. Shasta, stands mightily above lesser peaks and valleys of northern California. One-hundred mile views are the hiker's reward for climbing the 10,453-foot peak.

The peak is the near the southern end of the Cascade Range, which extends from California through Oregon and Washington to British Columbia. Lassen is also part of the Pacific Ocean ring of volcanoes called the Ring of Fire.

Lassen erupted many times from 1914 to 1917. A 1915 explosion known as the Great Hot Blast sent volcanic debris 5 miles into the sky. Ash fell as far away as Reno, Nevada.

One hike highlight is a look at the aptly named Devastated Area, a reminder of the volcano's power located just below the northeast summit.

To learn more about the great volcano, pick up an interpretive pamphlet at the trailhead or from park headquarters. Lassen Peak Trail begins just a mile north of the park's most popular hike—the nature trail to Bumpass Hell.

DIRECTIONS TO TRAILHEAD From Interstate 5 in Redding, follow Highway 44 east to Lassen Volcanic National Park. From Interstate 5 in Red Bluff, follow Highway 36 to the park. Highway 89 extends north-south through the national park and provides access to most of its prominent features, including the well-marked trailhead for Lassen Peak. Park visitor contact stations are located near the junction of highways 44 and 89 as well as highways 36 and 44.

THE HIKE The path begins its no-nonsense climb right away, switchbacking through a scattered stand of mountain hemlock. Even the first mile of the climb is scenic: look for Lake Almanor to the southeast, Brokeoff Peak and other park summits to the near west, the (often hazy) Sacramento Valley to the far west.

As you climb, you'll notice the hemlock are supplanted by the hardier whitebark pine, more tolerant of higher elevations and harsher alpine conditions.

The path levels some atop the summit ridgetop just west of the peak before you conquer Lassen Peak. Look northwest for awesome views of Mt. Shasta. Westward is the Coast Range. To the south are the northernmost peaks of the High Sierra.

(Ambitious hikers can follow the rough path leading through the lava flow to the peak's north rim for another fine view, particularly to the north.)

Massive Lassen Peak dominates the landscape for miles around.

■ TERRACE, SHADOW AND CLIFF LAKES

Terrace Lake Trail

To Terrace Lake is 1 mile round trip; to Shadow Lake is 1.6 miles round trip; to Cliff Lake is 3.4 miles round trip with 600-foot elevation gain

Lassen's lakes are many, but often they challenge the day hiker by virtue of their distance from a trailhead. Sometimes these lakes, beautiful though they may be, dash the would-be swimmer's expectations because "beach" access is poor or non-existent, and shallow waters are filled with snags.

In contrast to these hard-to-reach lakes, a trio of lovely lakes—Terrace, Shadow and Cliff—are easy to access and enjoyable for a swim. Enjoyable, that is, by midsummer when the water warms sufficiently for a pleasant dip.

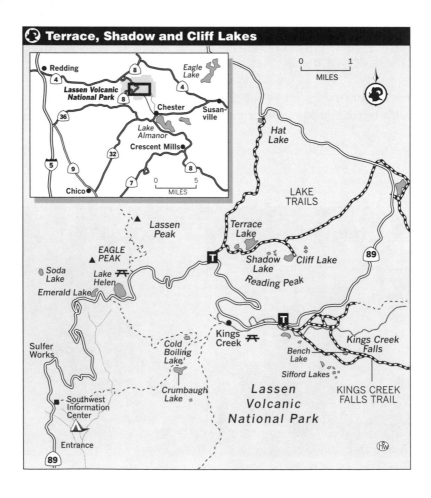

Lassen's lovely lakes reflect their shadow side.

The lakes were named by someone with a good geographical awareness because they reflect the lay of the land—and water. Long and skinny Terrace Lake is perched on a rock terrace. The "cliff" of Cliff Lake is really a very steep side of Reading Peak, which seems to rise right from water's edge.

Roundish Shadow Lake does receive its share of shadows. Of course, just about every other lake gets shadows, too, but Shadow Lake captures a big one: mighty Lassen Peak reflects upon its deep blue surface. A photo opportunity, indeed.

DIRECTIONS TO TRAILHEAD From the park's Southwest Entry Station, follow Highway 89 north for 9 miles to the signed parking area on the left (north) side of the road.

THE HIKE The path descends 0.25 mile over a wooded slope to a junction. A trail heads downhill (north) toward Paradise Meadows but you turn east (right) and drop another 0.25 mile to Terrace Lake.

The path skirts Terrace's south shore and you'll soon get a peek at, then descend to, Shadow Lake. After meandering along Shadow's southeast shore, the path descends to cross a creek, passes a couple small ponds, then forks. Take the right spur trail 0.25 mile to its end at Cliff Lake. At least as scenic as the lake's cliffs is a little island, topped with fir and hemlock.

■ KINGS CREEK FALLS

Kings Creek, Sifford Lakes Trails

To Kings Creek Falls is 3 miles round trip with 700-foot elevation gain; to Sifford Lakes is 5.25 miles round trip with 500-foot elevation gain

Kings Creek rises from Lassen Peak's south shoulder, spills through wooded glens and lush meadows, and rushes headlong over a rock outcropping to create Kings Creek Falls, one of the national park's most popular sights.

Twin cascades (split by rock) drop 50 feet or so into a rocky canyon. The attractiveness of the falls, as well as its close proximity (1 mile) to the main park road, contribute to the popularity of this jaunt.

Kings Creek Falls is certainly a worthy destination; however, the best part of this hike may be the journey itself. The path descends past corn-lily-dotted Lower Meadow (as opposed to Upper Meadow on the north side of Highway 89) and through woodsy areas cloaked in lodgepole pine, fir and hemlock.

Along with serving up lots of scenery, the trail itself is notable for a long series of stairsteps hewn from the granite banks of Kings Creek. The trail very closely parallels the creek.

Extend this walk—or escape the flocks of falls-bound visitors—by looping to Sifford Lakes. Swimming opportunities reward your efforts.

DIRECTIONS TO TRAILHEAD From the park's Southwest Entrance Station, travel 12 miles north on Highway 89 (2 miles past the Lassen Peak trailhead) to the signed parking area for Kings Creek. The path departs from the right (south) side of the highway.

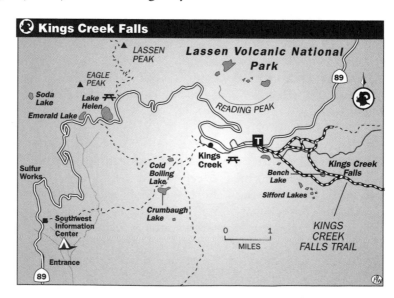

A picture-perfect hiker's path along meandering Kings Creek.

THE HIKE Begin a 0.25 mile saunter among towering fir and pine to the fringes of Lower Meadow. Past the meadow is a trail fork; left is the falls, right the return leg of Sifford Lakes Trail.

Continue to the falls (ignoring the "Horse Trail" that also leads to Kings Creek Falls) and begin a careful descent on a granite staircase. Step along past numerous cascades—referred to as The Cascades—on the ledge-like creek bank.

Just one hundred yards shy of the falls, look for Sifford Lakes Trail branching right. Continue to Kings Creek Falls and the fenced overlook. After admiring the falls, those opting for a longer hike will return to Sifford Lakes Trail and cross Kings Creek on a log footbridge. Bid adieu to Kings Creek, which flows out of the park and through Warner Valley before joining the North Fork of the Feather River.

Begin a steep but short 0.1 mile climb to the top of a minor ridge. The path levels as it continues along the base of a volcanic outcropping, punctuated by a couple of caves near its top.

About 0.6 mile from the Kings Creek crossing brings you to small and shallow Bench Lake, and another 0.4 mile reaches a trail junction. Fork right and walk 0.25 mile to the left-forking connector trail leading to Sifford Lakes.

It's a short half-mile to the first Sifford Lake, fine for swimming but not as pleasant as the second Sifford Lake, located 0.75 mile farther up the faint path. A couple more Sifford lakes are short cross-country walks from the second lake.

Retrace your steps back to the first Sifford Lake. South of this lake is a vista point offering a look down at the steaming landscape of Devils Kitchen. Return to the junction with the main trail and descend northwest a mellow mile to return to Kings Creek where it bubbles through Lower Meadow. You'll then follow Kings Creek Falls Trail 0.4 mile back to the trailhead.

■ LASSEN'S LAKES
Lakes trails
From Summit Lake to Upper Twin Lake is 6.4 miles round trip;
loop is 11.2 miles round trip with 800-foot elevation gain; loop
via Horseshoe Lake is 14.5 miles round trip

This hike tours Lassen's "Lake District," gentler country than the lava lands. The lakes are popular destinations for backpackers and day trippers.

Depending on your time and stamina, you can visit one, two or even a half-dozen lakes in a day. Largest of the lot on this loop is Horseshoe Lake.

Another highlight of the area is the meadows, sprinkled in season with lupine, blue penstemon, Indian paintbrush and many more wildflowers. King of the meadows is 3-mile-long Grassy Swale. "Swale" is a quaint British word for a wet, marshy hollow; it's a particularly fitting way to name this meadow.

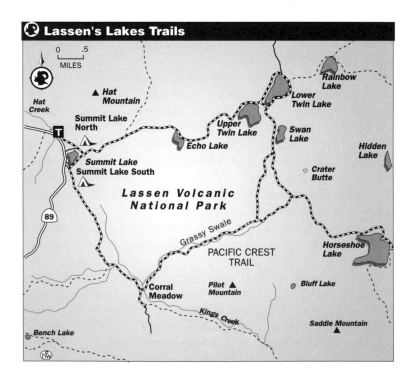

DIRECTIONS TO TRAILHEAD Summit Lake North (Ranger station, campground) is located on Highway 89 about in the middle of the park, some 13 miles from the Visitor Center and the junction with Highway 44. Park near Summit Lake's north shore.

THE HIKE From Summit Lake's north shore, cross the wooden footbridge over Hat Creek and begin a moderate ascent through a mixed forest of hemlock, lodgepole pine, and red and white fir. Best views are behind you: Chaos Crags over your left shoulder, Lassen Peak over your right.

A mile out, pass a left-forking trail that leads to Little Bear and Big Bear lakes. A modest 0.8 mile descent takes you to Echo Lake. Skirting the north shore, the trail soon leaves the lake behind and travels through meadows and past green ponds to Upper Twin Lake, 3.2 miles from the trailhead.

The path meanders past the lake's campsites 0.8 mile to a signed junction. The left branch travels the west shore of Lower Twin Lake. Bear right on the short connector trail leading to the Pacific Crest Trail, which you join, heading south.

You'll soon pass Swan Lake just east of the trail; it's your basic little backcountry lake and offers limited camping. The path then climbs a low divide and reaches a junction.

Those opting for a longer hike will leave the PCT here bound for Horseshoe Lake. On the way to the lake you'll spot 7,267-foot Crater Butte (climb it, if so motivated) rising some 500 feet above you to the southeast. The crater features a little lake inside.

A 0.75 mile descent brings you to another junction. Bear left and continue an easy mile to Horseshoe Lake.

After enjoying the lake's many charms, double-back a mile to the trail junction and fork left, following the creekside trail a short half-mile back to the PCT. Head south again, descending Grassy Swale alongside Grassy Swale Creek. Clouds of mosquitoes have been known to swarm along this stretch of trail, distracting hikers from the lovely meadow and wildflowers.

After a mile, the PCT crosses the creek, passing through the southern part of the swale, wet meadows and a forest of red fir. Now the trail reaches a confluence of creeks—Grassy Swale and Summit. After the merger, the two creeks continue their partnership under a new name—Kings Creek, which flows southeast. Cross Kings Creek (often a wet proposition, though you might find a log bridge). At some inviting west bank campsites, you bid adieu to Corral Camp and the PCT then join the signed trail heading to Summit Lake.

Ascend fairly steeply at first, then more moderately. After two creek crossings, you'll reach a junction 0.75 mile from Corral Camp. Bear right.

Two more miles of modest ascent take you from forest to meadow to the Summit Lake Campground road. Head north to the lake, then follow either the east or west shore trail back to the north shore trailhead.

■ DEVILS KITCHEN, BOILING SPRINGS LAKE
Devils Kitchen Trail, Boiling Springs Lake Trail
To Devils Kitchen is 4.4 miles round trip; to Boiling Springs
Lake is 2.5 miles round trip

Two unique hydrothermal areas beckon the hiker to a remote part of the park. From the Drakesbad trailhead, paths lead to Devils Kitchen and Boiling Springs Lake. Although this walk is not accessible from the park road (Highway 89) or main entrances, it's well worth the circuitous drive to the trailhead.

Bubbling mudpots along Hot Springs Creek gave Devils Kitchen its colorful name. A network of paths and footbridges links the hot attractions.

Steam escaping from below-ground fissures heats Boiling Springs Lake to a near-constant 125 degrees F. Its yucky, yellow-brown color is a result of miner-

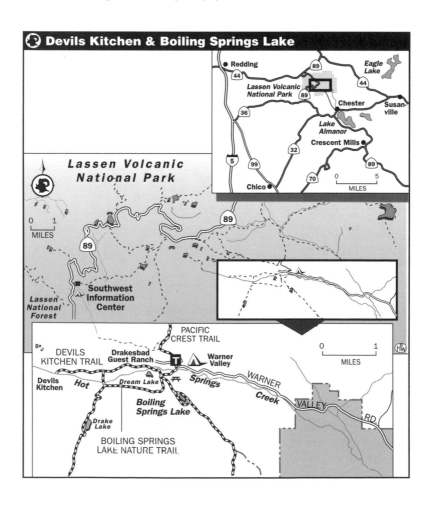

als, particularly iron oxide, in suspension. From steam vents waft hydrogen sulfide fumes, greeting hikers with a rotten-egg smell.

Boiling Springs Trail is an excellent path. The trail loops through an outstanding area that provides a great introduction to Lassen's plants and animals.

The natural hot springs along Hot Springs Creek were tapped for a health spa in the 1860s by pioneer Edward R. Drake. For nearly a century, Drakesbad was a private resort. Now Drakesbad Guest Ranch belongs to the national park and is operated by a concessionaire. Alas, the thermal pools at the ranch are for guests only.

DIRECTIONS TO TRAILHEAD From Highway 36 in Chester, turn north on Warner Valley Road. Drive 16 miles to Warner Valley Campground, then another 0.5 mile to the trailhead.

THE HIKE Head south on the Pacific Crest Trail, soon reaching and crossing Hot Springs Creek to a lodgepole-pine-shaded picnic area. A short walk farther brings you to a three-way trail junction. An upper and a lower trail lead to Devils Kitchen while the PCT heads south to Boiling Springs Lake.

The way to Devils Kitchen crosses Hot Springs Creek, then weaves through Drakesbad Meadow. Next the path enters a forested area before reaching the austere terrain of Devils Kitchen.

Explore a half-mile's worth of trails amidst steaming springs and fumaroles, then return the way you came.

From the above-mentioned three-way junction, Boiling Springs Trail (PCT) ascends gently through a Jeffrey-pine and white-fir forest. You'll circle the lake before retracing your steps back to the trailhead.

■ CINDER CONE
Cinder Cone Trail
5 miles round trip with 700-foot elevation gain; loop via Snag Lake is 14 miles round trip with 1,000 foot elevation gain

Cinder Cone is your basic volcano—a near-perfect cone around a central vent—straight out of the science textbooks.

Volcano experts believe Cinder Cone has erupted about five times since the mid-16th century; the latest eruption approximately 250 years ago. Fallen ash and cinders, testimony to an enormous eruptive power, spread over some 35 square miles around the volcano.

Equally impressive are the lava flows, particularly the aptly named Fantastic Lava Beds, on the south and east sides of Cinder Cone's base. The Painted Dunes, another lava flow sprinkled by hot ash and cinders, cooled to form the colorful dunes.

Over the centuries, many of the park's other cinder cones have become colonized by plants and stands of pine and fir. Not so Cinder Cone or Fantastic Lava Beds, whose fiery origins are not disguised by vegetation.

Cinder Cone Trail is definitely one of the most engaging nature trails in the national park system. Keyed to an excellent Park Service pamphlet, the trail boasts 44 numbered stops on the way to the top of volcano.

California- and Oregon-bound pioneers walked parts of this path in the 1850s. Imagine the reactions of emigrants as they traversed this bizarre landscape, struggling to cross one last mountain range in order to reach the relative comfort and safety of the Sacramento Valley.

Traveling by the 700-foot-high volcano is a fine family day hike. Walking on cinders and loose soil provides a good workout!

More ambitious hikers may extend this walk with a long circle tour of two of the park's largest lakes—Butte Lake near the trailhead and Snag Lake. From a vantage point atop Cinder Cone, hikers often suspect that Snag Lake is much easier to reach than it actually is. Remember that the cinder path is slow going in places.

DIRECTIONS TO TRAILHEAD From Highway 44, 11 miles east of Highway 89, turn south at the signed turn-off from Butte Lake. Follow the dirt road 6 miles to Butte Lake Campground. Park at the signed trailhead above the north shore of Butte Lake. The trail begins beyond the ranger station.

THE HIKE Walk along the edge of the Fantastic Lava Beds. You'll pass a right-forking trail leading to Prospect Peak, then reach a junction with the Cinder Cone summit trail, 1.4 miles from the trailhead.

After exploring the peak, descend the trail down the south side, traveling 1.5 miles through pine and fir forest to Snag Lake. Springs and wildflower-strewn meadows are part of the charm of the area. Walk 2.2 miles on the west, then south, and then east sides of the lake. Enjoy the forest and views through the trees of Cinder Cone and Fantastic Lava Beds.

From the lake, the path passes through a stand of aspen, then descends amidst lodgepole pine 3 miles to a trail junction. Veer left to Butte Lake, where the path closely follows the east shore 1.6 miles, then descends 0.6 mile west back to the trailhead.

Cinder Cone, a classic volcano situated in a park full of features fashioned by fiery origins.

One of California's most spectacular shoreline settings: Point Reyes.

CHAPTER FIVE

POINT REYES NATIONAL SEASHORE

Point Reyes is a great place to conduct your very own time-motion study of the San Andreas Fault. Evidence of both slow- and fast-moving forces can be found at the national seashore. Wave-torn rocks of the craggy coast match rocks in the Tehachapi Mountains more than 300 miles to the south. Many plants and shrubs found on the west side of the fault are pre-Ice Age relics not found on the east side.

Plates forming the earth's crust do not always creep quietly past each other, of course. In 1906 they clashed violently, and the result was California's worst natural disaster, the San Francisco earthquake. Point Reyes was shoved 16.4 feet to the northwest. A cow barn, located near the park rangers' headquarters, was ripped in two. A corner of the barn stayed on the foundation and the rest was carried 16 feet away.

Rangers at Point Reyes National Seashore encourage visitors to take a close look at the San Andreas. You can watch the seismograph, which constantly measures the earth's quivers, or take the self-guided Earthquake Trail (a memorable nature trail). One sees creeks and fences that were rearranged by the 1906 quake and the spot where, a colorful legend has it, an unfortunate cow was swallowed up by the heaving earth, leaving only her tail waving above ground.

Along with the earthquake-displaced land, the ocean is an overwhelming presence here. Point Reyes is bounded on three sides by more than 50 miles of bay and ocean frontage. The point, described as hammer-headed—or wing-shaped, by the more poetic—literally and figuratively sticks out and stands out from California's fairly straight-trending coast north of San Francisco.

British explorer Sir Francis Drake is said to have been the first to arrive on these shores, in 1579. Long before—and after—European discovery, the native Coast Miwok lived well off the land's bounty: elk, deer, fish, shellfish, acorns, berries and much more.

Since the 1850s, milk cows have grazed the lush grasses of the peninsula, and such dairy operations continue today. Butter produced here has been particularly prized by San Francisco foodies over the years.

As early as the 1930s, the National Park Service worked to purchase Point Reyes and add it to the park system. The price tag for Depression-mired America was too steep at that time, and then World War II interrupted all park plans.

During the post-war housing boom of the 1950s, real-estate developers sought to carve up the peninsula into golf courses, and residential and commercial parcels. The Park Service, Marin conservationists, and concerned Californians rallied to the peninsula's protection. In 1962, President John F. Kennedy signed into law the bill establishing Point Reyes National Seashore.

In hindsight, some conservationists believe that the drawn-out preservation process actually benefited Point Reyes because in the interim attitudes shifted a bit from parks-as-playgrounds to parks-as-nature preserves. Few roads or recreation facilities were constructed. The area's three tiny towns—Olema, Point Reyes Station, and Inverness—have remained very small. San Franciscans have an altogether different attitude toward their wilderness-next-door than, say, Bostonians have toward summer-crowded Cape Cod National Seashore.

Some 24,200 acres of the national seashore's wildest terrain was designated wilderness in 1985 and named for the late Congressman Phillip Burton. Burton, a longtime San Francisco representative, was a staunch wilderness advocate and an accomplished environmental legislator who greatly increased the size and number of America's wilderness areas.

The weather adds to the wilderness feeling of Point Reyes. High winds scour the beaches, and heavy fogs often blanket the peninsula. While Point Reyes is always memorable, it's not always postcard-pretty. Several drought years, combined with a severe 1995 fire that scorched some 12,000 acres, have left some sections of the national seashore forlorn and unattractive. Yet nature has its way of healing. What was a blackened slope in summer has become an emerald green grassland dotted with a host of wildflowers.

Point Reyes is a haven for birds; not surprisingly, it makes *Audubon* magazine's "Top Ten National Seashores" list. A diversity of habitats—seashore, forest, chaparral and more—is one reason the bird count exceeds 430 species. Because Point Reyes thrusts 10 miles into the Pacific, it lures many winter migrants. Limantour and Drake esteros (estuaries) are resting and feeding areas for many species of shorebirds and waterfowl.

Other wildlife-watching opportunities abound. A resident tule elk herd roams the Tomales Point area. Point Reyes Lighthouse is a premier spot for winter whale-watching. Migrating California gray whales swim close by the point.

When you are hiking, the awesome forces that shaped this land are often evident. You can hike along the earthquake rift zone, tramp along creeks flowing through the peninsula's fissures, and from the ridges look down at Olema Valley, the 1906 quake's epicenter.

More than a hundred miles of trail meandering through the 71,000-acre national seashore beckon the hiker to explore wide grasslands, Bishop pine and

Douglas fir forest, chaparral-cloaked coastal ridges and windswept beaches. The paths range from easy beach walks and nature hikes to rugged mountain rambles. Some excellent trail camps along or near the Coastal Trail suggest a weekend backpacking trip.

■ PALOMARIN
Coast Trail
From Palomarin to Bass Lake is 5 miles round trip; to Wildcat
Camp is 10.5 miles round trip with 600-foot elevation gain

For the homesick Brit or Scot, Point Reyes peninsula has more than a passing resemblance to the homeland. Inverness, Lands End, and Drakes Bay are some of the names on the land that pull on the heartstrings.

Along with its United Kingdom-like moors, weirs, glens and vales, Point Reyes has its "Lakes District." Five lakes –Bass, Pelican, Crystal, Ocean and Wildcat—were created in part by movement along the nearby San Andreas Fault. Earth slippage sealed off passage of spring-fed waterways, thus forming the little lakes.

The lakes are reached by a somewhat melancholy stretch of the Coast Trail, forever overhung, it seems, by dark, brooding clouds. Springtime travel is a bit

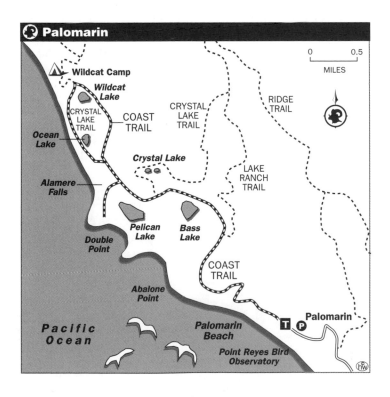

more cheery because the route is brightened by wildflowers: foxglove (causing more nostalgic sighs from our British friends), lupine, morning glory, cow parsnip and paintbrush.

The trail, with zigs, zags and roller-coasters along, as it serves up ocean vistas. Wildcat Beach and the meadowland around Wildcat Camp invite a picnic.

DIRECTIONS TO TRAILHEAD From Stinson Beach, drive 4.5 miles north and take the turn-off (Olema-Bolinas Road) to Bolinas. (This turn-off is rarely signed; Bolinas residents remove it.)

Follow this road to Mesa Road and turn right. You'll pass some Brave New World-looking radio towers, and the Point Reyes Bird Observatory, then reach a large trailhead parking area at road's end.

THE HIKE Coast Trail, an old farm road, ascends into a mature stand of eucalyptus, then contours out onto the cliff edge. The trail here, and in the miles to follow, is lined with coastal scrub—coyote bush, black sage, and coffee berry. Turning inland, the trail descends into a gully, then climbs again back to the blufftops. Coast Trail soon repeats this maneuver, this time climbing in and out of a larger gully.

You'll pass a junction with Lake Ranch Trail, which leads, among other places, to Five Brooks Trailhead off Highway 1. A short distance beyond this junction is Bass Lake, a tranquil spot shaded by Douglas fir.

Another trail junction offers the opportunity to take Crystal Lake Trail to another lake in the "Lakes District."

Triangular Pelican Lake, perched on a blufftop, is the next lake visited by Coast Trail, which descends to another junction. A side trail leads coastward to overlook Double Point, two shale outcroppings that enclose a small bay. Seals often haul out on the bay's small beach. Offshore stand Stormy Stacks, where California brown pelicans and cormorants roost.

Coast Trail crosses Alamere Creek, which cuts through a wild and wooded canyon on its way to the sea. During winter and spring, Alamere Falls cascading over the bluffs is an impressive sight.

A short distance beyond the creek crossing, the trail forks: the left fork, Ocean Lake Trail, and the right fork, a continuation of Coast Trail, both lead a bit over a mile to Wildcat Camp. The two trails skirt Ocean Lake and Wildcat Lake, and form a handy loop. From the camp, there's easy access to Wildcat Beach.

■ FIVE BROOKS
Stewart, Greenpicker Trails
To Firtop is 7.5 miles round trip with 1,000-foot elevation gain

Five Brooks is one of those downright weird landscapes rearranged by action along the very, very nearby San Andreas Fault. Two of the five brooks—Olema Creek and Pine Gulch Creek—are parallel watercourses, hardly a quarter-mile apart, and yet they flow in opposite directions!

Five Brooks is a favorite trailhead of the horsey set; equestrians like to ride up and down the long Rift Zone and Olema Valley trails, two paths that will never make it on to my "Top 20 Point Reyes Hikes" list. (Hikers with a strong interest in geology and earthquake faults will disagree with this assessment and likely find these trails fascinating.)

The favorite hiker's loop from Five Brooks is actually one of the few national seashore trails where the ocean is not an overwhelming presence; in fact, it's a no-show on this trail, where trees predominate.

And thank goodness for the tall trees. The 1995 Vision Fire ravaged the national seashore's conifer population, but the trees around Five Brooks escaped the conflagration.

Stewart and Greenpicker trails explore fittingly named Firtop, a fir-surrounded meadow rated "PG"—Picnicking Great. Stewart Trail, in previous lives, a logging road and a U.S. Army road, is now a wide hiking trail, occasionally used by National Park Service maintenance personnel who drive it to service Wildcat Camp.

DIRECTIONS TO TRAILHEAD From Highway 1, some 9 miles north of Stinson Beach and 3.5 miles south of Olema, turn

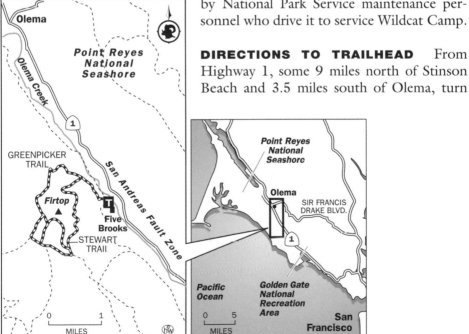

Pay attention to signs along the trail—especially when they issue such a strict warning!

west at the signed turn-off for Five Brooks and drive 0.25 mile to the large parking area.

THE HIKE Begin at the gated dirt road that soon leads past a shallow pond. After just a few minutes of walking, you'll spot the Douglas fir that will accompany you for much of the journey. Continue on your wooded way on the wide path that you'll share with mountain bikers and horseback riders.

About 1.8 miles out, you'll junction with Greenpicker Trail on your right as Stewart Trail swings south. After passing a connector to Ride Trail, Stewart Trail reverses direction again for the final ascent to Firtop.

From the signed junction up top, join right-forking Greenpicker Trail, a narrow path that descends mostly amongst the firs, to reunite you with Stewart Trail for the walk back to the trailhead.

■ BEAR VALLEY
Bear Valley Trail
From Bear Valley Visitor Center to Divide Meadow is 3 miles round trip; to Arch Rock is 8.5 miles round trip

Bear Valley is the busy hub of Point Reyes National Seashore. From the park Visitor Center, more than 40 miles of trail thread through the valley, and to the ridges and beaches beyond.

The National Park Service's Bear Valley Visitor Center is a friendly place, full of excellent history and natural-history exhibits. Film screenings, a seismograph, and dioramas tell the story behind the seashore's scenery.

Outside the Visitor Center, there is much to see, including a traditional Coast Miwok village. The family dwellings, sweat lodge, and other structures, were built using traditional native methods. Near the Visitor Center is the Morgan Horse Ranch, where Park Service animals are raised and trained.

Two park interpretive trails are well worth a stroll. Woodpecker Trail is a self-guided nature trail that introduces walkers to the tremendous diversity of the region's native flora. Earthquake Trail uses old photographs and other displays to explain the seismic forces unleashed by the great 1906 San Francisco earthquake. This well-done and entertaining geology lesson is particularly relevant because most of the land west of the San Andreas Fault Zone is within the boundaries of Point Reyes National Seashore.

Bear Valley Trail, a former wagon road, is surely one of the most popular paths in the national seashore. It passes through a very low gap in Inverness Ridge, and follows a nearly-level route to the ocean. First-time visitors will enjoy this easy trail that's highly scenic but sometimes suffers from overuse. (It's a gravel Park Service road that's traveled by bicycles, too.) Experienced hikers will enjoy Bear Valley Trail for the access it gives to a half-dozen more remote, less traveled trails.

DIRECTIONS TO TRAILHEAD Bear Valley Visitor Center is located just outside the town of Olema, 35 slow and curving miles north of San Francisco on Highway 1. A quicker route is by Highway 101, exiting on Sir Francis Drake Boulevard, traveling through the town of Fairfax and over to Olema. A left turn on Bear Valley Road takes you to the Visitor Center and trailhead.

THE HIKE Bear Valley Trail, an old ranch road, heads through an open meadow and passes a junction with Mt. Wittenberg Trail, which ascends Mt. Wittenberg. Beyond this junction, the trail enters a forest of Bishop pine and

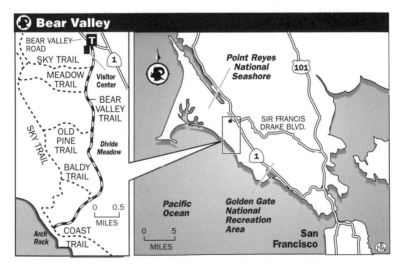

Bear Valley Trail is one of the most popular paths on the national seashore.

Douglas fir. Your path is alongside Bear Valley Creek.

Notice that the creek flows north, in the opposite direction of Coast Creek, which you'll soon be following from Divide Meadow to the sea. This strange drainage pattern is one more example of how the mighty San Andreas Fault can shape the land.

A half-mile along, you'll pass a second trail, Meadow Trail, and after another mile of travel, arrive at Divide Meadow. A hunt club, visited by Presidents William Howard Taft and Theodore Roosevelt, once stood here. During the early part of this century, meadows and nearby forested ridges abounded with deer, bear, mountain lion and game birds.

Well-named Divide Meadow divides Bear Valley Creek from Coast Creek, which you'll soon be following when you continue on Bear Valley Trail. Divide Meadow is a fine place for a picnic.

Shady Bear Valley Trail junctions with a couple more trails, including Old Pine Trail and Baldy Trail, that climb Inverness Ridge to the Sky Trail. Near the ocean, Bear Valley Trail emerges from the forest and arrives at an open meadow on the precipitous bluffs above Arch Rock. At low tide, you can squeeze through a sea tunnel at the mouth of Coast Creek.

Unpack your lunch, unfold your map, and plan a return route by way of one of Bear Valley's many scenic trails.

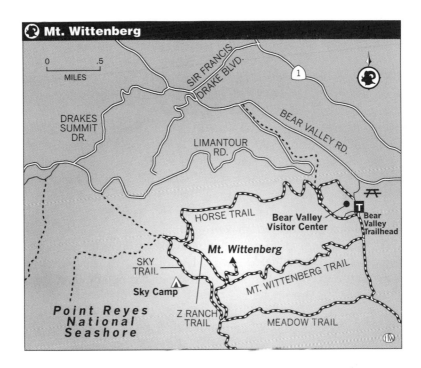

■ MT. WITTENBERG
Mt. Wittenberg Trail
To Mt. Wittenberg summit is 3.4 miles round trip with 1,300-foot elevation gain; return via Old Pine Trail is 6.6 miles round trip; return via Baldy Trail is 8.6 miles round trip

The highest summit on Point Reyes National Seashore, 1,407-foot Mt. Wittenberg, offers sweeping vistas of the entire Point Reyes Peninsula: Tomales Bay, Olema Valley, Bolinas Ridge. On clear days, look for distant Mt. St. Helena and Mt. Diablo.

Surely the least-used of the paths that begin from the seashore's busy headquarters, the Mt. Wittenberg Trail's stiff ascent apparently scares off most hikers. No need to be scared, although it is a serious workout to walk Wittenberg.

Rewards for the ascent include the aforementioned views and Sky Camp, an excellent picnic spot. Once you've gained the summit, you can join Sky Trail along Inverness Ridge, then choose one of a couple of different trails to return to Bear Valley.

DIRECTIONS TO TRAILHEAD Bear Valley Visitor Center is located just outside the town of Olema, 35 slow and curving miles north of San Francisco on Highway 1. A quicker route is by Highway 101, exiting on Sir Francis Drake

Boulevard, traveling through the town of Fairfax and over to Olema. A left turn on Bear Valley Road takes you to the Visitor Center and trailhead.

THE HIKE Begin on Bear Valley Trail and in 0.25 mile reach a right-forking junction at a large bay tree with signed Mt. Wittenberg Trail. Bear right and begin your march toward Inverness Ridge.

With sword ferns pointing the way, the path climbs past a mixed forest of tanbark oak and Douglas fir. After gaining more than a thousand feet in elevation, you reach the ridgecrest and a junction. Join the rightward path for a climb to the top of Mt. Wittenberg. Otherwise, head left and in 0.4 mile reach a four-way junction. For a somewhat mellow 1.5-mile descent back to Bear Valley, join east-trending Meadow Trail, which crosses a long meadow and then descends past bay trees and Douglas fir.

Sky Trail continues south a mile through a Douglas-fir forest and past a variety of berry bushes to meet Old Pine Trail, another fairly easy way back to Bear Valley. This trail descends 1.9 miles through a long meadow and past a small grove of old pine—Bishop pine.

Sky Trail continues its descent along forested Inverness Ridge another 1.4 mile to face "Baldy," a 1,034-foot rock knob. Baldy Trail drops a mile to Bear Valley; it's then 3 miles back to the trailhead.

■ MUDDY HOLLOW
Muddy Hollow Trail
From Muddy Hollow to Limantour Beach is 3.6 miles round trip; return via Estero Trail is 6 miles round trip

Sure, you can drive to Limantour Beach, but then you'd miss Muddy Hollow, Limantour Estero and much more.

Muddy Hollow and environs were among the fastest-healing portions of the national seashore in the aftermath of the devastating 1995 Vision Fire. The area's coastal scrub and chaparral environments, along with rolling grasslands, rebounded rapidly; however, much of the hillsides surrounding the hollow are still rather bleak. I've detailed an optional return route over those very hillsides, but if upon inspecting the hills, you want to pass, it's okay by me. The trails up there are infrequently maintained.

Muddy Hollow Trail meanders from a creekbank of red alders to the eastern tip of Limantour Estero to long, sandy, Limantour Beach.

Muddy Hollow is indeed muddy. Park service signs warn that the trail could be underwater in winter and spring.

DIRECTIONS TO TRAILHEAD From Olema, drive north on Highway 1 for 0.1 mile and turn left on Bear Valley Road. Drive 1.8 miles and turn left on

Limantour Road. Continue 5.75 miles to a signed dirt road. Turn right and drive 0.25 mile to the trailhead.

THE HIKE Follow the level dirt road, which narrows to more footpath-like proportions after 0.5 mile. The route parallels a red alder- and willow-lined creek whose waters account for making this hollow muddy.

You'll pass the hollow's fair-sized, freshwater pond, which attracts flotillas of ducks. At 1.4 miles, you'll meet right-forking Estero Trail. Muddy Hollow Trail

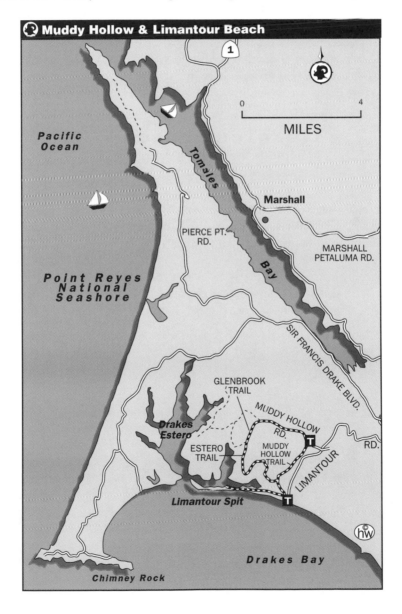

continues past Estero de Limantour and leads to a parking lot and to a beach access trail (paved) that extends to Limantour Beach.

For a different return trip, double-back to Estero Trail, which travels between two bodies of water and soon ascends a hillock. Look over the wetlands, Muddy Hollow and Limantour Beach, then continue through the coastal scrub. About 1 mile along Estero Trail, cross Glenbrook Creek and ascend moderately north. Over-the-shoulder vistas unfold of Point Reyes and Drakes Bay. Two miles along Estero Trail, you'll meet, and join, Glenbrook Trail as Estero Trail veers west toward Drakes Estero.

Proceed 0.7 mile to Muddy Hollow Road. You'll head southeast on the road, which passes left-forking Bucklin Trail after 0.5 mile and left-forking Bay View Trail after another 0.5 mile. Reminders of the devastating 1995 Vision Fire are particularly present around here in the form of blackened trees. Follow Muddy Hollow Road across Glenbrook Creek and return to the trailhead.

See Map on Page 75

■ LIMANTOUR BEACH
Limantour Spit Trail
To end of Limantour Spit is 4 miles round trip

Many coast walkers claim Limantour Beach is the Bay Area's best for walking. Certainly Limantour's walking possibilities seem limited only by the imagination. Sandy Limantour Beach invites long walks, Limantour Estero attracts birdwatchers to its shores, and long Limantour Sand Spit offers splendidly scenic passageway between the ocean and the estero.

Curious sand spit sojourners want to know: where does the spit come from? Pacific waves, arising from the northwest, hammer the head of Point Reyes;

Dunes at Limantour Beach.

greatly deflected, the waves end up approaching land from the south. This odd swell contributes sand to Limantour Spit.

Along Limantour Spit Trail, hikers get an egret's-eye view of pickleweed- and eelgrass-fringed Limantour Estero. Black brandts, pelicans and many more bird species feed and rest at the estero.

In 1841, José Yves Limantour sailed from Mexico and ran aground on the spit that now bears his name. Limantour's place in history, however, comes not from his poor navigation (his Mexican ship overshot San Francisco) but from his shady real-estate dealings.

Limantour claimed to have received 600,000 acres worth of land grants from Mexican governor Micheltorena (1842-1845). During the state's early American period in the 1850s, the city of San Francisco recognized the validity of these claims and Limantour sold much of "his" land (in downtown San Francisco no less) before the federal government determined his documents to be fraudulent and Limantour fled to Mexico.

Whether along San Diego Bay, Morro Bay or Drakes Bay, spit-walking is a special experience because the walker is treated to both Pacific and estuary environments. With its mudflats, grassy islands and ever-changing patterns of water meeting land, Limantour Spit is a hike that bears repeating.

DIRECTIONS TO TRAILHEAD From Olema, drive north on Highway 1 for 0.1 mile and turn left on Bear Valley Road. Drive 1.8 miles and turn left on Limantour Road. Continue to road's end at a parking area.

THE HIKE From the parking lot, follow the paved trail toward Limantour Beach. Fork right on the dirt path leading up the spit.

The trail serves up equal measures of Pacific and estero views as it skirts Estero de Limantour. After about a mile, the path peters out, and you wander over to the beach.

The second mile is a wonderfully wild excursion—particularly after a winter storm, when there's apt to be all manner of flotsam and jetsam cast upon the beach. From spit's end you'll witness a meeting of Estero de Limantour and Drakes Estero.

■ CHIMNEY ROCK
Chimney Rock Trail
To Chimney Rock Overlook is 2.8 miles round trip

So compelling is Point Reyes Lighthouse, most visitors don't bother with the walk to Chimney Rock Overlook, which offers a panoramic view nearly equal to that of the lighthouse. You'll travel a spring wildflower-lined path, glimpsing an old U.S. Coast Guard Lifeboat Station. While you might

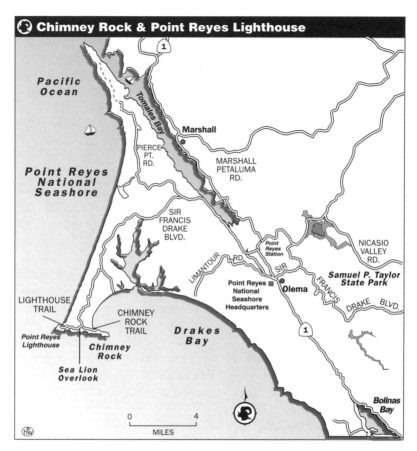

Chimney Rock & Point Reyes Lighthouse

not be able to discern which offshore rock resembles a chimney, you will be able to view the coastline all the way to San Francisco on a clear day.

In spring, expect lots of wildflowers, including lupine, poppies and Douglas iris. Experts have counted five dozen species.

From December to February, don't miss the short walk to Elephant Seal Overlook. The enormous, boisterous creatures re-colonized isolated Point Reyes beaches in the early 1980s. This is one of the best places to safely observe them.

A short walk leads to the Point Reyes Lifesaving Station, which was constructed in 1927 and continued in operation until 1968. Notwithstanding the mighty beacon of nearby Point Reyes Lighthouse, many shipwrecks occurred and there were many calls for the Coast Guard, whose brave men saved dozens of lives.

DIRECTIONS TO TRAILHEAD From Highway 101 in Olema, drive north a short distance, then turn left on Sir Francis Drake Highway and proceed 17.5 miles to the signed turn-off for Chimney Rock. Turn left and drive another mile to the parking area and signed trailhead.

THE HIKE   From the parking lot, follow the trail across the grassy cliffs. Savor a view of the sparkling white cliffs back of Drakes Beach. Detour over to an overlook of Point Reyes Peninsula and, on especially clear days, the Farallon Islands. Back on the main path, continue your wind-blown way to the clifftop vista point. Sea stacks and the surging surf are part of the dramatic seascape, though there is not a good viewing angle of Chimney Rock.

See Map
on Page
78

■ POINT REYES LIGHTHOUSE
Lighthouse Trail
To lighthouse is 1.2 miles round trip
with 400-foot elevation gain

Some lighthouses welcome sailors to port; some lighthouses warn them of danger. Point Reyes Lighthouse was most certainly built to warn vessels away from a treacherous coastline that was the death of many ships.

Congress voted construction funds for a light back in 1852 but legal tussles with coastal bluff landowners delayed installation until 1870. Meanwhile, many more ships ran aground.

From past experience, lighthouse keepers had learned that placing a light too high atop California's coastal cliffs diminished the light's fog-penetrating effectiveness; thus, the Point Reyes Lighthouse was built about halfway down the 600-foot bluffs.

Thanks for the light! By some accounts, Point Reyes is the foggiest point on the Pacific Coast.

The odd placement of the station greatly increased its construction costs, as well as the costs of supplying it during its century of service. Nasty weather, isolation from the world, and the relentless bellow of the foghorn made the lot of the lighthouse keeper a difficult one and contributed to drinking and discipline problems. Some keepers went outright bonkers.

By some accounts, Point Reyes is the foggiest point on the Pacific Coast, and supposedly second only to Rhode Island's Nantucket Island in the entire U.S. When the foggy curtain lifts, however, the lighthouse observation platform is a superb place from which to watch for migrating California gray whales. During the winter months, bring your binoculars and scan the horizon for the passing gentle giants.

The lighthouse Visitor Center is open Thursday through Monday, 10 a.m. to 4:30 p.m., weather permitting. Inquire at the center about tours of the facility.

DIRECTIONS TO TRAILHEAD   From Highway 1 in Olema, drive north a short distance, then turn left on Sir Francis Drake Highway and drive 18.5 miles to road's end at the parking lot for Point Reyes Lighthouse.

THE HIKE   A path and 308 stairs (like walking up and down the staircase of a 30-story building) comprise the route to the lighthouse.

■ DRAKES BEACH
Drakes Beach Trail
2 to 3 miles round trip

Historical controversy as thick as the summer fog envelops Drakes Bay. Is this really the place where English explorer Sir Francis Drake landed his *Golden Hinde* in 1579? Or did he come ashore at another location in San Francisco Bay? Bodega Bay? Tomales Bay? Coos Bay? Santa Barbara?

Drakeologists, academic and amateur, have created a virtual cottage industry over the years in their debates about who landed where and why. Certainly the tall white cliffs back of Drakes Beach match the description recorded in Drake's journal and are convincing evidence advanced by the pro-Drakes Bay majority.

Whether you're a Drakes Bay believer or not (or even if you couldn't give a whit about something five centuries removed from the present), you'll enjoy a saunter along the bay. South-facing Drakes Beach is more sheltered from the wind than the national seashore's west-facing beaches and is fringed by a bay instead of the open ocean; this adds up to an altogether calmer walking experience. Drakes Beach is accessible for 2 miles or so to the west; most of its eastern stretch is accessible only at low tide.

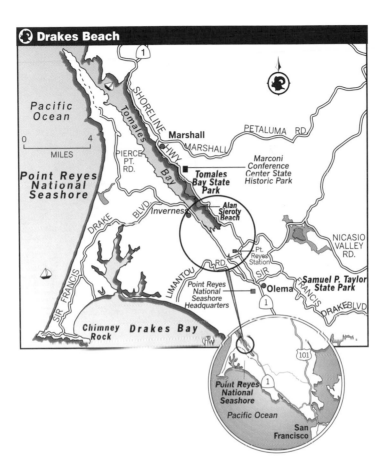

For an excellent overview of the great Drake debate, check out the excellent interpretive exhibits at the Ken C. Patrick Visitor Center, housed in a handsome redwood building with a beach-facing deck. The Park Service does an excellent job of discussing Drake's voyage in its many cultural and political manifestations.

Observe a moment of silence for Visitor Center namesake Ranger Patrick, the first National Park Service ranger shot and killed in the field. Deer poachers shot him on Mt. Vision; the chief culprit was sentenced to life in prison, his cohorts given lesser sentences.

Drakes Beach Café is a park concession and the only food service within the national seashore boundary, so the hungry hiker might fear the worst. However, visitors from both the Bay Area and far away, praise the quality of food served at the café. Get a great overview of Drakes Bay from the Peter Behr Overlook, located 0.25 mile by paved path south of the Visitor Center.

Take a walk along Drakes Beach, possibly the landing point of Sir Francis Drake.

DIRECTIONS TO TRAILHEAD From the hamlet of Olema, head 0.1 mile north on Highway 1 to Bear Valley Road. Turn left and proceed 2.25 miles to Sir Francis Drake Highway. Turn left and drive 13.5 miles to the signed turn-off for Drakes Beach. Turn left and go 1.5 miles to road's end and the large parking area near the Visitor Center.

THE HIKE You can wander east past a little lagoon and continue (best at low tide) toward Drakes Estero. The way southwest is an enjoyable saunter of 2 miles or so.

■ DRAKES ESTERO
Estero Trail
From Estero Trailhead to Drakes Estero
is 8 miles round trip with 500-foot elevation gain

This coast walk will keep you glued to your field glasses. No, the route isn't difficult to follow; you'll want the field glasses to help you observe the abundant wildlife around Drakes Estero. The many fingers of Drakes Estero, Marin County's largest lagoon, is patrolled by canvasbacks, ruddy ducks and American wigeons. Great blue herons, willets, godwits and many, many more shorebirds feed along the mudflats. You might see deer, either the native black-tailed or the "imported" white fallow browsing the grassy ridges. Harbor seals and sea lions often swim into the estero.

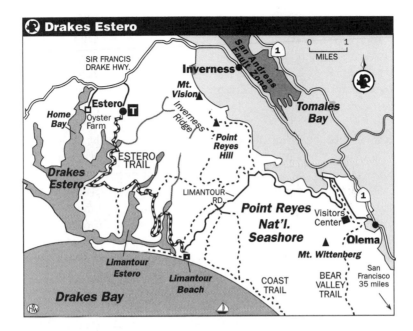

Drakes Estero

SIR FRANCIS DRAKE HWY.

Inverness

Mt. Vision

Estero
T
Home Bay
Oyster Farm

Inverness Ridge

Point Reyes Hill

San Andreas Fault Zone

1

0   1
MILES

Tomales Bay

ESTERO TRAIL

Drakes Estero

LIMANTOUR RD.

Point Reyes Nat'l. Seashore

Visitors Center

1

Olema

Mt. Wittenberg

Limantour Estero

Limantour Beach

COAST TRAIL

BEAR VALLEY TRAIL

San Francisco 35 miles

Drakes Bay

You won't need binoculars to sight the most common animal found in these parts—cows. Both Herefords and Black Angus graze the headlands. This is cow country, and has been since the 1850s. Schooners maneuvered into Drakes Estero, took on a cargo of fine butter, and returned to San Francisco, a ready market for dairy products produced on Point Reyes.

The estero you'll visit, as well as the beach and bay you'll overlook, are named for that pirate/explorer in the service of Queen Elizabeth I, Sir Francis Drake.

While walking along the estero, debate that age-old question: Did Sir Francis in June of 1579 sail his *Golden Hinde* into Drakes Bay or into San Francisco Bay? Is he really the discoverer of San Francisco Bay or does that honor fall to other sailors, more than two hundred years earlier?

The bay where Drake set anchor had chalky cliffs, and reminded the Englishman of the cliffs of Dover. Drake's description of this bay points to Drakes Bay. To mark his discovery, Drake left a brass plate nailed to a post. This plate was supposedly found in 1936 and was originally considered genuine. Metallurgical tests later called in question its authenticity, and in 2003 the plate was confirmed to be a hoax, part of an elaborate and playful scheme dreamed up by local historians.

Old ranch roads form a nice trail system on the west side of Inverness Ridge. Estero Trail is the most dramatic of these pathways, and offers fine vistas and superb wildlife watching opportunities.

DIRECTIONS TO TRAILHEAD　From Highway 1 in Olema (where there's a well-marked turn-off for the Point Reyes National Seashore Bear Valley Visitor Center), proceed 2 miles north and veer left onto Sir Francis Drake Highway. The highway follows the west side of Tomales Bay, passes through the town of Inverness, then heads left (west). You'll pass a junction on your left with a road leading toward Mt. Vision. Keep looking left and you'll see the signed road leading to Estero parking area. Follow this narrow road to the signed trailhead.

THE HIKE Estero Trail, an old ranch road, climbs gently. As you climb look over your left shoulder and admire Inverness Ridge, highlighted by, from west to east, Mt. Vision, Point Reyes Hill, and Mt. Wittenberg.

The trail turns to the left and passes a stand of pine, once the nucleus of a Christmas tree farm. Soon the path crosses a causeway, which divides Home Bay from a pond. Birdwatchers will sight large numbers of shorebirds in the mudflats of Home Bay.

The trail rises above the estero, descends to another pond, and ascends again. About 2.5 miles from the trailhead, you come to a signed junction. Sunset Beach Trail continues well above the estero, and ends at a couple of small ponds, backed by Drakes Bay and the wide Pacific.

Estero Trail swings east and after 0.5 mile comes to a junction. You can head south on Drakes Head Trail down to Limantour Estero, or you can follow Estero Trail all the way to Limantour Beach.

■ ABBOTTS LAGOON
Abbotts Lagoon Trail
From Abbotts Lagoon to Point Reyes Beach
is 3.2 miles round trip

Something about Abbotts Lagoon personifies the word melancholy. Maybe it's the lagoon itself, a large, moor-like environment that compares to some of those I've visited by trail in Scotland. Then there are lonely, wind-swept grasslands and the (perpetual, it seems) gray skies. It's the kind of place you photograph in black and white.

While a bit on the somber side, the lagoon and lands beyond are by no means dreary and depressing; in fact, the landscape encourages reflection—an inward journey to accompany a fine outer one.

On a weekday excursion, your thoughts may very well be your only companion on this rather lightly visited trail. A low ridge hides Abbotts Lagoon from the sight of passing motorists on Pierce Point Road; this positioning seems to discourage drop-in visitation of the kind that occurs elsewhere along the coast of the national seashore.

Gray-hued the lagoon may be, but it's anything but lifeless. Lots and lots of birds, both migratory and year-around residents, congregate in an upper fresh-

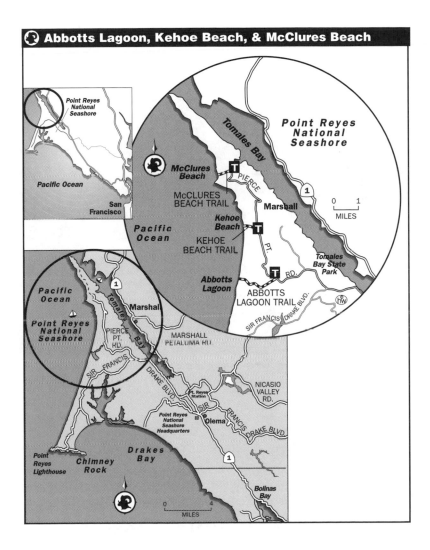

Abbotts Lagoon, Kehoe Beach, & McClures Beach

water lagoon and a more brackish lower lagoon. Look for the western grebe and its pint-sized cousin, the pie-billed grebe, as well as lots of coots and terns.

DIRECTIONS TO TRAILHEAD From the hamlet of Olema, head north just 0.1 mile on Highway 1, then turn left on Bear Valley Road. Proceed 2.25 miles and fork left on Sir Francis Drake Highway. Drive 5.5 miles to Pierce Point Road, fork right and continue another 3.2 miles to the signed Abbotts Lagoon Trail and gravel parking lot on the left (west) side of the road.

THE HIKE The wide, level trail heads across open fields. A bench encourages quiet contemplation of the lagoon. A mile's walk leads to a footbridge that bisects the upper and lower lagoons or as more lyrical naturalists refer to it—the

Bring your own romance to this lonely, wind-swept beach; you'll likely enjoy a private sojourn at this lightly visited lagoon.

wings of the lagoon. Soon you'll reach low sand dunes and walk across them to the ocean shores of Point Reyes Beach. Seals and sea lions have been known to snooze on this beach.

Walk to your heart's content for miles, up-coast or down.

See Map on Page 85

■ KEHOE BEACH
Kehoe Beach Trail
1 mile or more round trip

Capping the far north end of Point Reyes Beach, remote Kehoe Beach is well worth the short walk. The beach is backed by bluffs, bedecked in spring by wild hollyhock, phacelia, baby blue-eyes and California poppies.

DIRECTIONS TO TRAILHEAD From Olema, head north just 0.1 mile on Highway 1, then turn left on Bear Valley Road. Proceed 2.25 miles and fork left on Sir Francis Drake Highway. Drive 5.5 miles to Pierce Point Road, fork right and continue another 5.5 miles to roadside pullouts for the Kehoe Beach Trailhead, located on the left (west) side of the road.

A short walk to a wild beach where birds migrate and seals congregate.

THE HIKE The path to the beach skirts Kehoe Marsh, a freshwater habitat attractive to birds, both resident and migratory. The mellow path crosses the wetland, passes a tiny lagoon, crosses the dunes and descends to the beach. Harbor seals have been known to haul out on Kehoe Beach, which is walkable for a short mile north and several miles south.

■ MCCLURES BEACH
McClures Beach Trail
To McClures Beach is 1 mile round trip

Way out on the northwestern shore of Point Reyes lies a beach that's positively theatrical: great granite cliffs, enormous rocks, huge waves. Exposed to the full fury of the Pacific, McClures Beach resounds with waves like rolling thunder that strike the rocks and sea stacks at land's end and toss great plumes of spray skyward.

Margaret McClure, whose family owned a dairy, was once of the first property owners to permit public access to a Point Reyes-area beach. She donated the beach and a portion of the nearby bluffs to the public for parkland back in the 1940s.

DIRECTIONS TO TRAILHEAD From the hamlet of Olema, head north on Highway 1 for just 0.1 mile before turning left on Sir Francis Drake Highway and proceeding 5.5 miles north and west to a junction with Pierce Point Road. Turn right (north) and continue 9 miles to signed parking for McClures Beach on the west side of the road.

THE HIKE From the parking area, join the sandy, creekside trail for the brief descent to the beach. Look offshore for the unusual sea scooter, a small, black sea duck with a bright orange and white bill that surfs the waves. Pelicans, cormorants and murres are among the many seabirds that perch on the rocks near shore.

The most intriguing part of the 0.8-mile-long beach is at the south end. Head toward the sea stacks, sculpted from McClures' cliffs by the relentless surf. At low tide, you can squeeze through a narrow rock passageway and emerge at a dramatic little pocket beach.

■ TOMALES POINT
Tomales Point Trail
From Upper Pierce Ranch to Lower Pierce Ranch is 6 miles round trip with 300-foot elevation gain; to Tomales Point is 8 miles round trip with 400-foot gain

When the fog settles over the dew-dampened grasslands of Tomales Point, walkers can easily imagine that they're stepping onto a Scottish moor, or wandering one of the Shetland Islands.

The point's rich pasture caught the eye of Solomon Pierce, who began a dairy in 1858. Pierce and his son Abram produced fine butter, which was shipped to San Francisco from a wharf they built on Tomales Bay. For seven decades, the point remained in the Pierce family.

The walk begins at Upper Pierce Ranch, where the family house, barn and outbuildings are now maintained by the Park Service. The path, an old ranch road, wanders over the green hills, which are seasonally sprinkled with yellow

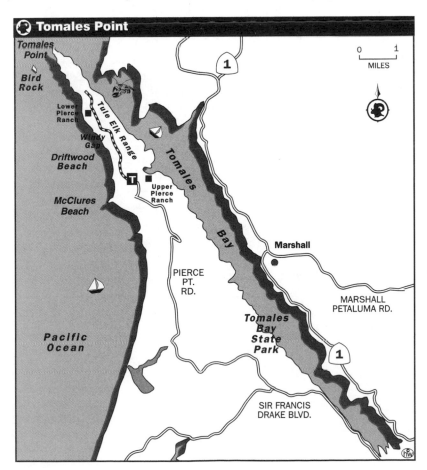

poppies and tidy tips, orange fid-
dleneck, and purple iris. A small
pond and an eucalyptus grove
mark the site of Lower Pierce
Ranch.

Be on the lookout for the tule
elk herd that wanders the bluffs.
A large elk population once
roamed the Point Reyes area, but
by the 1860s, hunters had eliminated the animals. In 1977, the
National Park Service relocated
some elk onto Tomales Point
from the Owens Valley.

Dramatic views of the Point
Reyes area are seen from Tomales

Tule elk: Local residents enjoy the scenery.

Point, the northernmost boundary of Marin County and Point Reyes National
Seashore.

DIRECTIONS TO TRAILHEAD Drive north on Sir Francis Drake Boulevard
past the town of Inverness. Shortly after Sir Francis turns west, bear right
(north) on Pierce Point Road, and follow this road 9 miles to its end at Upper
Pierce Point Ranch. Tomales Point Trail shares a trailhead with the 0.5-mile-
long path leading to McClures Beach.

THE HIKE From the old dairy buildings at Upper Pierce Ranch, the trail
climbs north across the coastal prairie. Views of the beach and surf are superb.
The wide path climbs and descends at a moderate rate.

As you crest the ridge and meander over to its eastern side, you'll begin to
get a view of Tomales Bay, as well as Hog Island and the village of Dillon Beach.
The old ranch road descends to the site of Lower Pierce Ranch, and you'll pass
a pond and a eucalyptus grove.

Soon the road becomes a trail, and a mile past the ranch, arrives at a high
vista point that looks down on Bird Rock, The rock is occupied by cormorants
and by white pelicans.

A faint path, and some cross-country travel, will take you to the very top of
Tomales Point, for stirring views of Bodega Head and Tomales Bay.

6

MUIR WOODS
NATIONAL MONUMENT

John Muir

"This is the best tree-lover's monument that could possibly be found in all the forests of the world," wrote John Muir upon learning a redwood preserve was dedicated in his name. "You have done me great honor and I am proud of it."

Most of the million-plus visitors a year who walk in the woods would agree with the great naturalist. Without a doubt, the national monument is a must-see for visitors from around the state and around the world.

Muir Woods, administered by the Golden Gate National Recreation Area, definitely draws an international crowd. While walking the trails, expect to hear a half-dozen languages praising the tall trees—though something about these cathedrals of redwoods quiets even the most effusive visitor.

The great naturalist John Muir may have provided the inspiration for setting aside these redwoods, but it was Congressman William Kent who provided the necessary funds and political juice. In 1905 Kent purchased 300 acres of virgin redwoods, just in time to save them from the loggers' axes. He then persuaded President Theodore Roosevelt to declare the grove a national monument and name it for Muir. In later years, Kent donated more acreage, improved roads and brought a branch line of the Mt. Tamalpais Railroad to the woods.

Shortly after President Franklin Roosevelt died in 1945, representatives of the fledgling United Nations (then headquartered in San Francisco) met in this solemn grove of redwoods to honor America's thirty-first President.

Tips to beat the crowds: Arrive early (before 9 a.m.) or late (after 4 p.m.). Visit on weekdays rather than weekends. As in other popular parks, a mile's walk leaves most other visitors behind.

Six miles of trail cross the park. The main, nearly flat trail along Redwood Creek is paved. Several bridges over Redwood Creek enable the casual walker to make several loops. Muir Woods is linked by trail to Mt. Tamalpais State Park above, and Highway 1, Stinson Beach and Muir Beach below.

■ MUIR WOODS
Main, Bootjack, Ben Johnson Trails
2-mile and 6-mile loops

A nature trail with numbered stops keyed to the park map begins at Bridge Two, visits Cathedral Grove, crosses Redwood Creek at Bridge Three, and then returns via Bohemian Grove. A pleasant extension continues along Redwood Creek before looping back to the heart of Muir Grove.

DIRECTIONS TO TRAILHEAD   Muir Woods is 12 miles from the Golden Gate Bridge. From Highway 101 northbound in Mill Valley, take the Highway 1/Stinson Beach exit. After exiting, stay in the right lane as you go under Highway 101. You are now on Shoreline Highway (Highway 1). Head west 2.7 miles to Panoramic Highway, turn right and drive .8 mile to Muir Woods Road. Turn left and proceed 1.6 miles to the main parking area for Muir Woods on your right. If the main parking lot is full, there is another one about 100 yards southeast.

THE HIKE   From the parking area, walk north to the information kiosk and Visitor Center. Pay the small entrance fee. Cross the bridge to the west side of Redwood Creek.

Visitors from across the nation and around the world stroll through the redwoods that honor America's foremost naturalist.

In winter, reflect that your journey up-creek appears to be much easier than that of the steelhead and salmon struggling upstream to spawn.

Your northbound trail soon brings you to Bohemian Grove, where California's premiere men's club retreated in the 1890s. The Bohemians considered building a rough-it-deluxe camp here but opted for the more temperate environs along the Russian River.

Now you embark on the monument's nature trail, keyed to an interpretive pamphlet. Stay with the nature trail to its end, then cross Redwood Creek on a footbridge to the east side of Redwood Creek and Cathedral Grove.

Head north 0.25 mile to reach the William Kent Memorial Tree, which, to most visitors' surprise, is

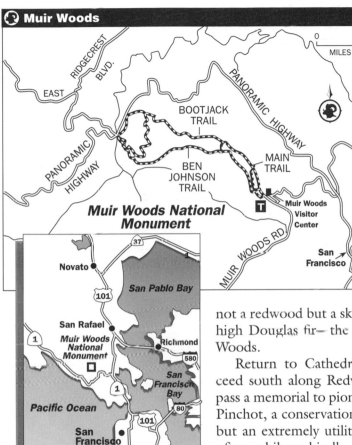

not a redwood but a sky-scraping 273-foot high Douglas fir— the tallest tree in Muir Woods.

Return to Cathedral Grove and proceed south along Redwood Creek. You'll pass a memorial to pioneer forester Gifford Pinchot, a conservationist in his own right but an extremely utilitarian one, who was often philosophically at odds with the visionary John Muir.

For a longer loop, follow Muir Woods' Main Trail, which becomes Bootjack Trail and continue along Redwood Creek through the forest to Van Wyck Meadow. Here you'll join the historic World War I-era TCC (Tamalpais Conservation Club) Trail heading south, then briefly west to Sapleveldt Trail. Switchback down to Ben Johnson Trail, which leads back to the heart of Muir Woods. Main Trail or Hillside Trail returns you to the Visitor Center.

■ OCEAN VIEW
Ocean View, Lost, Fern Creek Trails
3-mile loop

Ocean View Trail, formerly Panoramic Trail, does, in fact, offer ocean views and panoramic vistas, but you have to work for them. This fairly steep pathway leaves the Muir Woods crowds behind as it climbs to Panoramic Highway.

A Park Service sign warns that Ocean View Trail is steep and does not loop. Steep it is, but it does loop when linked with Lost Trail and Fern Creek Trail.

Lost Trail was so-named because it was buried by a landslide back in the 1930s. A Young Adult Conservation Corps crew uncovered and rehabilitated the path in 1976.

This trio of trails is a winning combination. They connect to other trails in the national monument and to Mount Tam's many trails.

DIRECTIONS TO TRAILHEAD Muir Woods is 12 miles from the Golden Gate Bridge. From Highway 101 northbound in Mill Valley, take the Highway 1/Stinson Beach exit. After exiting, stay in the right lane as you go under Highway 101. You are now on Shoreline Highway (Highway 1). Head west 2.7 miles to Panoramic Highway, turn right and drive .8 mile to Muir Woods Road. Turn left and proceed 1.6 miles to the main parking area for Muir Woods on your right. If the main parking lot is full, there is another one about 100 yards southeast.

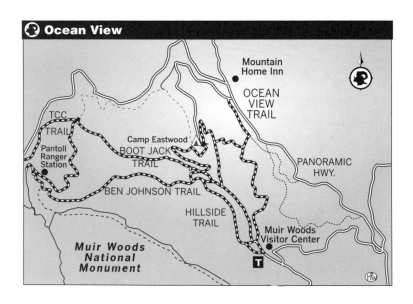

THE HIKE Walk past the information and Visitor Center on the paved trail along Redwood Creek. Look right for signed Ocean View Trail and begin your ascent among redwoods on the east side of the creek canyon. After a 1.3-mile climb, you'll reach the signed junction with Lost Trail.

Ocean View Trail continues another 0.25 mile to a junction with Redwood Trail. Bear left here and follow the trail (or Panoramic Highway, which it parallels) to Mountain Home Inn, where you can buy a cool one and savor the view from the establishment's redwood deck.

After your refreshment, retrace you steps on Redwood Trail back to Ocean View Trail. For a change of scenery on the return, head west on Lost Trail and descend 0.4 mile through Douglas fir and redwoods to Fern Creek Trail. Turn left and return to the "main" paved pathway that travels among the redwoods through the heart of Muir Woods National Monument back to the Visitor Center and parking areas.

GGNRA coastal trails offer hikers an urban-rural-wilderness collage.

CHAPTER SEVEN

GOLDEN GATE NATIONAL RECREATION AREA

Some of San Francisco's best walks are coast walks, which explore the northern and western edges of San Francisco's shoreline. A good part of this shoreline—28 miles worth in San Francisco and in Marin County—is under the jurisdiction of Golden Gate National Recreation Area.

An intrepid walker could explore much of the urban shoreline in one long day. One could begin at Fort Funston, walk along Ocean Beach, visit Cliff House, Lands End, Baker Beach, and Fort Point and the Golden Gate. The tireless walker could then continue along the city's north shore, heading bayside past Crissy Field, and then along Golden Gate Promenade to park headquarters and Fort Mason.

Surprisingly, such a lengthy shoreline walk would explore only one part of the 76,000-acre Golden Gate National Recreation Area, by some accounts the world's largest national park in an urban area. In addition to its San Francisco shoreline, the park also includes the Marin Headlands north of the Golden Gate Bridge and the San Francisco Bay Discovery Site atop Sweeney Ridge, south of the city in San Mateo County.

The Presidio, recently transferred to the National Park Service from the U.S. Army, is being converted from an Army base into a unique area combining educational and cultural facilities with nature trails and beaches. America's most infamous prison site, Alcatraz Island, is also part of Golden Gate National Recreation Area.

The land now comprising GGNRA had long been under government ownership. American military occupation dating from the 1840s restricted development. As the Army's properties became obsolete for modern defense, they were transferred to the National Park Service.

The old slogan, "Parks are for people," definitely applies to GGNRA. More than 20 million visitors a year are believed to set foot in the area. Many of these visitors have a grand time without realizing they did so on national park land.

A lunch at Cliff House, a walk along Lovers' Lane through the Presidio, a theater performance at Fort Mason—these are just a few of the many pleasures available within the boundaries of the park.

While San Francisco's shore is every bit a part of one of America's most beloved cities it also offers a feeling of remoteness as well. Preserving the waterfront as public domain during the Real Estate Go-Go years of the 1970s and 1980s, provided San Francisco with a terrific greenbelt sprinkled with historical and cultural attractions.

Walking GGNRA offers an urban-rural-wilderness collage; natural history and social history are often part of the same walk. From the forested ridges, take in San Francisco's skyline; from the city, look toward the bold Marin Headlands.

Walkers with an eye for architecture will admire steep-pitched Victorians in the Presidio, and out in Olema Valley. The elaborate brick masonry of Civil War-era Fort Point, the Sutro Bath ruins, and many more buildings offer an insight into San Francico's rich history.

The famed Golden Gate Bridge, namesake and centerpiece for the National Recreation Area, can be admired from below at Fort Point and from above on the ridgetops of the Marin Headlands.

You can walk through 200 years of military history, from the days of Spanish/Mexican occupation to 19th-century gun emplacements to 1960s Nike missile sites. Walk along Baker Beach past concrete bunkers built during World War II to defend the Golden Gate Bridge from attack.

Coastal Trail travels through Golden Gate National Recreation Area, Mount Tamalpais State Park and Point Reyes National Seashore. The path (sometimes called part of Coast Trail, Pacific Coast Trail or California Coastal Trail) offers fine hiking to remote backcountry camps.

You can begin your walk in the city, cross the Golden Gate Bridge and head for Marin Headlands Hostel or one of several hike-in camps. From the Marin Headlands, the Coastal Trail more or less follows the shore northwest, from Rodeo Beach to Tennessee Valley to Muir Beach. The path continues to Mt. Tamalpais State Park and through Point Reyes National Seashore.

You could hike two, three, four days or more on Coastal Trail. And if you're creative with a bus map you can even figure out how to arrange transit back to San Francisco.

■ PHLEGER ESTATE
Crystal Spring, Richards Road, Miramonte Trails
From Huddart County Park to Phleger Estate is 4.2 miles round trip with 200-foot elevation gain; loop via Raymundo and Mt. Redondo Trails is 6.6 miles round trip with 600-foot elevation gain

Woodsy Woodside, one of the Bay Area's priciest and most rustic residential areas, has a park that seems very much in keeping with its neighborhood. You half expect a gated entry or valet parking for the Phleger Estate.

Prominent San Francisco attorney Herman Phleger owned this land of steep canyons and second-growth redwoods at a time when property located 40 miles south of San Francisco was quite rural and removed from city life. Phleger managed to commute by auto over poor roads to offices in the city during the 1930s.

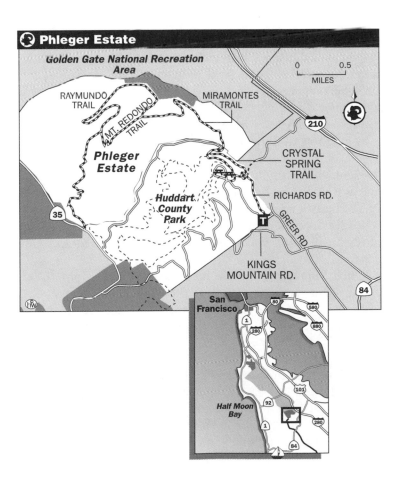

Interstate 280 makes the commute from Woodside lots easier these days—at least when traffic is light. But Woodside and the remote Phleger Estate retain an air of tranquility.

We can be thankful that Phleger's heirs sold the 1,227-acre parcel for considerably under market value and it became the southernmost unit of the Golden Gate National Recreation Area in 1995.

Don't look for highway signs directing you to the Phleger Estate or to trailhead parking. The only convenient hiking access to the national parkland is by way of adjacent Huddart County Park.

While the Phleger Estate is an island on the land, accessible only to hikers, Huddart County Park is not exactly a well-kept secret, and boasts lots of popular picnic areas.

There is much to discover in this northeastern pocket of the Santa Cruz Mountains. Deep and steep ravines, frequently wrapped in fog, support dense stands of redwood. Higher and drier slopes are cloaked in oaks. The estate's main trail traces West Union Creek, which just happens to lie directly on the San Andreas Fault.

DIRECTIONS TO TRAILHEAD From Highway 280 in Woodside, take the Highway 84 (Woodside Road) exit and head west through Woodside for 1.7 miles to Kings Mountain Road. Turn right and travel 1.5 miles to Huddart County Park (small entry fee per vehicle). Leave your car in the first parking lot, just past the entrance station.

You'll locate the trailhead, signed with seven destinations no less, above the parking lot by a couple of information boards.

THE HIKE The wide path, lined by a split-rail fence, winds through redwood and madrone as it skirts the Zwierlein Picnic Area. In 0.2 mile you'll join Crystal Spring Trail, sticking with this well-signed path as it passes several trail junctions, then junctions Richards Road. Bear left and a short 0.1 mile ascent up the dirt road will bring you to signed Miramonte Trail and entry to the Phleger Estate.

Join fern-lined Miramonte Trail as it travels alongside Union Creek. Watch for the abundant deer gamboling through the woods and a multitude of banana slugs slithering across the path. An impressive sign, topped by an iron Native Amercan figure astride a horse, marks the 1995 dedication site of the Phleger Estate, and plaques list the many notables who contributed to the preservation of this parkland.

The path continues along bubbling Union Creek before abruptly and briefly turning south and ascending above the creek. Soon the trail changes direction again and heads west to a T-intersection with Mt. Redondo and Raymundo trails. Turn right on Raymundo Trail and begin your counter-clockwise tour of the mountain. You'll saunter along Union Creek for a bit, then climb above it to another junction marked with a sign and an iron Native American figure.

Unless you're training for a trek to Nepal, ignore Lonely Trail, which ascends 1,000 feet in elevation to Skyline Boulevard. Instead, bid adieu to Raymundo Trail as it gives way to Mt. Redondo Trail and join this pleasant path as it dips to a trickling creek, crosses it, and descends back to the junction with Miramonte Trail. From this junction, retrace your steps back to the trailhead.

■ SWEENEY RIDGE
Sweeney Ridge Trail
From Skyline College Trailhead to Discovery Site is 4 miles round trip with 600-foot elevation gain

Unlike most California coastal locales, San Francisco Bay was discovered by walkers, not sailors. The bay's infamous fog, and its narrow opening had concealed it from passing ships for two centuries when Captain Gaspar de Portolá sighted it on November 4, 1769.

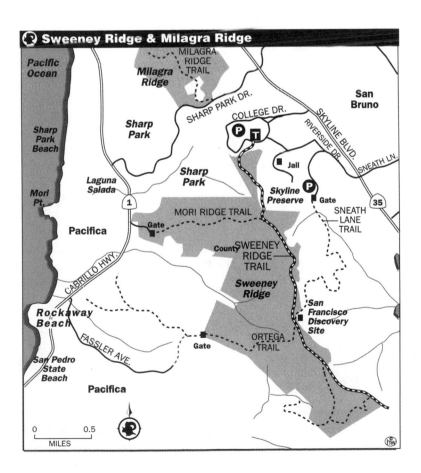

The actual discovery site is atop Sweeney Ridge above the town of Pacifica. Portolá was, at first, miffed by his discovery because he realized that his expedition had overshot its intended destination of Monterey Bay. He soon realized, however, that he had discovered one of the world's great natural harbors, and he figured it would be an ideal place for his government to build another presidio. Portolá's discovery aided Captain Ayala, who was then able to sail his San Carlos into the bay.

It was quite a conservation battle to save Sweeney Ridge. The late Congressman Phillip Burton, aided by many Bay Area conservationists, succeeded in placing a thousand acres of the ridgetop under protection of the Golden Gate National Recreation Area.

The ridge is often cloaked in morning fog, and in the afternoon, the wind really kicks up. When it's foggy, the coastal scrub and grasslands are bathed in a strange, sharp light. Sweeney Ridge is particularly attractive in spring, when lupine, poppies, cream cups, and goldfields color the slopes.

And the view is magnificent: Mt. Tamalpais and Mt. Diablo, the Golden Gate and the Farallon Islands, plus dozens of communities clustered around the bay.

Sweeney Ridge is the name of the trail you'll use while walking the ridge itself. Four trails lead to Sweeney Ridge: Baquiano Trail and Mori Ridge Trail lead eastward to Portolá's discovery site, while Sneath Lane Trail and Sweeney Ridge Trail climb southward to the ridgetop.

I prefer the two southward approaches; they offer more of a feeling of surprise when you climb Sweeney Ridge and behold San Francisco Bay.

DIRECTIONS TO TRAILHEAD To start this hike at Skyline College, take Highway 35 to San Bruno. Turn west on College Drive, following it to the south side of campus. Look for parking area #2.

To begin this jaunt at Sneath Lane, take Highway 280 or 35 to the Sneath Lane exit in San Bruno. Follow the lane westbound to its end at a small parking area. Paved Sneath Lane (closed to vehicle traffic) climbs Sweeney Ridge.

THE HIKE From Skyline College, you'll join a fire road that rounds a coastal-scrub-dotted hill and in 0.75 mile reach the foundations of an old Nike missile site. The trail drops steeply into a ravine, then begins an equally steep climb out of it.

At the one-mile mark, Sweeney Ridge Trail is joined by Mori Ridge Trail coming in from the right. You'll keep to the left with a wide fire road, which travels 0.5 mile to an old radar station that was linked with the Nike missile site. From here, the now paved fire road leads a mellow 0.5 mile to the San Francisco Bay Discovery Site.

Return the same way or descend via paved Sneath Lane Trail. If you choose the Sneath Lane route, you'll need to continue another 0.25 mile beyond the trailhead on Sneath Lane, then make a left on Riverside Drive. After another

0.25 mile, make a right on the road near the parking area for the county jail, and soon reach parking lot #2 at the Skyline College trailhead.

■ MILAGRA RIDGE
Milagra Ridge Trail
From College Avenue to summit is 2 miles round trip.

In a word, this hike is a breeze. Strong winds whisk over Milagra Ridge, buffeting hikers and delighting two other kinds of visitors—kite fliers and remote-control glider operators.

The northwest-southeast trending ridge angles steeply downward toward Pacifica and the Pacific Ocean. On clear days (savor them in this often-foggy locale), ocean views are fantastic.

Milagra was once an even more prominent ridge, but its summit was flattened in the 1950s by the military in order to install a Nike missile site. Milagra's missiles were controlled from a facility on Sweeney Ridge.

Milagra Ridge is crucial habitat for the rare Mission Blue and San Bruno elfin butterflies. These two species survive only in the very particular environment on this ridge, on Sweeney Ridge, and on the slopes of San Bruno Mountain.

The National Park Service closely monitors recreational activity to aid survival of the butterflies. Hiking the Milagra Ridge, one puzzles how a light-as-air butterfly has adapted to an environment noted for such strong winds.

The National Park Service is also concerned about several endangered plants including the San Francisco wallflower and the coast rockcrest that cling to life on this coastal-terrace-prairie ecosystem. This concern for both butterflies and this special flora has led the agency and volunteers to close some habitat-disturbing trails on Milagra Ridge and to line others with cable and post fencing.

Please hike only on posted pathways and avoid habitat recovery areas.

DIRECTIONS TO TRAILHEAD From Interstate 280 in San Bruno, exit on Westborough Boulevard and head west. Continue past Skyline Boulevard (Highway 35) as Westborough becomes Sharp Park Road. At College Drive (a major entrance to Skyline College on the left) turn right and drive a very short distance to road's end and the Milagra Ridge trailhead. Very limited roadside parking is available.

THE HIKE A paved road (accessible to the disabled) heads right for the ridgetop. The road, part of Bay Area Ridge Trail, is one way to go; a dirt path leading up the ridge is another.

Milagra's open ridge offers a feeling of scale and expansiveness far greater than this park unit's size (just 232 acres) might suggest. The ridgetop is honeycombed with trails. You'll find the old Nike site at the northwest edge of the ridge. When the foggy curtain parts, enjoy the stunning coastal views.

■ THORNTON BEACH
Thornton Beach Trail
From Thornton Beach to Fort Funston is 3.5 miles round trip

Thornton Beach is the luckless locale where California's infamous San Andreas Fault leaves land and enters the Pacific. A quiver along this fault precipitated a 1957 quake that annihilated a length of Coast Highway.

Cliff collapse here was a problem for the entire 20th century. The tall bluffs along Thornton Beach and above Devils Slide to the south were the favored route of the proposed Ocean Shore Railroad, intended to link San Francisco and Santa Cruz in the early 1900s. Construction scars at the base of Devils Slide are still visible, reminders of this unstable land and of the never-completed railway.

The bluffs above Thornton Beach have taken a beating in more recent years—from winter storms of 1982, the earthquake of 1989, El Niño generat-

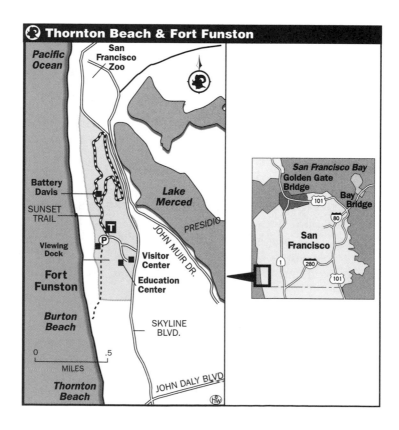

ed storms of 1998. Resultant landslide damage has been extensive, and parts of the bluffs are closed to hikers.

Thorton Beach is much more inviting than its resume of natural disasters might suggest. A sand strand invites beach walkers and an adjacent, wind-protected valley offers fine picnicking. A part of the Bay Area Ridge Trail linked Thornton Beach with Fort Funston in 1992.

You'll enjoy walking over a dune crest below Thornton's much-eroded bluffs. Over the years, earthquake-triggered landslides have exposed many fossilized bones and shell specimens, some dating from the Pliocene Epoch, more than a million years ago.

The beach was once owned by county supervisor Robert S. Thornton; eventually it came into public domain as Thornton State Beach. These days Thornton Beach is the southernmost shoreline of GGNRA.

DIRECTIONS TO TRAILHEAD The entrance to Thornton State Beach is at the intersection of Skyline Boulevard (Highway 35) and John Daly Boulevard in Daly City. Park alongside Skyline Boulevard and walk down to the beach. Those approaching via southbound Skyline Boulevard should turn right on signed Olympic Way before reaching the Skyline/John Daly intersection. Those approaching via northbound Skyline Boulevard should turn left on unsigned Olympic Way, the first left after the Skyline/John Daly intersection. Follow Olympic Way to its fenced dead-end at the entrance to Thornton Beach.

THE HIKE Join the unsigned narrow path (Bay Area Ridge Trail) or a wider one leading south over the bluffs. The two trails soon join and a single path descends toward the beach. When you reach a terrace above the beach, you have three choices: descend a steep narrow path to the beach, continue on Bay Area Ridge Trail along the crest of a long high dune between a ravine and the beach; walk south in the ravine.

Most enjoyable in this walker's opinion is the Bay Area Ridge Trail, which winds atop the dune crest past coyote bush, blackberry bush and beach lupine. The path meets up with the ravine trail at what remains of Thornton State Beach's amenities—two concrete picnic tables nestled among Monterey pine and cypress.

Continue south on the signed, sandy track and soon reach a para-glider launch site atop a dune. From here, the path drifts nearer the beach. Walk the strand—Phillip Burton Memorial Beach, named for the late conservationist Congressman whose efforts led to the creation of Golden Gate National Recreation Area—or continue with the dune trail to Fort Funston. Beach Access Trail leads up to Fort Funston.

See Map
on Page
104

■ FORT FUNSTON
Sunset Trail
To Battery Davis and return by the beach is a 2.5-mile loop

Bold, wind-swept headlands and soaring sand dunes characterize Fort Funston, an unusual stretch of shoreline that extends south from Ocean Beach. Sunset Trail, the California coast's first wheelchair-accessible pathway, explores this unique pocket of the Golden Gate National Recreation Area.

For the first half of the 20th century, the military outpost named for Frederick Funston guarded the Bay from potential assaults from air and sea. When Funston was founded in the early 1900s, it resembled a West Coast-style frontier fort.

Over the years, ever-more powerful armaments were added—most notably Battery Davis, a heavily reinforced gun emplacement built in 1938. The barrels alone of the battery's 16-inch guns tipped the scale at 146 tons apiece. Military experts, pleased with the construction, established Battery Davis as the model for all 16-inch gun emplacements built around the U.S.

During World War II, Fort Funston became a base for even heavier weaponry. A Nike missile site was constructed atop the bluffs.

With the military long departed, Fort Funston is now a lively destination for hikers, dog walkers, equestrians, bird watchers and naturalists. Former barracks house the Fort Funston environmental education center, which hosts armies of schoolchildren. Disturbed dunes have been revegetated with native plants.

The skies above the old fort are filled with friendly aircraft. Tall bluffs combined with dependable Pacific breezes make Fort Funston one of North America's more renowned hang-gliding spots. A wooden observation deck

Fort Funston's sand dunes and beach make for a fine outing.

perched on a hillside by the parking lot offers good views of the hang-gliders (though Park Service signs warn onlookers of the dangers of crashing "power-less flight vehicles"), as well as GGNRA's enticing shoreline. Fort Funston is also known locally as a haven for dogs, and sunny weekends may draw many more pooches than people to play on the beach.

Paved Sunset Trail visits Battery Davis. Hikers can add to this short walk by joining other Funston paths or by making a longer loop back to the trailhead via the beach. The beach route is best at low tide.

DIRECTIONS TO TRAILHEAD From San Francisco, head south on Great Highway, continuing as the highway becomes Skyline Boulevard at Lake Merced. About 0.4 mile south of John Muir Drive, turn west off Skyline into the Fort Funston parking lot.

THE HIKE Walk north on Sunset Trail, which leads over sand dunes and through coastal scrub flora to Battery Davis, located about 0.5 mile from the trailhead. Picnic tables and benches are conveniently situated en route.

Continue north until Sunset Trail's paved part ends and continue on the footpath as it skirts fenced-off bank-swallow habitat and bends oceanward above Skyline Boulevard. Join the footpath over the yellow lupine- and beach-strawberry-dotted dunes down to the beach.

Walk south, perhaps in the company of horseback riders, along the usually windy beach. A conglomeration of cement and pipe belonging to the local water treatment plant extruding from the bluffs is the only obstacle.

You'll spot an unsigned path leading directly toward the observation plat-form and a steep horse trail leading up the bluffs, both of which will get you back to the trailhead. However, it's better to continue down the beach a bit far-ther and join Beach Access Trail which heads inland toward the Visitor Center, then north to return you to the trailhead.

■ LANDS END
Coastal Trail
From Cliff House to Golden Gate Bridge is 6 miles round trip

San Francisco is known as a city of walkers. Whether this reputation is due to its relatively healthy, vigorous upscale population, or to the city's ter-rible traffic and scarcity of parking, is open for debate.

This walk, a scenic and historic journey from Cliff House to the Golden Gate, explores a part of San Francisco's diverse shoreline.

Today's Cliff House, perched above Ocean Beach, is the fourth structure erected on this site. In 1863, the first roadhouse was built; it catered to the wealthy, high-toned carriage crowd. Along came millionaire and philanthropist Adolph Sutro, who had moved to San Francisco after making his fortune as an

engineer during Nevada's silverstrike era. Sutro thought that the city's working-class residents would enjoy a seaside diversion of public pools. He built a steam railway from downtown to the coast; the ride to Cliff House cost a nickel.

After the original Cliff House, called Seal Rock House, burned down, Sutro replaced it with a six-story gingerbread-style Victorian mansion. This, too, burned to the ground in 1907. Sutro again rebuilt, this time constructing a rather utilitarian structure.

After many years of planning and two years of renovation, the latest incarnation of Cliff House re-opened in 2004. This new and greatly updated Cliff House boasts two bars, two restaurants and a terrace available for sunset wedding ceremonies and other private parties. Architectural elements from the 1909 design, as well as some inspiration from the old Sutro Baths, were incorporated into Cliff House IV.

Coastal hikers, and anyone else who takes inspiration from Lands End, will appreciate the expanded panoramic vistas from three publicly accessible observation decks. Seal Rocks, frequented by seals and noisy sea lions, the Marin Headlands and the wide blue Pacific are all part of the wonderful views.

Fishermen lined up for the catch of the day on Seal Rock, near the Cliff House.

DIRECTIONS TO TRAILHEAD From Highway 101 (Van Ness Boulevard) in the city, turn west on Geary Boulevard and follow it to its end. As the road turns south toward Ocean Beach, you'll see Cliff House on your right.

THE HIKE After you've enjoyed the many attractions of Cliff House, walk northeast a short distance to the Greco-Roman-like ruins of the Sutro Baths. Six saltwater swimming pools and a freshwater plunge were heated by a complex series of pipes and canals. Museums, galleries and restaurants were also part of the complex built by Adolph Sutro in 1890. The popularity of public spas gradually waned and, in 1966, fire destroyed all but the cement foundations of the baths.

Wander north over to the Merrie Way parking area and join Coastal Trail. For a time you'll be walking on the abandoned bed of the old Cliff House and Ferries Railroad. The trail winds through cypress and coastal sage, and hugs the cliffs below El Camino del Mar.

Coastal Trail leads along the Lincoln Park Bluffs. If it's low tide when you look down at the shoreline, you might be able to spot the wreckage of some of the ships that have been dashed to pieces on the rocks below. This rocky, precipitous stretch of coast is known as Lands End.

You'll get great views from the Eagle Point Lookout, then briefly join El Camino Del Mar through the wealthy Seacliff residential area. A quarter-mile of travel (keep bearing left) brings you to sandy China Beach, the site of an encampment for Chinese fishermen a century ago. The beach is also known as James Phelan Beach for the politician-philanthropist, who left part of his fortune to help California writers and artists.

Backtrack to Sea Cliff Avenue, following the westernmost lanes of this fancy residential area, and continue north a short half-mile to expansive Baker Beach. At the south end of the beach is the outlet of Lobos Creek.

In his autobiography, Ansel Adams recalled the many delightful days he spent as a child exploring Lobos Creek. These childhood adventures were the great nature photographer's first contact with the natural world.

At the north end of Baker Beach is Battery Chamberlain, a former coastal defense site, complete with a "disappearing" 95,000-pound cannon. Occasionally park interpreters demonstrate how the cannon could be cranked into its cement, tree-hidden bunker.

Follow the beach service road up through the cypress to Lincoln Boulevard. Coastal Trail is a bit sketchy as it follows the boulevard's guard rail for a half-mile of contouring along the cliffs. The trail meanders among cypress and passes more military installations—Batteries Crosby, Dynamite, and Marcus Miller. Beyond the last battery, Coastal Trail leads under the Golden Gate Bridge. Just after the trail passes under the bridge, you can follow a path to historic Fort Point.

■ PRESIDIO
Ecology Loop Trail
2 miles round trip

San Francisco's historic Presidio occupies some 1,500 acres of real estate in one of America's most desirable—and expensive—cities. After a century and a half of use as a military post, the U.S. Army transferred ownership of the Presidio to the National Park Service in 1994. Of the many Army bases across the U.S. shut down during the decade of such closures, the Presidio was the only military installation to become part of the park system.

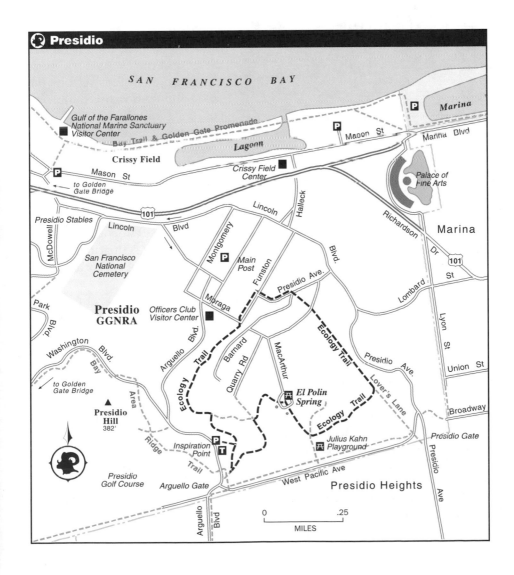

View of Alcatraz from the Presidio.

The Park Service manages the Presidio in partnership with the Presidio Trust, a federal government corporation. With the trust managing the interior and the majority of the buildings, and the Park Service responsible for the coastal areas, the agencies team to enhance natural areas, renovate and maintain buildings, upgrade the Presidio trail system, and offer visitor programs.

The Park Service and the Presidio Trust aim to rehabilitate the best of the Presidio's historic buildings, as well as restore the woodlands and native dune vegetation. The Presidio hosts an astonishing number (280) species of native plants. More than 200 species of birds have been sighted in this urban refuge, which offers habitat to a variety of mammals and reptiles.

A little more than a decade after its formation, the urban national park reached a milestone: it began to pay for itself. Some 2,500 residents rent housing ranging from converted barracks to renovated officers' quarters. A free shuttle system connects residents from the Presidio's 21 neighborhoods to nearby public transit.

The Presidio is now home to a significant number of quality profit-making and nonprofit enterprises. Filmmaker George Lucas' Letterman Digital Arts Center opened for business in 2005 on the site of the old army hospital. The Thoreau Center for Sustainability houses 50 community and environmental organizations.

Not everyone is altogether pleased by such developments, though most of the local citizenry and visitors seem to be taking the Presidio's extreme makeover in a stride. As buildings are restored so, too, are landscapes, including hiking trails, wildlife habitat and the unique urban forest.

One of the most spectacular transformations on the Presidio is the 100 acres of Crissy Field shoreline, consisting of a restored salt marsh, walking and biking paths, and native plants stretching from the foot of the Golden Gate Bridge to the Marina Green. Between 1998 and 2000 individuals and groups from schools, corporations and civic organizations planted more than 100,000 native plants in an area formerly occupied by military buildings and asphalt.

Several periods of architecture are represented in the Presidio, ranging from red brick barracks, circa 1895, built in the Georgian style, to a Spanish Revival-style theater. Some experts rate the Victorian-era officers' homes along Funston Ave. among the best examples of that period in San Francisco.

Environmentally conscious before his time Army Major W.A. Jones is credited with initiating a forestry program in the 1880s that transformed the forlorn, windswept sand dunes into the wooded preserve it is today. Thousands of trees, native and not, were planted under the direction of the Army Corps of engineers: Acacia, eucalyptus, Monterey pine, redwood, madrone and many more species. Some areas were planted in straight rows and now appear like companies of soldiers standing in formation.

Once landscaped, the Presidio proved to be one of the most highly desirable stateside locations for a soldier to be assigned to. Although the base was used mainly as a medical facility and administration center, during World War II its coastal batteries were activated in order to defend the Golden Gate Bridge against possible enemy attack.

Even before the Presidio became part of Golden Gate National Recreation Area, San Franciscans in the know enjoyed limited public access. Now the walker can wander at will over a 28-mile-long network of paved roads, sidewalks and footpaths.

The Visitor Center, located at the former Officers' Club (Building 50 at Moraga Avenue), is your source for Presidio information, including books, free maps and brochures. It's open daily from 9 a.m. to 5 p.m.

An excellent place to begin a walking tour is near Inspiration Point, at the southeastern corner of the Presidio, on the Ecology Trail. This loop trail explores architecture and military history and also offers a nice walk in the woods. If you have young ones in tow, pick up a copy of *Kids on Trails,* a free children's tour guide to activities along the Ecology Trail.

DIRECTIONS TO TRAILHEAD From the Presidio's Arguello Gate entrance, just north of Arguello Blvd. and Jackson St., drive a few hundred yards to the paved parking area on the right, at Inspiration Point. The trailhead is on the east side.

THE HIKE At the parking area walk down a set of wooden steps and turn left to join the Ecology Trail, a wide dirt trail (fire road). After passing Inspiration Point itself, you'll make a gradual descent through groves of Monterey pine and eucalyptus. The buildings of the Main Post lie ahead. The Presidio's oldest existing structures, dating back to 1861 and the Civil War, are found on the Main Post, as is the Visitor Center, located in the former Presidio Officers' Club.

Now the path is paved. Pass Pershing Hall—a bachelor officers' quarters, and continue along the sidewalk on Funston Ave. Officers' Quarters, a splendid row of Victorians that housed officers and their families, is another historic area on Funston Ave.

Turn right at Presidio Ave. and continue over a footbridge. Cross MacArthur and continue on to paved Lovers' Lane. The lane has been a favorite of romantic walkers ever since the 1860s, when it was used by off-duty soldiers to walk into town to meet their sweethearts.

A gradual uphill grade leads near the historic site of El Polin Springs, used by Spanish soldiers more than two hundred years ago. During the summer, archeology students conduct ongoing excavations of the site.

The slope above the springs is serpentine grasslands, and is home to many rare or threatened plants, including the endangered Presidio clarkia. More than two dozen varieties of trees can be seen along the trail. Continue up the trail to the base of Inspiration Point, and follow your route back to the parking lot.

■ ALCATRAZ ISLAND
Agave Trail
1 mile round trip

Once the island was populated with the likes of Al "Scarface" Capone, George "Machine Gun" Kelly and a couple of hundred more incorrigibles. Now the isle's most distinguished residents are the black-crowned night heron, the double-crested cormorant and a few thousand Western gulls.

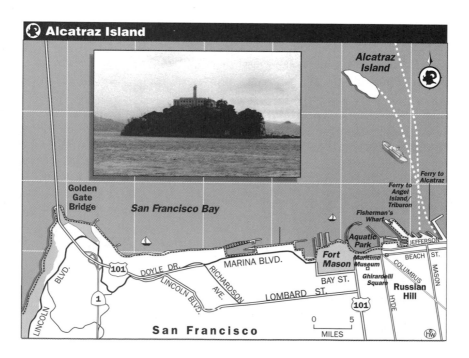

The birds, with National Park Service encouragement, have taken over Alcatraz. Allowing the birds to recolonize "The Rock" is part of a Park Service program to restore some semblance of the natural world to an island long synonymous with of America's best-known maximum security prison.

The so-called "Bird Man of Alcatraz" (Robert Stroud) would certainly be delighted. (The 1962 movie was inaccurate; Stroud raised birds and wrote a book on bird diseases at Leavenworth Prison, but was not allowed to keep birds during the 17 years he was incarcerated on Alcatraz.)

Not everyone is happy with the isle's change from crookery to rookery. The old prison is one of San Francisco's most popular tourist attractions and many visitors (avid bird-watchers excepted) complain about the walls and walkways splattered and splotched with bird droppings, the one-time military parade ground littered with mounds of white and gray feathers, and the malodorous bird guano. National Park officials are faced with the nearly impossible task of managing "historical resources"—the prison, "natural resources" (the birds) and the thousands of tourists who flock to the isle.

The Pacific Coast's first lighthouse was installed on the island in 1854. Alcatraz later served as a military prison for Civil War, Native American and World War I prisoners. From 1934 to 1963 The Rock imprisoned some of America's most infamous "public enemies."

Native American activists took over the island in 1969, claiming sovereignty on the basis of an 1868 U.S. treaty with the Sioux nation and attempting to establish an educational and spiritual center. U.S. Marshals evicted the group in 1971. Alcatraz became part of the Golden Gate National Recreation Area and was opened to the public in 1973. It has been a popular attraction ever since.

Visitors can tour the prison's cell house with the help of a 35-minute audio tour (small fee) and view a short video shown in the Casement Theater. Ranger-led walks emphasize such topics as Natural History, Prison Guard Life and Escape Attempts.

Agave Trail offers a walk on the wild side of the island. It takes hikers near tidepools and a sea lion haul-out, and offers great views of flocks of sea birds.

The trail takes its name from the island's dense population of the spiny succulent. The agaves were strategically planted during the isle's prison era to discourage any would-be rescuers from coming ashore.

Autumn is the best time for a visit. Agave Trail is open only from mid-September through January. The trail is closed the balance of the year in order to protect the nesting sites of the western gull and other fowl. The fall season typically offers the clearest Bay views, as well as relief from the hordes of summer tourists.

DIRECTIONS TO TRAILHEAD Alcatraz Island is accessible by ferries, which depart from Fisherman's Wharf. Reservations (a week ahead), are suggested for weekend and summer visits in particular. Signed Agave Trail begins just south of the ferry dock at an inviting picnic ground.

THE HIKE   The path meanders past eucalyptus (favored by nesting black-crowned night herons) and across a hillside spiked with the trail's namesake agave.

Movie fans might recognize locations from Clint Eastwood's *Escape from Alcatraz* and *The Rock*, the latter a 1996 action thriller starring Sean Connery and Nicholas Cage as unlikely heroes who attempt to thwart terrorists who've taken over Alcatraz and are threatening San Francisco with chemical weapons.

The trail descends toward the water and, at low tide, some intriguing tide-pools, then ascends sandstone steps to serve up dramatic vistas of the bay, Bay Bridge, Treasure Island and metro San Francisco.

Back up top is a parade ground hewn out of solid rock by military prisoners of the 1870s. Agave Trail passes the ruins of a guardhouse and junctions the main trail to the cellblock. Walkers can continue to the isle's old lighthouse.

■ GOLDEN GATE PROMENADE
Golden Gate Promenade
From Aquatic Park to Golden Gate Bridge is 4 miles one way

Surely one of the most memorable shore walks in San Francisco is along Golden Gate Promenade. Along the 4-mile path extending from Aquatic Park to Golden Gate Bridge is a rich diversity of historical, architectural and cultural attractions complemented by a sandy beach, vast waterfront green, and inspiring vistas of the Golden Gate Bridge and Marin Headlands.

Golden Gate Promenade even has its own logo: a blue and white sailboat emblem. Along the promenade you can witness several periods of military history from the early airfield at Crissy Field to that Civil War-era brick fortress Fort Point.

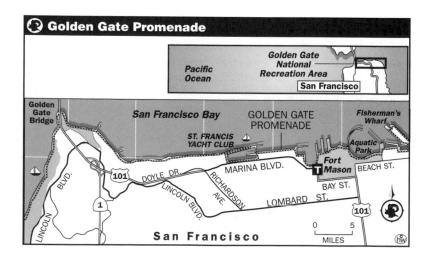

The promenade is a popular place to exercise. San Franciscans jog, cycle, walk, run and triathlon here. Some stop at the exercise stations en route. Rare is the time when the area isn't filled with athletic Bay Area residents pursuing their aerobic conditioning.

You can begin this walk from a couple of different locales, ranging from east to west: Fisherman's Wharf, Aquatic Park or Fort Mason. The latter option has much to recommend it for the first-time visitor. Golden Gate National Recreation Area headquarters is at Fort Mason, and the parking is pretty good here, too. Obtain a map from the white, three-story, one of many historic buildings at Fort Mason.

Fort Mason (well worth a walk all by itself) has evolved into the north shore's culture capital. The piers and warehouses of Fort Mason Center host theater performances, live radio shows, environmental education seminars, and many kinds of recreational activities.

Sunbathers enjoy snuggling into one of the hollows of grassy Marina Green to get out of the wind, which is considerable—to the delight of kite flyers. The winds stirring the bay across from Crissy Field have made the waters here a premiere sailboarding locale.

Don't miss another national park system attraction off the promenade. San Francisco Maritime National Historic Park, once part of the Golden Gate National Recreation Area, is now an independent unit that includes a museum and a collection of historic ships.

The maritime museum is housed in a onetime 1930s bathhouse, built in the form of a luxury ocean liner. Stainless steel railings and portholes add to the nautical look of the structure. Inside are exhibits interpreting a century and a half of California seafaring—from the ships that carried gold-seeking '49ers to whaling boats, yachts and ferries.

DIRECTIONS TO TRAILHEAD   Park in the large lot at Fort Mason, at the intersection of Marina Boulevard and Beach Street.

THE HIKE   From Fort Mason, you may walk along Marina Boulevard or across Marina Green, but the paved pathway along the bay shore is the best way to go.

At St. Francis Yacht Harbor, notice the sea wall, which offers a great stroll; at its end, is a wave organ which (when the tide is right) serenades walkers with the sounds of San Francisco Bay.

The promenade joins Marina Boulevard for a time, passing some Mediterranean-style haciendas and—nearing that glorious reminder of the 1915 Panama Pacific Exposition—the Palace of Fine Arts and its superb, hands-on science exhibits—the Exploratorium.

Resuming a more bay-side route, Golden Gate Promenade leads along Crissy Field. Besides nostalgia for the early days of aviation, Crissy Field also boasts the north shore's most pristine stretch of beach. The low dunes bordering the beach are dotted with native grasses.

The promenade zigzags around a parking lot and fishing pier before nearing Fort Point. With so much to see, your return route will be as fascinating as the first half of your walk.

See Map on Page 116

■ GOLDEN GATE BRIDGE
Golden Gate Trail
Across the Golden Gate from Fort Point to Vista Point is 3 miles round trip

It's known as one of the world's engineering marvels, the proud emblem of a proud city, and "The Bridge at the End of the Continent." The Golden Gate Bridge is all of this—and a great walk: one of those must-do-once-in-a-lifetime adventures.

The technically inclined revel in the bridge's vital statistics: its 8,981-foot length, cables that support 200 million pounds, twin towers the height of 65-story buildings. Statisticians have calculated everything from the number of gallons of International Orange paint required to cover 10 million square feet of bridge, to the number of despondent souls who have leaped from bridge to bay.

For all its utilitarian value, the bridge is an artistic triumph. As you walk the bridge, try to remember how many set-in-San Francisco movies and television shows have opened with an establishing shot of the bridge.

The bridge spans over 400 square miles of the landlocked harbor of San Francisco Bay, which is really three bays—San Francisco and the smaller San Pablo and Suisun bays to the north and northeast. Geographers describe the bay as the drowned mouth and floodplain of the Sacramento-San Joaquin rivers.

Ninety percent of California's remaining coastal wetlands are contained in San Francisco Bay and its estuaries. Shoreline development and industrial pollutants have damaged fish, shellfish, and bird populations. Fortunately, a great many people care about the bay, and are working hard to save and rehabilitate one of the state's most important natural resources.

For centuries, high mountains and heavy fogs concealed one of the world's great natural anchorages from passing European ships. It was a coast walker—Sergeant Jose Francisco Ortega, of the 1769 Portolá overland expedition—who first sighted San Francisco Bay. (See Sweeney Ridge Walk in this chapter.)

Guarding the Golden Gate is Fort Point, a huge Civil War-era structure built of red brick. The fort, similar in design to Fort Sumter in South Carolina, was built for the then-astronomical cost of $2.8 million, and was intended to ensure California's loyalty to the Union.

Fort Point, now part of Golden Gate National Recreation Area, boasts several fine military exhibits, including one emphasizing the contributions of African-American soldiers. Visitors enjoy prowling the three-story fort's many

Take in the world-class views of the Golden Gate Bridge from above Fort Point.

corridors and stairwells. From 1933 to 1937, the fort was the coordinating center for the bridge construction.

While the walk across the bridge is unique, and the clear-day views grand, the trip can also be wearing on the nerves. A bone-chilling wind often buffets bridge walkers, and traffic vibrating the bridge also seems to reverberate throughout one's entire being. Anyone afraid of heights should definitely avoid this walk!

To best enjoy the bridge walk, start well away from it, perhaps even as far away as Fisherman's Wharf, Fort Mason, or Marina Green. It's a pleasing bayside stroll past the yacht harbor and Crissy Field, and along Golden Gate Promenade to Fort Point.

DIRECTIONS TO TRAILHEAD Don't try to drive as close as you can to the bridge. First-time visitors invariably miss the viewpoint parking area just south of the toll plaza and before they know it, they end up in Sausalito. Fort Point's parking lot is one good place to leave your vehicle, as are other parking lots along the bay.

THE HIKE From Fort Point, a gravel, then paved, road leads up to a statue of visionary engineer Joseph Strauss, who persuaded a doubting populace to build the bridge.

As you start walking along the bridge's east sidewalk, you'll get a great view of Fort Point. Pause frequently to watch the ship traffic: yachts, tankers, tug boats, ferries, passenger liners. Literally everything necessary for modern life, from California almonds to Japanese cars, passes in and out of the bay by freighter.

Splendorous clear-day views include the cities of the East Bay, and the bold headlands of Marin, which form the more rural part of Golden Gate National Recreation Area. You'll spot Treasure, Alcatraz and Angel islands and, of course, the San Francisco skyline.

The bridge's second high tower marks the beginning of Marin County. Vista Point is the end of your bridge walk. Here you'll witness tourists from around the world photographing each other and proclaiming their admiration for the Golden Gate in a dozen foreign languages.

■ RODEO LAGOON
Rodeo Lagoon Loop Trail
To Rodeo Beach is 1.5 miles round trip

R odeo Valley is the mother of all trailheads for the Marin Headlands, the jump-off place for explorations of beaches, military history and the bold beauty of the headlands themselves.

Sweeping grasslands, pebbly beaches, and ridgetops with dramatic vistas beckon the hiker. To learn more about Marin's military past and its considerable environmental attractions, stop at the Marin Headlands Visitor Center.

The Visitor Center is housed in what was once the Fort Barry Chapel, an interdenominational gathering place built in 1941 that held Catholic, Protestant and Jewish services for servicemen preparing to go to war. The center offers

Rodeo Lagoon's easy loop trail offers grand views of the hilly headlands.

displays interpreting the area's history from the native Coast Miwok era to modern times, as well as a fine little gift shop and bookstore.

Rodeo Lagoon Trail is the easiest of introductions to the headlands; in fact, it's about the only flat trail around. Gaze up at the headlands back of the Visitor Center. Kind of hilly, huh?

On the way to Rodeo Beach, the trail skirts the mostly freshwater lagoon, home to flotillas of ducks, as well as pelicans, egrets, herons and kingfishers. The pebbly, often windy beach is a favorite of kite fliers and a treat for rockhounds who marvel at the black agates, jasper and other stones strewn about the shore.

The cliffs above the beach offer a fine vantage point for a look at the harbor seals and sea lions swimming in the surf and resting on the rocks. Very strong currents and extremely cold water discourage all swimmers and all but the boldest surfers.

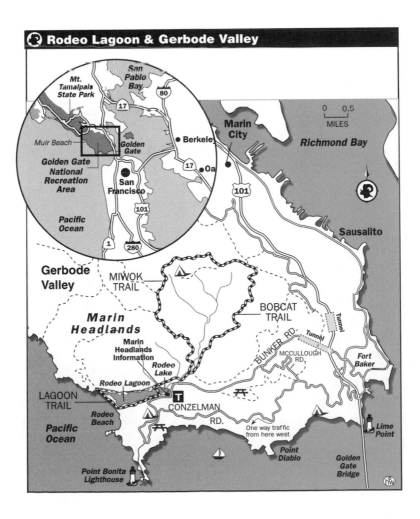

While something in our hikers' genes attracts us to loop trails, you might want to pass on the return leg of the Rodeo Lagoon Loop; it travels too close to Bunker Road for hiking pleasure.

DIRECTIONS TO TRAILHEAD From Highway 101 northbound, just north of the Golden Gate Bridge, exit on Alexander Avenue. Turn left and go under 101, then briefly back-track south to Conzelman Road. Bear right and drive a mile to junction McCullough Road. Turn right and proceed 0.8 mile to Bunker Road. Turn left and drive 2 miles to the parking area for the Marin Headlands Visitor Center. Join signed Lagoon Trail on the west side of the parking lot.

THE HIKE The wide gravel path meanders westward alongside the lagoon, which is fringed with cattails and thickets of willows. Picnic tables near the wetland offer a place to relax.

You soon reach the beach, a narrow barrier that separates the lagoon from the Pacific. Only in winter do storm waves surge over this beach into the lagoon. The resultant mix of saltwater-freshwater is an ideal habitat for many plants and birds.

Follow the hiking trail a bit up the bluffs to admire the coast and rock islands. Largest of the rock isles is guano-crested Bird Island, occupied by a multitude of gulls and brown pelicans.

See Map
on Page
121

■ GERBODE VALLEY
Bobcat, Miwok Trails
Loop around Gerbode Valley is 6.4 miles
round trip with 800- foot elevation gain

Just a mile back from the coast, northeast of Rodeo Valley, lies a land that many hikers adjudge to be GGNRA's wildest. Lovely Gerbode Valley, named for Marin Headlands preservationist Martha Gerbode, is the centerpiece of the park's backcountry.

In the mid-1960s, developers intended to construct enough houses, stores and roads to support a city of 18,000 people on this wild land. Thanks to the efforts of conservationists, the land passed from military to National Park Service administration and stayed out of the hands of developers.

From the ridgetops above the valley, the hiker gains great views of the bay from Tiburon to the Golden Gate Bridge towers, as well as to the north of mighty Mt. Tam.

The Park Service intends to restore this compelling area to an even more natural condition by replacing foreign grasses, introduced long ago during California's Spanish days, with native species.

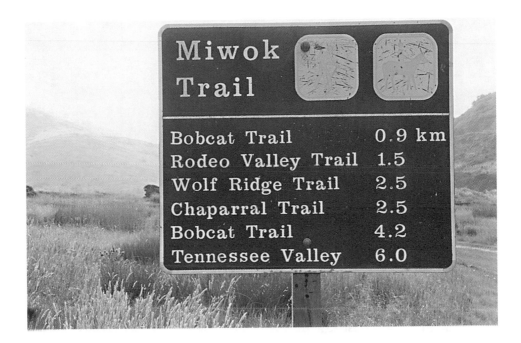

By all accounts, Bobcat Trail may be well-named; hikers have reported many sightings of the creatures in what is excellent habitat for the animals. Other wildlife includes coyote, deer, rabbits and the occasional fox.

A spider web of trails explores the Gerbode Valley, as well as adjacent hills and valleys. For a fine circle tour, take Bobcat Trail on a mellow climb to the ridgeline, then descend via Miwok Trail.

DIRECTIONS TO TRAILHEAD From Highway 101 northbound, just north of the Golden Gate Bridge, exit on Alexander Avenue. Turn left and go under 101, then briefly backtrack south to Conzelman Road. Bear right and drive a mile to junction McCullough Road. Turn right and proceed 0.8 mile to Bunker Road. Turn left and drive 2 miles to the parking area for the Marin Headlands Visitor Center. Join signed Lagoon Trail on the west side of the parking lot.

THE HIKE Rather than heading toward the beach, take Lagoon Trail on a stair-stepping descent north. You briefly parallel Bunker Road, then cross it. Join the wide path (Miwok Trail) to the right (east) of a long warehouse and walk a flat 0.5 mile to a signed junction. Miwok Trail heads north, but you join Bobcat Trail, which first leads east and then, after meeting Rodeo Valley Trail, climbs northeast.

Better and better valley views unfold as you climb. As you approach the ridgecrest, you'll hear the spooky sound of the wind vibrating the high-tension power lines.

Out of this world: VORTAC aids in air-traffic control

Bobcat Trail turns west atop the ridgecrest and offers views of Highway 101, Sausalito and Richardson Bay. Now you step toward a scene straight out of an old science fiction flick: a white-space-capsule-like metal cone pointed skyward.

Greetings, Vortac. It's a directional homing device for aircraft, what the Federal Aviation Administration calls, without regard to brevity, A Very High Frequency Omni-Range and Tactical Air Navigation Aid.

At about 3.5 miles from the trailhead, you say good-bye Vortac and join signed Miwok Trail as it winds around the fenced-off Vortac's summit perch. Miwok Trail turns south and descends past junctions with Old Springs and Chaparral trails. It's an easy descent back to the junction with Bobcat Trail.

Retrace your steps back to the trailhead or follow the north leg of Rodeo Lagoon Trail to Rodeo Beach.

■ TENNESSEE VALLEY
Tennessee Valley, Coastal Trails
From Tennessee Valley to Tennessee Cove is
4 miles round trip; to Muir Beach is 9 miles
round trip with 800-foot elevation gain

It was a dark and stormy night...when the side-wheel steamship Tennessee, with 600 passengers aboard, overshot the Golden Gate and ran aground off this isolated Marin County cove. No lives were lost on that foggy night of March 6, 1853, but the abandoned ship was soon broken up by the surf. The vessel is remembered by a point, a cove, a valley and a beach. Very occasionally a bit of the Tennessee's rusted remains are visible.

Although only a few miles north of San Francisco, Tennessee Valley, walled in by high ridges, seems quite isolated from the world. Until 1976 when it became part of the Golden Gate National Recreation Area, the valley was part of Witter Ranch.

Tennessee Valley Trail meets Coast Trail about a half-mile from Tennessee Beach. The walk through Tennessee Valley to the shore is suitable for the whole family. More intrepid walkers will join Coastal Trail for an up-and-down journey to Muir Beach. (See Muir Beach Walk.)

DIRECTIONS TO TRAILHEAD   From Highway 101 north of the Golden Gate Bridge, take the Highway 1 offramp. Follow the highway a half-mile, turn left on Tennessee Valley Road, and follow it to the trailhead and parking area.

THE HIKE   Tennessee Valley Trail begins as a paved road, farther on becomes gravel, and farther still becomes a footpath. The route descends moderately alongside a willow- and eucalyptus-lined creek. A mile out, take the left-forking trail, which forbids mountain bikes.

About 0.5-mile from Tennessee Cove, the trail intersects Coastal Trail. Continuing on Tennessee Valley Trail will take you past a small lagoon, located just inland from Tennessee Beach. A trail circles the lagoon and leads back to Tennessee Valley Trail.

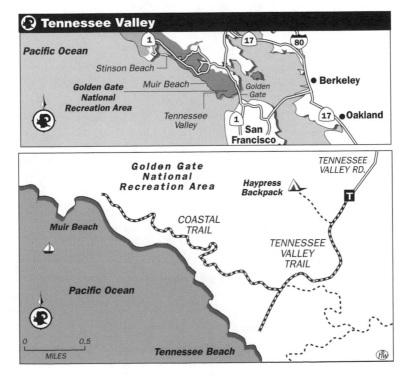

The Marin Headlands Hostel, less than ten minutes from the Golden Gate Bridge, welcomes hikers from around the world.

A right at the above-mentioned fork connects to Coastal Trail. As you ascend north, pause to look behind at Tennessee Valley. Coastal Trail flattens out a bit, then descends to Pirate's Cove. The trail marches up and down the coastal bluffs, and passes a junction with Coyote Ridge Trail. You'll get a grand view of Muir Beach and Green Gulch. From this junction, you'll descend rather steeply to Muir Beach.

■ MUIR BEACH
Coyote Ridge, Green Gulch Trails
5 miles round trip with 800-foot elevation gain

Golden Gate National Recreation Area boasts two major beaches in Marin, Stinson and Muir, the latter a semi-circular strand enclosed by a forested cove.

Green Gulch Trail and Coyote Ridge Trail both begin and end at Muir Beach and are of approximately the same length. Green Gulch Trail tours an organic farm-Zen center that permits (caring and respectful) hikers to travel its

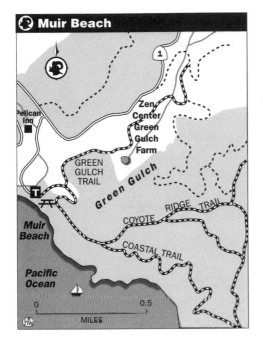

paths. Coyote Ridge Trail climbs the grassy hills above the beach and offers great coastal views.

DIRECTIONS TO TRAILHEAD From Highway 101, 5 miles north of the Golden Gate Bridge, exit for Mt. Tamalpais/Muir Woods. Follow Highway 1 nine winding miles to the Muir Beach parking lot. Expect a crowded lot on sunny summer days.

THE HIKE Cross a wooden bridge over the marshy mouth of Redwood Creek and head southward on Coastal Trail. After two hundred yards, you'll junction with Green Gulch Trail. Join it if you wish, but I prefer to take a counterclockwise route for this hike and continue with a mellow climb along Coast Trail, getting a gull's-eye view of Muir Beach.

Three-quarter mile from the trailhead, bear left on Coyote Ridge Trail and begin a fairly steep 1.2-mile ascent. Stay left at a fork, curving north and then west toward Green Gulch. You'll descend the gulch past the Zen nursery, organic farm and meditation center, returning to the Coastal Trail and back to Muir Beach.

■ BOLINAS RIDGE
Bolinas Ridge Trail
To Jewell Trail junction is 2.5 miles round trip; to Shafter Trail Junction is 10 miles round trip with 700-foot elevation gain

Bolinas Ridge, a long finger of land bordered by Highway 1 and Point Reyes National Seashore on the west, is perhaps the Golden Gate National Recreation Area's most remote landscape.

Ridge hikers are treated to dramatic vistas of the wooded slopes to the east and Olema Valley to the west. Bolinas Ridge separates Olema Valley from the forested state parks—Mt. Tamalpais and Samuel P. Taylor to the east.

Olema Valley has the infamous distinction of being the epicenter for the 1906 San Francisco Earthquake. The quake, one of the most severe in American history, resulted from the intense horizontal movement that occurred along the San Andreas Fault.

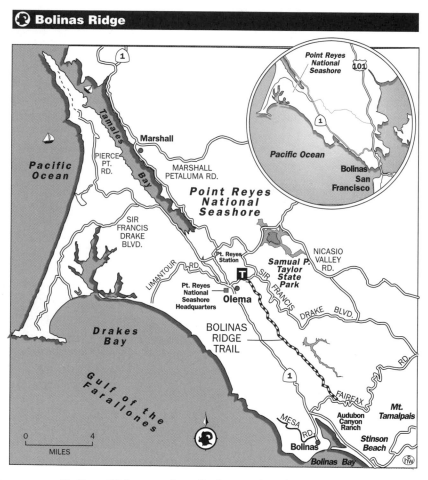

Bolinas Ridge

Long ago, Bolinas Ridge was heavily forested with redwood and Douglas fir; these trees, however, were logged and milled into lumber used to build San Francisco. The ridge these days is mostly grass-covered, dotted with coast live oak and some remnant groves of Douglas fir.

Bolinas Ridge Trail, true to its name, travels the ridgetop some 15 miles from Olema to trail's end at Bolinas-Fairfax Road. You could make this a long one-way day hike with a car shuttle, or do as most hikers do—hike to one of the ridgetop's excellent viewpoints and turn around as time and energy dictates.

The trail is a popular mountain bike route; however, Bolinas Ridge Road is a wide path and hiker-biker conflicts are minimal on this route.

DIRECTIONS TO TRAILHEAD From Highway 101 in San Rafael, exit on Sir Francis Drake Boulevard and drive west 17.5 miles to the trailhead on the left side of the road. Park carefully along the highway.

THE HIKE Join the ascending dirt road, which curves south through rolling grassland. Before long, views open up to the east of Olema Valley and behind you of Tomales Bay and Point Reyes Peninsula.

A mile and a quarter of walking brings you to a junction with Jewell Trail, which drops east to Lagunitas Creek. Continue along the ridgetop a short distance farther for grand views west of forested Inverness Ridge. After another mile along the ridge, you'll walk in the company of Douglas fir growing on eastern slopes.

Get above it all on GGNRA's ridge trails.

Four miles out, you'll reach more open terrain, then over the next mile will gain the ridgetop's high point, reach excellent vistas, and meet the Shafter Trail. This junction is a good turnaround point.

If you're game, Bolinas Ridge Trail dips and climbs, but is a fairly mellow route all the way to Bolinas-Fairfax Road.

John Muir's stately Victorian housed his "scribble den" where the environmentalist wrote his finest work.

8

JOHN MUIR
NATIONAL HISTORIC SITE

■ MUIR FARM AND MT. WANDA

John Muir Nature Trail
0.25-mile loop around Muir Orchard;
3-mile loop of Mt. Wanda with 400-foot elevation gain

John Muir at work in his "scribble den."

Most of us picture John Muir in one of two ways: as a young man exploring the High Sierra and the wonders of Yosemite or as America's revered elder naturalist, author and founder of the Sierra Club.

We don't often think of Muir in his middle years—the 1880s and 1890s—a time of great creativity and happiness for him, when he married, raised two daughters and managed a fruit ranch on the outskirts of Martinez, California.

In 1880, Muir married Louie Strentzel, daughter of famed horticulturist Dr. John Strentzel. Muir reportedly began work in the family orchards and vineyards the day after the wedding. He was determined to prosper, both to provide for his family and to bank sufficient funds to cover the costs of his many nature explorations and decidedly non-remunerative conservation activities.

Muir proved to be a talented horticulturist himself and, for more than a decade, combined dedication to family and farm work in the autumn, winter and spring months with wilderness exploration in the summer.

John Muir National Historic Site preserves his family home, as well as a part of his ranch, where he lived from 1890 until his death in 1914. It is altogether fitting that a man often referred to as "The Father of National Parks" is honored at a site administered by the National Park Service.

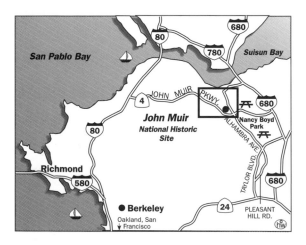

Allow an hour to an hour-and-a-half to walk the Orchard Trail and to tour the Muir Home. The home is a handsome example of the upper middle-class Victorian lifestyle. Particularly intriguing are the parlors where the Muirs entertained and the Sierra Club Exhibit Room. Another highlight is John Muir's study (his "scribble den," as he called it) where he wrote many magazine articles and books about America's wildlands.

John Muir's home, grounds and the park Visitor Center are open Wednesday through Sunday, 10 a.m. to 4:30 p.m.

In 1993, the park acquired 325 acres of rolling ranchland, site of many a Muir family walk. The park's two highest points, 660-foot Mt. Wanda and 640-foot Mt. Helen are named after Muir's two daughters. In a journal entry dated April 12, 1895, Muir recorded: "Another lovely day, mostly solid sunshine. Took a fine fragrant walk up the West Hills with Wanda and Helen, who I am glad to see love walking, flowers, trees and every bird and beast and creeping thing."

John Muir Nature Trail, an interpretive trail keyed to a brochure available from the Visitor Center, along with a couple of connecting fire roads, explore what park rangers call The Mt. Wanda Area. This wild side of the park is open every day from sunrise to sunset.

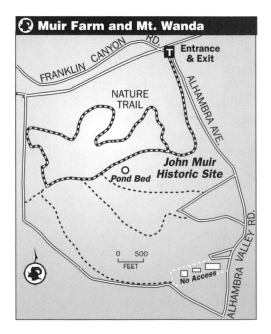

DIRECTIONS TO TRAILHEAD
From Highway 4 (John Muir Parkway), some 9 miles east of I-80 and 4 miles west of I-680, exit on Alhambra Avenue and drive north to John Muir National Historic Site.

While it's only a five-minute walk from the park Visitor Center to the Mt. Wanda trailhead, I suggest, for reasons of safety, that you make a very un-Muir-like short drive to the Caltrans Park and Ride lot located at the corner of Alhambra Avenue and Franklin Canyon Road.

THE HIKE From Franklin Canyon Road, join the signed fire road and begin a steady climb above the John Muir Parkway and the Topeka/Santa Fe railroad trestles. As you climb views open up to the east of mighty Mt. Diablo, towering above surrounding suburban sprawl. To the north, you can view the town of Martinez, as well as the Carquinez Straits between San Pablo Bay and Suisun Bay.

About 0.75 mile from the trailhead, you'll reach the signed beginning of the 1.3-mile-long John Muir Nature Trail. The educational (although a tad bit overly earnest) path delivers lessons about local geology, creeks, flora and fauna.

Mt. Wanda's most compelling natural resources are its grand diversity of oaks—coast, live, valley, blue and black, as well as its grassy meadows.

The nature trail ends at a junction with a fire road. You can close the loop and return to the trailhead by turning left on the road. Other connecting fire roads allow you to extend your walk a bit, if you choose.

Tao House was home to Eugene O'Neill and Carlotta Monterey from 1937 to 1944.

Eugene O'Neill, who won four Pulitzers and the Nobel Prize, penned five plays in his Tao House office overlooking the scenic countryside.

CHAPTER NINE

EUGENE O'NEILL NATIONAL HISTORIC SITE

■ EUGENE O'NEILL NATIONAL HISTORIC SITE
Starview, Amigo, Williams Trails
From Starview Drive to Eugene O'Neill NHS
is 3 miles round trip with 300-foot elevation gain

When Eugene O'Neill, one of America's most distinguished playwrights of the 20th century, was awarded the Nobel Prize for Literature in 1936, he used the prize money to build Tao House, his estate in the hills above Danville, California. In his seven years of residence in the hilltop retreat, O'Neill wrote his final plays, the often autobiographical masterworks *Long Day's Journey into Night*, *The Ice Man Cometh*, *Hughie* and *A Moon for the Misbegotten*.

O'Neill's house is open for twice-daily guided tours. Reservations are required. Most visitors board a National Park Service shuttle van from Danville to O'Neill's home. Few visitors realize that it's possible to take a short hike from adjacent Las Trampas Regional Wilderness to the historic site. Rangers welcome hikers but point out that tour reservations are still required in order to set foot in the O'Neill house.

Tao House reflects O'Neill's interest in Eastern thought and the passion of his wife, actress Carlotta Monterey, for Asian art and décor. The house is an unusual, even odd, blend of Spanish-California Mission architecture with Chinese style and design elements.

O'Neill's study is particularly intriguing to the many admirers of the playwright. His workplace, restored to near perfection with original and period furnishings, features a fireplace and private porch—a perfect place to write.

And write he did, in strict seclusion; Carlotta was a wary gatekeeper who allowed very few people to disturb her husband's work schedule. While O'Neill wrote, Carlotta pursued her own creative vision with Tao House. Deep blue ceilings, mirrors and "opium" couches are among her decorating touches. Outdoors, the garden walkway zigzags this way and that—a Chinese-influenced

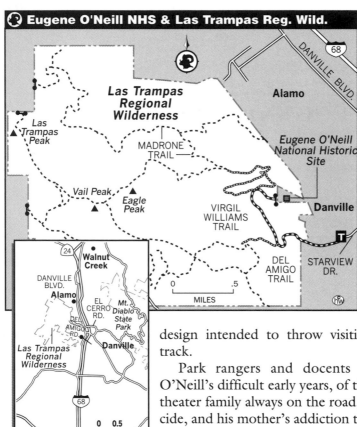

Eugene O'Neill NHS & Las Trampas Reg. Wild.

Las Trampas Regional Wilderness

Alamo

Las Trampas Peak

MADRONE TRAIL

Eugene O'Neill National Historic Site

Vail Peak

Eagle Peak

VIRGIL WILLIAMS TRAIL

Danville

DEL AMIGO TRAIL

STARVIEW DR.

0   .5

MILES

Walnut Creek

DANVILLE BLVD.

Alamo

EL CERRO RD.

Mt. Diablo State Park

DEL AMIGO RD.

Danville

Las Trampas Regional Wilderness

0   0.5

MILES

design intended to throw visiting evil spirits off-track.

Park rangers and docents tell the story of O'Neill's difficult early years, of the itinerant life of a theater family always on the road, of alcoholism, suicide, and his mother's addiction to morphine. By the 1920s, however, O'Neill had overcome his desperately unhappy youth to completely re-invigorate American theater with three Pulitzer-Prize winning plays: *Beyond the Horizon, Anna Christie* and *Strange Interlude*. Still, family tragedy intruded: within three years of his first successful play on Broadway, his mother, father, and then his older brother died. These great losses, and resultant feelings of guilt and mourning, plagued the playwright for the rest of his life. At Tao House, O'Neill became ever-more autobiographical. The Tyrone family in *Long Day's Journey into Night* (for which O'Neill received a fourth Pulitzer Prize, posthumously) is almost a non-fiction account of his own family.

Looking out at the beautiful hills and valleys surrounding Tao House, it's easy for the visitor to conclude that this California scene was no inspiration for, and had no relation to, O'Neill's work. Park Superintendent Glenn Fuller feels differently. "Tao House and these surroundings provided a setting conducive to reflection and the deep probing of the past that was so integral to his work."

O'Neill was afflicted with a rare degenerative nerve disorder that caused tremors in his hand. As his condition worsened he was literally unable to put pencil to paper; this resulted in a creative shut-down, and he never completed another play after 1943.

World War II on the homefront resulted in a manpower shortage and a loss of the kind of help the O'Neills required—drivers, housekeepers, etc.—necessary to maintain a life at Tao House. The O'Neills moved to Boston, where the great playwright died in 1953.

Eugene O'Neill National Historic Site is open 8 a.m. to 4:30 p.m. every Wednesday through Sunday with the exception of major holidays. Home tours (at 10 a.m. and 12:30 p.m.) are free and the National Park Service provides a shuttle van (also free) from Danville (pickup location provided at the time of reservation).

DIRECTIONS TO TRAILHEAD From Interstate 680, exit on El Cerro Road and go west to Danville Boulevard. Turn right and go one block. Turn left on Del Amigo Road and ascend about 0.5 mile to Starview Drive. Bear left and continue to the trailhead. Park on Starview Drive and not on the private road.

To reach downtown Danville, exit Interstate 680 on Diablo Road and follow it west. Turn left onto Hartz Avenue to the heart of Danville, where shops and restaurants are located.

THE HIKE From the trailhead at the end of Starview Drive, follow Starview Trail 0.4 mile west to Del Amigo Trail, then another 0.2 mile to a junction with Virgil Williams Trail. Turn right (north) and walk 0.7 mile to a junction with Madrone Trail. A fire road leads down to Eugene O'Neill National Historic Site.

Classic hikes to world-renowned destinations beckon nature lovers from around the globe to tramp Yosemite's trails.

CHAPTER TEN

YOSEMITE NATIONAL PARK

K nown the world over for its great granite cliffs and domes, enormous waterfalls and giant sequoias, Yosemite is everything a national park should be and more. Such well known Yosemite Valley destinations as Vernal Fall, Nevada Fall and Yosemite Falls, Half Dome and Happy Isles are magnets for hikers. Equally attractive are many more sights outside the valley: Mt. Dana, Tuolumne Meadows, Cathedral Peak, Hetch Hetchy, the Mariposa Grove of Big Trees and many more.

The park boasts a magnificent High Sierra backcountry, one that (by rather severe Sierra standards anyway) is quite accessible. Well marked trails lead to wildflower-festooned alpine meadows, lovely lakes and tarns, trails and cross-country routes to peaks.

Most people, when asked to link a person to a place and that place is Yosemite, say, "John Muir." It is altogether fitting and proper that we do this. The great naturalist's pioneering work in glacier theory and passionate efforts to make Yosemite a park have long been admired and will be appreciated by generations to come.

I, however, associate Yosemite with a far-less-known nature writer by the name of Joseph Smeaton Chase. Who?

Chase was a British-born, Los Angeles social worker who ventured into California's backcountry during the first two decades of the 20th century and left us a trio of nature classics: *California Desert Trails, California Coast Trails,* and *Yosemite Trails.*

His first book, *Yosemite Trails,* published in 1912, describes three long outings in the park from the Wawona, Hetch Hetchy and Tuolumne areas. Chase reveled in the majesty and solitude of the backcountry: "As we moved quietly along I was free to notice the thousand and one things that make up the silent conversation of the trail."

Chase got good reviews from the Eastern and foreign press and raves from such California publications as *Out West* magazine: "If you have wanted all your life to make a trip to Yosemite and cannot go, the next best thing is to read *Yosemite Trails* by J. Smeaton Chase. You will forget while reading it that you are not there, and when you have finished you will find a way to go."

With all due respect to Chase's book, it seems, in hindsight, that critics and readers responded more to the park than his prose. Yosemite has that kind of

Theodore Roosevelt—America's first environmentalist president—loved the wild lands of Yosemite. He signed the bill preserving the park in 1906.

effect on people: Bigger than words. Larger than life. A visit stays with you forever.

My visits to Yosemite were baby-boom typical. My parents took me as a tiny tike in the 1950s, and as a teen in the 1960s. We camped in Yosemite Valley, stayed in the creaky little Curry cabins, floated on inner tubes in the Merced River, hiked to Mirror Lake when it was still a lake, watched the evening Firefall from Glacier Point, enjoyed ranger talks and naturalist-led walks.

As a young adult (the word is used hesitantly) I hung out with the hippies in Tuolumne Meadows and after graduation from college, hiked the Yosemite backcountry and the John Muir Trail from Yosemite Valley to Mt. Whitney.

These days I bring my own family to Yosemite to enjoy the same scenic grandeur and experiences (minus the discontinued Firefall!) that I enjoyed while growing up.

But my family—and everyone else who visits Yosemite these days—certainly has more company than ever before. Park visitation increased from about a million visitors a year in the 1950s to two million a year in the 1960s to four million a year in the 1990s. Then and now such heavy visitation sometimes results in summer traffic jams in Yosemite Valley, and crowding at overlooks, concessions, Yosemite Village and on the shuttle bus system.

In fact, traffic and crowding in Yosemite Valley have been among the National Park Service's worst problems for decades. Plans to reduce auto traffic in the valley by extensive use of buses, as well as other management plans to reduce congestion, have been a challenge to implement. Yosemite Valley's "remodeling" program was accelerated by a severe 1997 flood, which swamped buildings, washed away roads and ruined campgrounds. When the Park Service carries out its intentions to ease traffic and reduce commercial facilities, the pay-off will be a richer park experience for hikers and visitors of all kinds.

Unlike the motorist, diner or souvenir shopper, the hiker feels fewer effects of Yosemite's crowds. With the exception of the heavily trafficked "waterfall trails" and a couple other valley footpaths, the hiker is far less likely to feel the impact of such crowding.

Yosemite's trails are for the most part well-engineered, well maintained and well-signed. Opportunities for summer solitude may be few on the major trails, but the farther away from a roadhead one hikes, the greater the opportunity for tranquility. "Well-used" is a better characterization of most Yosemite trails than "overused." The journey on these pathways is often as pleasurable as the famed destinations they reach.

John Muir' suggested hikes in his 1912 Yosemite guidebook were 25 miles long. One can only imagine hikers of that era were of sturdier stock—or else few followed in Muir's footsteps.

Individual trails have individual stories:

• The trail up Mt. Dana was constructed at the behest of esteemed Yosemite botanist Dr. Carl Sharsmith, who designed a route that minimized human impact on the mountain's fragile flora.

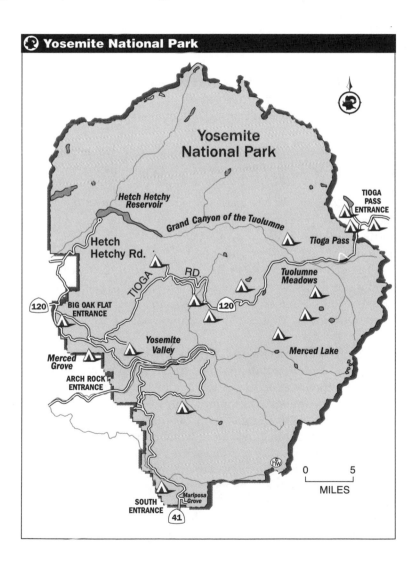

- Yosemite Falls Trail, like some other early (1870s) paths, was privately built and operated as a toll trail.
- Mirror Lake was once auto-accessible; now the road to the lake is a walking path.

Some Yosemite Valley trails are accessible all year. While the park has glaciated peaks that rise to more than 13,000 feet in elevation, Yosemite Valley is less than a mile high and some park areas are even below 3,000 feet. In spring, Yosemite's waterfalls are at their most majestic. In summer, alpine slopes burst into bloom. Autumn is a favorite time for a walk. The "Range of Light" is particularly dramatic and the aspens glow like fire in the wind.

At any moment on any hike in Yosemite National Park you might just notice what nature writer Chase called "the thousand and one things that make up the silent conversation of the trail."

■ MARIPOSA GROVE
Mariposa Grove trails
4.8-mile loop with 1,000-foot elevation gain

Mariposa is by far the largest of Yosemite's three groves of giant sequoias. A walk among the world's largest living things is one to remember.

Expect lots of company in Mariposa Grove. The enormous trees—combined with easy access, close proximity to the park's south entrance, a gift/snack shop, and a tram tour no less—really draw a crowd.

The magnificent sequoias of Mariposa Grove, along with the wondrous Yosemite Valley, prompted President Abraham Lincoln to set aside Yosemite as a reserve and grant it (temporarily) to the state of California for its protection. It's not exaggeration, therefore, to say that this grove of giant sequoias inspired the very first steps toward the establishment of our entire system of national parks.

At times, Mariposa Grove rivaled Calaveras Grove and the groves of big trees in Sequoia National Park in popularity. The modern visitor can visit named trees that have captured the imagination of generations of visitors.

No visit of a century ago was complete without a stage ride through a drive-through tree. Thousands of wagons, then cars drove through Wawona Tunnel Tree, from 1881 when a tunnel was bored through it, until 1967 when it fell. California Tunnel Tree, another sequoia with a tunnel through its midsection, still stands—though its drive-through days are over.

Grizzly Giant, a 200-foot tall behemoth that measures 30 feet in diameter, is estimated to have sprouted some 2,700 years ago; it's believed to be the oldest sequoia in Mariposa Grove.

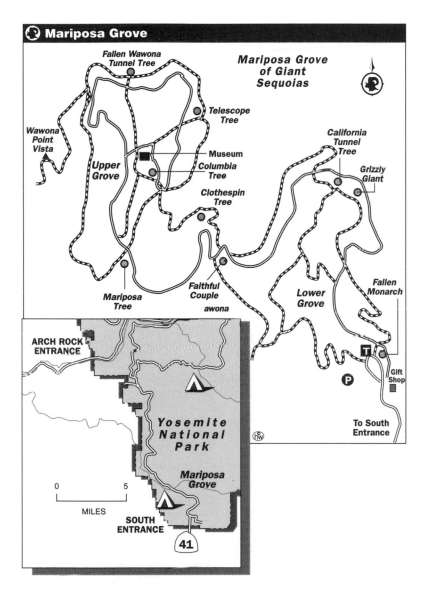

Mariposa Grove

Mariposa Grove
of Giant
Sequoias

Fallen Wawona
Tunnel Tree

Telescope
Tree

California
Tunnel
Tree

Wawona
Point
Vista

Museum

Columbia
Tree

Grizzly
Giant

Upper
Grove

Clothespin
Tree

Mariposa
Tree

Faithful
Couple

Lower
Grove

Fallen
Monarch

awona

ARCH ROCK
ENTRANCE

Yosemite
National
Park

Gift
Shop

To South
Entrance

Mariposa
Grove

0   5

MILES

Mariposa
Grove

SOUTH
ENTRANCE

41

It's easy to guess, by observing the spacing of the Three Graces, the Faithful Couple and the Bachelor Tree how these trees got their names.

You might spot some sequoias with blackened bark. In years past, the Park Service resolutely suppressed all wildfires. However, with the realization in the 1970s that sequoia reproduction depends on fire, the occasional lightning-caused blaze has been allowed to burn, and some controlled burns have been proscribed in order to simulate natural conditions.

To learn more about sequoia ecology and history, check out the exhibits at the Grove Museum. The museum is located in the Upper Grove on the site of Yosemite guardian Galen Clark's 1864 cabin.

DIRECTIONS TO TRAILHEAD From Highway 41 at Yosemite's South Entrance Station, drive east 2 miles to Mariposa Grove.

THE HIKE At the start of the trail, pick up a copy of the Park Service's "Mariposa Grove of Giant Sequoias" pamphlet from the dispenser and begin walking the gentle path. You'll soon visit the Fallen Monarch, the Bachelor and Three Graces, and at the 0.8-mile mark, the Grizzly Giant that leans perilously like the Leaning Tower of Pisa. Not far from old Grizzly is the one-time drive-through California Tunnel Tree; it's the unofficial "tourist turnaround;" from here to the Upper Grove, you'll proceed with less company.

Your path steepens, passes a trail leading to Clothespin Tree, and climbs to a junction with the tram road and a meeting with the Upper Loop Trail 1.5 mile from the trailhead. Bear right and walk among the sequoias. Keep an eye out for the famed and fallen Wawona Tunnel Tree. After visiting this curiosity, meet the tram road, then join the Museum Trail, which descends to the museum.

Continue past the museum to rejoin the Upper Loop Trail. On your return visit the odd, fire-fashioned Clothespin Tree and the sequoia twosome known as the Faithful Couple. Revisit the Grizzly Giant and retrace your steps to the trailhead.

■ WAWONA MEADOW
Meadow Trail
3-mile loop

For years—20 or so anyway—I resisted walking Wawona Meadow. Wawona Hotel and its lovely setting appealed to me in an Adirondack-Mountains-resort sort of way: wide green lawns, white-painted Victorian buildings, wicker chairs on the verandas. The hotel and adjacent small golf course seemed a tad too much civilization to possibly have any interesting hiking nearby.

Then along came our baby Sophia and suddenly family-friendly Wawona Meadow and Yosemite's flattest trail had new appeal for two hikers pushing a jogger stroller.

We're glad we finally discovered Wawona Meadow, one of Yosemite's few year-round trails. Wildflowers—lupine, larkspur and more—color the meadow in spring and early summer. In autumn, the meadow's bordering deciduous trees don their fall colors. Deer frequently can be seen browsing the meadow.

Wawona was originally known as Clark's Station, named for Yosemite pioneer Galen Clark, discoverer of nearby Mariposa Grove. In 1857, doctors gave him but a couple months to live and sent him to the mountains in hopes of miracle cure. In testament to nature's healing powers, Clark lived to serve as guardian of Yosemite's giant sequoias for 50 years and to author his first book, *Indians of the Yosemite,* at the age of 90.

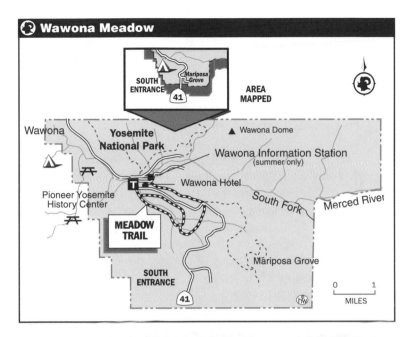

Wawona Meadow

SOUTH ENTRANCE

Mariposa Grove

41

AREA MAPPED

Wawona

Yosemite National Park

▲ Wawona Dome

Wawona Information Station
(summer only)

T ●

Wawona Hotel

Pioneer Yosemite History Center

South Fork

Merced River

MEADOW TRAIL

Mariposa Grove

SOUTH ENTRANCE

41

0　　　1
MILES

Galen Clark, one of Yosemite's first guardians.

Clark's Station served as a stage stop and Yosemite gateway for many years. To learn more about the park's Wild West-flavored history, check out the Pioneer Yosemite History Center located in Wawona on the east side of Highway 41.

DIRECTIONS TO TRAILHEAD   From Yosemite's South Entrance, follow Highway 41 north 7 miles into the park to the Wawona Hotel, The signed path begins across the highway from the hotel parking lot.

THE HIKE   The trail, an old dirt road, angles across the golf course and soon meanders south amidst the trees bordering Wawona Meadow. It's a gentle ascent on the pine-needle-strewn road in the company of oaks, pines and cedars. Bordering the meadow is an old fence that once served to confine sheep and cattle.

Enjoy an equally gentle descent along the east side of the meadow. Fewer trees here mean you'll have good views of the meadow's wildflowers in season, and of the abundant deer all year.

The looping pathway returns you to Highway 41 near Wawona Hotel.

■ TAFT POINT
Taft Point Trail
From Glacier Point to Taft Point is 2.2 miles
round trip with 200-foot elevation gain

A short trail designed for viewing what geologists calls fissures sounds like a real yawn. But this isn't just any trail and these fissures aren't just any fissures.

Yosemite's fissures are The Fissures, deep cracks in the cliff edge. And through The Fissures is the floor of the Yosemite Valley, a half-mile below.

Down there is really down there. Clamp your clammy palms over the simple handrail, lean over the precipice and see the valley, an odd angle on Upper Yosemite Falls, and go eyeball to eyeball with El Capitan.

The trail is kid-friendly, but the destination is not. Bring your children on the hike, but hold on to them at all times around Taft Point.

DIRECTIONS TO THE TRAILHEAD   Taft Point shares a trailhead with the path to Sentinel Dome. The parking area is located on the north side of Glacier Point Road, some 15 miles from its intersection with Wawona Road and about 1.5 miles before road's end.

THE HIKE   From the parking lot, the trail leads 50 yards, then angles west in the company of lodgepole and Jeffrey pine and soon crosses Sentinel Creek.

A half-mile out, the path passes a junction with Pohono Trail, which traces the rim of Yosemite Valley to Glacier Point.

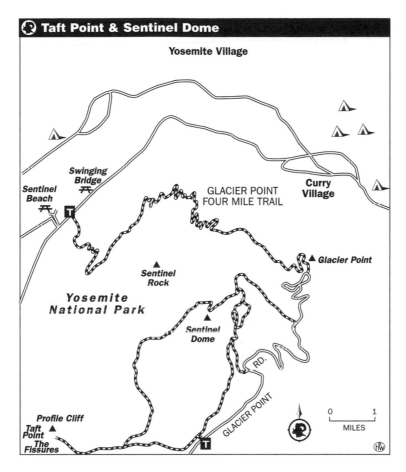

Taft Point & Sentinel Dome

Yosemite Village

Swinging Bridge

Sentinel Beach

GLACIER POINT FOUR MILE TRAIL

Curry Village

Glacier Point

Sentinel Rock

Yosemite National Park

Sentinel Dome

RD.

Profile Cliff

Taft Point

The Fissures

GLACIER POINT

0   1
MILES

The path meanders past a seasonal profusion of corn lilies, then leaves the trees behind on a descent of rocky slopes. Just shy of a mile out, the trail reaches the first of The Fissures. Unlike the clefts at Taft Point, these are unprotected by guardrails, so watch your step. Continue another 0.1 mile to Taft Point.

■ SENTINEL DOME

Sentinel Dome Trail
From Taft Point to Sentinel Dome is 2.2 miles
round trip with 400-foot elevation gain

Rarely does a hiker get so grand a view for so little gain or pain. A mere 400-foot elevation gain and a mile-long walk gets you to the top of 8,122-foot Sentinel Dome for a spectacular view of Yosemite Valley.

Some hikers contend the dome top view is better than the one just up the road at Glacier Point. Certainly it's a whole lot less crowded along Sentinel Dome's trail than along Glacier Point's guardrail.

Older hikers who remember the famous gnarled Jeffrey pine atop the dome will be saddened to learn of the tree's demise in the late 1970s. A victim of drought or pawing by tourists or both, one supposes. The tree remains photogenic, however, in a driftwood sort of way.

DIRECTIONS TO TRAILHEAD From Highway 41 at Chinquapin, follow Glacier Point Road 13 miles to a parking area. (This turnout is 2 miles short of road's end at Glacier Point.)

THE HIKE Begin a mellow ascent over open granite slopes. You'll then pass through a pine-and-white-fir forest before intersecting an old road that once allowed motorists to reach the base of Sentinel Dome.

The wide path ascends from forest to exposed granite on the back side of the dome, passing a junction with trails that lead to Glacier Point and Yosemite Valley. No pathway climbs Sentinel Dome but the route up its wide backside is quite apparent.

■ GLACIER POINT
Glacier Point-Panorama, John Muir Trails
9 miles one way with 3,200-foot elevation loss

Panorama Trail delivers the promise in its name: fabulous views of Half Dome, Liberty Cap and Clouds Rest. Each turn in the trail brings the hikers another dramatic vista. Even Yosemite icons Vernal and Nevada falls, so difficult to glimpse simultaneously from the valley floor, can be seen in a new light—together—from Panorama Trail.

These super views make this hike the park's best one-way trip down to Yosemite Valley's Happy Isles. A car shuttle is necessary or, better yet, board one of the regularly scheduled buses to Glacier Point.

Glacier Point was the launch pad for Yosemite's after-dark, crowd-pleasing Firefall. Piles of burning embers were pushed over the edge to create a spectacle that was popular for nearly a hundred years before it was halted in 1968.

While your descent to Yosemite Valley may not be as dramatic as the Firefall, it will be one to remember. On the way to Happy Isles you'll get a great at-the-brink view of Illilouette Fall, visit Nevada and Vernal falls, and travel the historic John Muir Trail.

DIRECTIONS TO TRAILHEAD Follow Glacier Point Road all the way (16 miles) to its end at Glacier Point. The signed path begins at the east end of the parking area.

THE HIKE After a brief climb, the trail forks—Pohono Trail to the right and our Glacier Point-Panorama Trail to the left. Descend among red fir, blackened

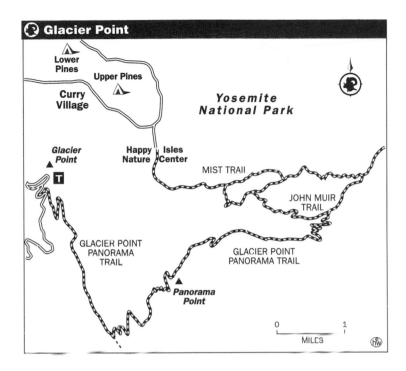

but not killed by a 1987 wildfire, enjoying the first of the panoramic views between singed trunks.

At 1.7 miles, the path passes a junction with Buena Vista Trail and soon offers a short connector trail leading to a viewpoint for Illilouette Fall. After another 0.25 mile descent the path leads over a bridge over Illilouette Creek, then ascends Panorama Cliff above the fall. With the climb come more fabulous views, including a heart-stopper from Panorama Point.

The trail begins a mellow descent, leveling out as it heads eastward to a junction with Mono Meadow Trail. A mile-long switchbacking descent through the forest brings you to a junction with John Muir Trail. Continue a bit farther for an eye-popping look to the brink of Nevada Fall, then

Half Dome stands, much as it does today, as Theodore Roosevelt and John Muir ride past on horseback.

return to the JMT for the hike to Vernal Fall. (See Vernal and Nevada falls walk description.)

After crossing the Merced River on a bridge, the John Muir Trail delivers you to Happy Isles. Walk or take the shuttle bus to Curry Village.

See Map
on Page
149

■ GLACIER POINT
Four-Mile Trail
To Glacier Point is 9.6 miles round trip with
3,200-foot elevation gain

Four-Mile Trail is a Yosemite classic, the original route to Glacier Point. When first constructed in the 1870s, it extended 4 miles, but after an overhaul in the 1920s and the addition of some switchbacks it now measures 4.8 miles. No matter, the original trail name is still with us.

In my very early (Boy Scout) days of hiking Yosemite, Four-Mile Trail seemed far longer than its name suggested. We scouts were more than a little surprised (to put it mildly) to struggle up the trail and find Glacier Point Hotel (then in its very last days; it burned in 1969) and hordes of tourists who had driven to the point.

You mean we could've driven up to Glacier Point?

Walking up to it means you'll appreciate the view more, our scoutmaster assured us.

Took me a long time—three decades in fact—before I really appreciated our scoutmaster's wisdom. Indeed the Yosemite Valley panorama does seem more satisfying after a hike with a 3,200-foot elevation gain. Now I'm a strong advocate for hiking up to Glacier Point. Okay, you can catch a ride up and walk down, but at least experience Four-Mile Trail one way or another.

These days Glacier Point offers restrooms, a snack bar, the old Geology Hut, a new amphitheater and a 0.25- mile paved pathway. And of course the same stunning view that has wowed generations of Yosemite visitors still remains.

For the hiker ascending Four-Mile Trail, the views begin with the meandering Merced River, then all the postcard panoramas of Upper Yosemite Falls, El Capitan Half Dome, Vernal Fall and much, much more.

Get an early start; parts of the path travel through clusters of manzanita and chinquapin and can be quite hot on a summer afternoon.

DIRECTIONS TO TRAILHEAD From Southside Drive in Yosemite Valley, head 1.2 miles west of Yosemite Village to mile-marker V18 and the pullouts alongside the road.

To reach Glacier Point, head out of the valley about 9 miles south on Highway 41, then follow Glacier Point Road 16 miles east to the parking lot and trailhead. A tour bus runs from Yosemite Lodge to Glacier Point.

THE HIKE As if to disguise its charms, the first 25 percent of Four Mile Trail is simply a mellow meander across the valley floor followed by a moderate ascent among oak and manzanita. For us impatient hikers, it seems to take a long time to leave traffic noises behind.

About 1.5 miles out, the real climb begins—first through more oak woodland, then among incense cedar and white fir. It's about 2.3 miles of very steep ascent, rewarded by ever-more expansive vistas of Yosemite Valley and a bird's-eye view of Yosemite Falls.

Finally, you finish all those switchbacks and the last mile is a cooler, calmer climb and contour amidst sugar pine and white fir to Glacier Point.

■ VERNAL FALL, NEVADA FALL
Mist Trail, John Muir Trail
From Happy Isles to Vernal and Nevada falls
is a 6-mile loop with 2,000-foot elevation gain;
add another 2 miles without shuttle bus

Two famous falls and two famous footpaths are the highlights of this popular hike that many consider Yosemite's most scenic.

Vernal Fall is a cascade of uncommon beauty—a 317-foot Merced River spill that plunges over bold granite cliffs. Mist billows from the crashing water, rainbows arch toward the heavens.

Another Merced River-fed creation—Nevada Fall—also commands attention. More than one mountaineer has remarked upon the resemblance of the 594-foot falls to an avalanche of snow.

Mist Trail is a memorably steep ascent on a stair-stepped trail. En route hikers are bathed in the considerable spray of Vernal Fall. Linking the two falls with the Happy Isles Trailhead is the John Muir Trail, which extends another 210 miles or so to Mount Whitney.

The Park Service's latest reconstruction of the mile or so of trail between Happy Isles and the base of the Mist Trail stairs included the installation of a functioning drainage system. Thus, the seven-foot wide path is considerably less slick these days now that water is channeled off the trail.

Yosemite Valley visitors who are short of time should at least make the 1.6-mile round-trip pilgrimage to Vernal Fall Bridge. En route, you'll get views of two more falls—Illilouette and Upper Yosemite.

For a hike up Mist Trail, wear rain gear. On a warm summer day, however, you could just get wet, then dry out on the sunny rocks above the falls.

In spring, Yosemite's waterfalls are at their most majestic and Yosemite Valley is relatively uncrowded. Often March and April are particularly good months to hike the valley, which, because of its fairly low elevation (4,000 feet or so), usually does not have much snow on the ground during early spring.

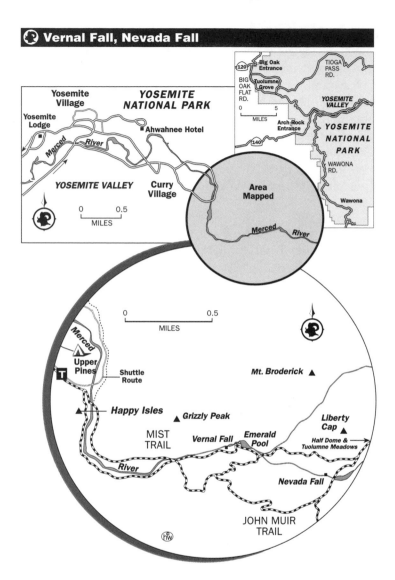

DIRECTIONS TO TRAILHEAD   Park in the Curry Village day-use lot and take the shuttle bus to the stop for Happy Isles. If you take this hike during the off-season, you'll have to walk a mile from Curry Village to the trailhead.

THE HIKE   Head out on a paved pathway, soon crossing a bridge over the Merced River. Ascend amidst oak and bay, and reach Vernal Fall Bridge after 0.8 mile.

Climbing onward, you'll choose Mist Fall Trail at a junction and ascend mist-slickened stairs carved into the rock. Passing close to Vernal Fall, you'll emerge from the mist and begin tramping a dirt trail to the top of the falls and a viewpoint.

Up-river you climb, past Emerald Pool and Silver Apron, a beautiful, broad, river-washed rock formation that resembles a fan. A mile-and-a-half out, you'll junction with John Muir Trail and follow it toward Nevada Fall. Again you follow the Merced, on a mellow 0.5 mile ascent to the base of Nevada Fall.

You'll cross the Merced on a bridge, and begin your return to Happy Isles on the John Muir Trail, carefully negotiating some slippery switchbacks. Nearing the Merced again, you'll meet a bridle trail, but stick with the footpath, bearing right to return to this walk's first junction with the Mist Trail. Bear left and retrace your steps to Happy Isles.

■ HALF DOME
John Muir, Half Dome Trails
From Happy Isles to Half Dome summit is 16.5 miles round trip with 4,800-foot elevation gain

To the non-climber of yesteryear, and even today, Half Dome seems impossible to ascend.

In his 1870 *Yosemite Guide-Book*, California's leading geologist Josiah Whitney pronounced Half Dome "perfectly inaccessible" and described it as "the only one of all the prominent points about the Yosemite which never has been and never will be trodden by the human foot."

First to surmount Half Dome was George Anderson who, in 1875, doggedly drilled his way to the top—securing eyebolts every five feet or so, standing on the last bolt while drilling the next. John Muir followed fast on the heels—and eyebolts—of his fellow Scot.

Today, Yosemite's icon summit is scaled by rock climbers using several different routes. And Half Dome can be conquered by experienced hikers, too.

The very long day hike begins in Happy Isles where the John Muir Trail begins. Past Vernal Fall and Nevada Fall you climb, then on through Little Yosemite Valley.

The final assault on the summit requires climbing at an almost 45-degree angle up slick granite with the help of twin cables that hikers grip to haul themselves to the top.

Depending on weather conditions, the Park Service installs the cables in mid-May and removes them in early October. Bring gloves to wear for the cable part of the climb.

The acrophobic and out-of-shape should hike elsewhere. Even the most experienced hikers should remember that mid-afternoon summer thunderstorms in Yosemite are common. The last place you want to be in an electric storm is atop Half Dome, forced to make a hurried descent over slippery rock while holding on to wet metal cables. Get an early start on this trail. You want to top Half Dome and begin your descent by early afternoon—just in case a thunderstorm blows into the valley.

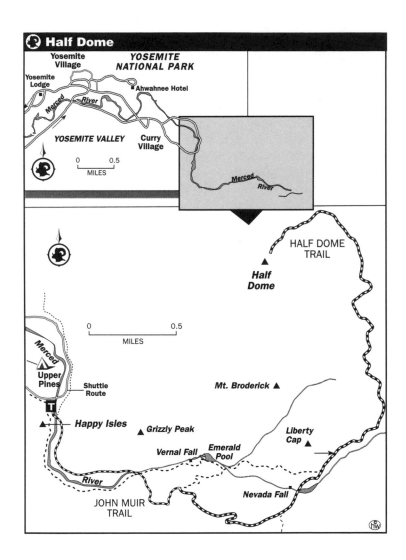

Up top, there's a lot of top—a very broad summit indeed. From the 8,842-foot dome you get 360-degree vistas: up and down Yosemite Valley, Clouds Rest and Cathedral Peak, the jagged Sierra crest.

DIRECTIONS TO TRAILHEAD Leave your car in the large lot at Curry Village. Take the shuttle bus to Happy Isles.

If you're getting an early start (before shuttle service begins at 7 a.m.), you must hike up-valley about 0.8 mile from Curry Village day-use parking to Happy Isles along the shuttle bus route. This increases your already long hiking day to 18 miles round trip.

THE HIKE Beginning at the beginning (more often the end, actually) of the Happy Isles-to-Mt. Whitney John Muir Trail, hike along the Merced River. You soon cross the river on a wide bridge and ascend on a paved pathway.

One mile along, cross the river again below Vernal Fall and reach a fork. Two trails climb to Nevada Fall. Mist Trail shaves almost a mile from the distance, but is a strenuous, stair-stepping route. The right fork—the JMT—makes a more moderate ascent via well-engineered switchbacks.

The Muir and Mist trails reunite 2.7 miles from Happy Isles and you continue climbing above and parallel to the Merced River, traveling into Little Yosemite Valley. At the 4.5-mile mark, the trail divides again (the right fork leads to a campsite), then reunites again in 0.25 mile.

A bit more than 6 miles out, bid adieu to the JMT and bear left on Half Dome Trail, climbing wooded slopes toward the great rock. About 0.75-mile from the top, you begin the final ascent, first climbing granite steps, then topping a minor dome before descending briefly to a saddle, where you find the cables. Get a grip on the cables (and yourself) and climb to the top.

Make your way carefully over to the dome's very highest point, located at the north end. Enjoy the view, but stay away from the cliff edge.

■ MIRROR LAKE
Mirror Lake Trail
From Shuttle Bus Stop to Mirror Lake is 2 miles round trip; with optional Tenaya Creek loop is 4.8 miles round trip

Once upon a time, Half Dome's reflection in Mirror Lake was beautiful to behold, a living postcard admired by generations of Yosemite Valley visitors.

Such reflections are rare now, and will soon be no more.

Never a deep body of water, it was a pond naturally enclosed by a rockfall. In 1890, humans enhanced the little lake's reflective qualities by constructing a dam.

Mirror Lakes usually dries up at summer's end. In years past at this time the Park Service dredged the lakebed, hauling away tons of sand and gravel. The excavated material was spread on winter roads to gain autos better traction on the snow.

In 1971, this practice was stopped, and each year since, silt has accumulated to make Mirror Lake ever-smaller. These days Mirror is quite literally just a shadow of its former self, a gravelly lake bottom fringed by a meadow with a branch of Tenaya Creek flowing through it.

Mirror Meadow, er, lake, nevertheless remains a popular destination for day hikers. The setting, even sans reflection, still inspires, and kids enjoy frolicking in and along Tenaya Creek.

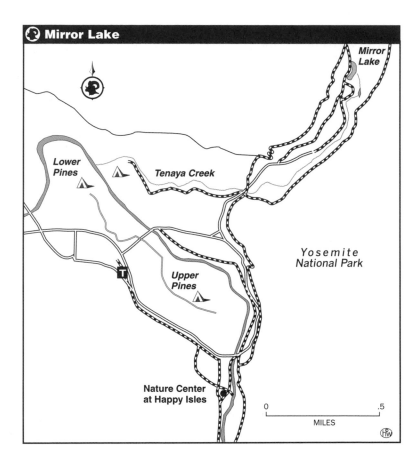

In the old days, a parking area for autos (later a shuttle bus stop) was situated close to the shores of Mirror Lake. Now the shuttle bus stops a mile from the lake and you may choose to walk the distance along a paved road or hoof it along a bridle trail.

Beyond the lake, you can extend your walk by tramping up and down the narrow canyon cut by Tenaya Creek. The extra distance rewards with a bit of forested solitude.

DIRECTIONS TO TRAILHEAD   Take the Yosemite Valley shuttle bus to stop #17, Mirror Lake.

THE HIKE   Saunter (usually with lots of company) along the paved road, soon crossing Tenaya Creek on a stone bridge. The road winds with the river, climbing gently to Mirror Lake.

At the bridge you can lose some of the crowd by joining the dirt bridle trail that travels through a very mixed forest of oak, Douglas fir, incense cedar and big-leaf maple to the lake. Despite the guided platoons of rental horses (stand

Mirror Lake in days gone by was a place for reflection—both literally and spiritually.

aside to let them pass) and plethora of road apples, the bridle trail is an enjoy-able and altogether more peaceful walk than the paved route.

Once at the lake, such as it is, locate the bridle trail on the north side and begin walking on a meandering trail that leads away from the lake.

You'll travel amidst forest and ferns, passing a junction with the trail leading to Tenaya Lake, then reaching a wooden bridge that spans frisky Tenaya Creek. Now you follow the Bridle Trail along the south side of the creek. Look up from your nearly level trail to admire Basket Dome and Half Dome. Continue past the Mirror Lake site 0.25 mile, cross Tenaya Creek on a footbridge, then rejoin the paved road leading back to the shuttle bus stop.

■ YOSEMITE VALLEY
Yosemite Valley Loop Trail
5.5-mile loop

Two generations of so-called hiking authorities have repeated two words of advice about the floor of Yosemite Valley: "Stay away."

I disagree.

Considering the crowds and congestion that often overwhelm Yosemite Vil-lage and its asphalt arteries, the valley's trail system offers a surprisingly, and refreshingly, natural experience. To be sure Yosemite's heart-of-the-valley trails are very well used; however, they're not overwhelmed by hikers. And you just might find that traveling in company with hikers from across the nation and around the world is a unique experience, too.

Hiking Yosemite Valley's floor delivers a view lost to most motorists. When you get away from what John Muir termed "blunt-nosed mechanical beetles"

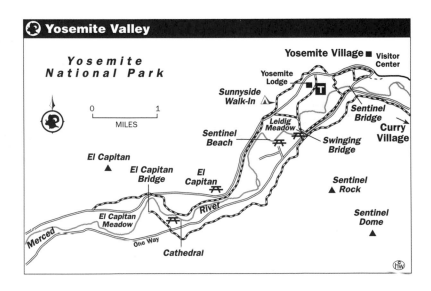

Camping has long been one of the favorite activities in Yosemite National Park.

and set out afoot, the scale and grandeur of all that stone meeting sky—Royal Arches, North Dome, Clouds Rest, Half Dome and more—seems to increase exponentially.

For purposes of a hiker's quick geographical orientation, Yosemite Valley can be said to begin on the west where Bridalveil Fall cascades from the valley's south wall. The valley extends east as far as Washington Column, the stone pillar positioned above where Tenaya Creek and the Merced River converge.

Veteran valley hikers all have their favorite loops, long and short. Some divide the hiking into east valley and west valley segments. Others characterize Yosemite Valley floor walking as the Village Loop or the Lodge Loop. Hiking options are limited only by the finite number of bridges over the Merced River.

I've described a middle-distance jaunt. Families with young hikers might enjoy a shorter Sunnyside Camp-Yosemite Chapel-Sentinel Bridge loop. Lengthen the described loop by continuing west to Bridalveil Meadow and Bridalveil Fall or by meandering east via the network of paths connecting The Ahwanee, Curry Village and Yosemite Village.

This valley walkabout begins near historic Yosemite Lodge. The U.S. Army established its headquarters here in the park in 1906 and constructed barracks, bath houses and tent houses. When the Army left in 1914, facilities were converted to visitor accommodations. The drafty, rustic tent cabins were used by generations of park visitors.

This hike begins at today's much-upgraded Yosemite Lodge; however, the actual trailhead is located across Northside Road by Sunnyside Walk-in Campground. Older hikers may recall that this campground was drive-in, not walk-in, until 1976. True, other valley campgrounds of the era were noisy and crowded, but Sunnyside was particularly cacophonic.

DIRECTIONS TO TRAILHEAD   Day-use parking is available at Yosemite Lodge. Walk from the lodge to the parking lot for Sunnyside Walk-in Campground, located almost directly across Northside Road from Yosemite Lodge. March north to the camp parking lot. Just 50 yards after the asphalt ends you'll intersect your chosen pathway. Turn left and begin your excursion.

THE HIKE   Follow the path southwest through a mixed woodland 0.3 mile to cross Northside Drive. Head south along the edge of Leidig Meadow. The meadow was named for hoteliers Isabella and George Leidig, who constructed an inn situated below Sentinel Rock in 1869. Enjoy grand views of Half Dome, Cloud's Rest, Washington Column, and much more. You'll get another chance to partake of the vistas on the return leg of this hike.

The path heads west to meander between North Side Road and the willow- and cottonwood-cloaked north bank of the Merced River and passes Sentinel Beach Picnic Area at the 0.75 mile mark and aptly named Yellow Pine Picnic Area shortly thereafter.

Another mile of sojourning along the Merced leads to El Capitan Picnic Area. Observe mighty El Capitan, which towers 3,593 feet above the Merced River. Rock climbers can frequently be seen ascending the monolith, believed to be the largest block of exposed granite in the world.

Continue another 0.5 mile west along the Merced to Devils Elbow, which doesn't sound named for fun, but actually is kind of Yosemite's Riviera—a sandy beach with plenty of flat rocks for sunbathing.

Cross the river via the road over El Capitan Bridge and resume trail-walking southeast toward Cathedral Picnic Area. Carefully cross Southside Drive, head briefly south, then east, on a two-mile stretch of trail in the shadow of the valley's south wall. Savor magnificent views of the valley's north wall, including Upper and Lower Yosemite falls.

A bit more than 4.5 miles along, your path crosses Sentinel Creek and after another 0.25 mile passes a junction with Four-Mile Trail (see page 150) that ascends to Glacier Point. Another 0.25 mile brings you to Swinging Bridge Picnic Area.

Return to Yosemite Lodge by joining the paved bike path that skirts Leidig Meadow.

■ YOSEMITE FALLS
Yosemite Falls Trail
6.6 miles round trip with 3,200-foot elevation gain

Truly it's a wonder—a three-tiered cascade combining the 1,430-foot upper Yosemite Falls, the 675-foot middle falls, and 320-foot lower Yosemite Falls. That adds up to a total height of 2,425 feet—highest in North America.

Most Yosemite Valley visitors pay homage to Yosemite Falls, third highest waterfall in the world, by walking a short distance to the base of the lower falls. Another trail—a much more difficult one—leads to the top of the upper falls. Looking up Yosemite Falls from its base offers one perspective; watching it spill over the brink from the top is another memorable experience.

The path to upper Yosemite Falls, one of the park's oldest, was originally built as a private sector endeavor in the 1870s and operated as a toll trail. Hikers paid fees at the trailhead before making the ascent.

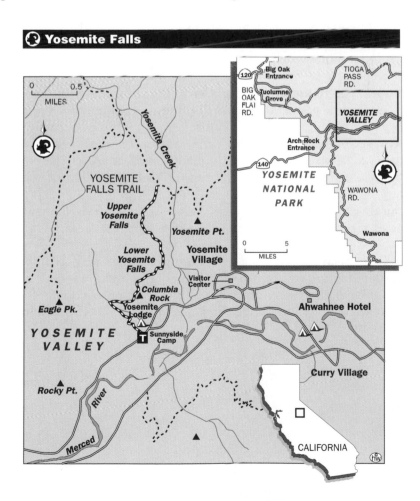

Yosemite Falls Trail climbs the airy heights to the precipice of Upper Yosemite Falls, rewarding the hard-working hiker with magnificent views of Yosemite Valley. The trail's steepness scares off some hikers, but many more remain undaunted and make the climb. Expect company—sometimes more than you'd prefer—en route.

Best time to visit is in springtime when snowmelt swells the falls to their most spectacular. In summer, or in drought years, the falls flow with far less vigor.

Be sure to check out the new and very much improved area around the base of the falls. The National Park Service added a mile of new trail, granite walls, a stone amphitheater and five new bridges over Yosemite Creek. Dozens of interpretive signs highlight the area's ecology and history, and there's even a shrine offering homage to John Muir, who lived at the base of the falls in 1869 and 1870.

And be sure to thank heaven—or at least donors to the $13.5 million Yosemite Falls Project, completed in 2005, the largest private-public project in park history—for what you don't see anymore: a bus parking lot the size of a football field and 50 diesel-belching buses disgorging thousands of visitors, who shuffled along an ugly asphalt path to get to one of the world's foremost scenic wonders.

DIRECTIONS TO TRAILHEAD Park across the road from Yosemite Lodge. Locate the trail by the gas station near the east edge of Sunnyside Campground.

THE HIKE Wasting no time, the path climbs steeply in the company of oaks, zigzagging upward via more than 40 tight switchbacks. A mile later, gain a viewpoint at Columbia Rock. Savor the view of Yosemite Valley located 1,000 feet below.

After another 0.5 mile, the path nears Lower Yosemite Falls. Soon after, it's more switchbacks and before long you leave behind the trees for a rockier world.

At the 3-mile mark, you'll reach a junction with Eagle Peak Trail, but bear right (east) and descend toward Yosemite Creek. You'll spot a short connector trail that you may follow (very carefully) to a precipitous overlook. The main path crosses the creek on a footbridge and ascends 0.75 mile to Yosemite Point and terrific views.

■ TUOLUMNE GROVE
Tuolumne Grove Trail
From Tioga Road To Tuolumne Grove is
2.5 miles round trip with 500-foot elevation gain

Tuolumne Grove stands tall for hikers. In Yosemite days of old, park visitors drove Big Oak Flat Road right up to the towering sequoias. Now paved, 6-mile-long "Old" Big Oak Flat Road is closed to vehicle traffic and travelers must walk a mile to admire the grove.

Tuolumne Grove's modern orientation to travelers afoot extends to its most famed attraction—Dead Giant. This gargantuan sequoia stump was tunneled in 1878 in order that horse-drawn wagons, and later automobiles, could drive through it. Nowadays Dead Giant is a "Walk Through" tree.

Travelers from around the world hike to Tuolumne Grove and you may hear exclamations of wonder in many languages. However, the steep return climb from the grove is often more hike than these visitors expected and the sentiments expressed on the way back are best left untranslated.

Walk through Dead Giant—the stump was tunneled in 1878 and is still standing today.

DIRECTIONS TO TRAILHEAD Tuolumne Grove is located in the Crane Flat area of the park. The trailhead is located off Tioga Road just 0.5 mile north of its intersection with Big Oak Flat Road.

THE HIKE Descend through a mixed forest on the paved road. About a mile out, a sign welcomes you to Tuolumne Grove and two more minutes of walking bring you to the first giant sequoias.

A signed right fork leads to the Dead Giant. Walk on through and descend to a picnic area situated in close company with more huge sequoias. From the picnic area, a 0.25 mile dirt trail loops through the tall trees.

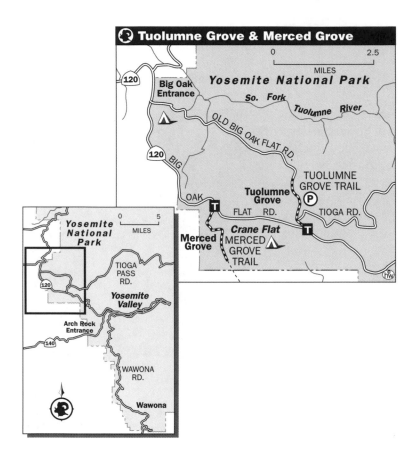

■ MERCED GROVE

Merced Grove Trail

To Merced Grove is 3 miles round trip
with 400-foot elevation gain

Tucked into a remote western pocket of the park, Merced Grove is by far less visited than Mariposa and Tuolumne, Yosemite's other sequoia groves. By tree count (20 or so), it's the smallest grove and it requires the longest walk in order to reach it.

Thus the hiker looking for solitude among the sequoias might just find it in Merced Grove or, at least be assured that the trail will be shared with only a few kindred spirits.

The path to the grove is a dirt road, one of the first carriage roads created during the early horse-and-buggy days of the national park. In later years grove visitors drove their autos down the road to Merced Grove.

In the quiet serenity of the ancient forest, wild creatures live as they always have. Tread lightly for a possible glimpse.

Now the road is for hikers only. Park rangers haven't posted any interpretive signs or built any facilities in the grove, so the hiker comes away with the same feeling of wonder and discovery that the grove's first visitors may have had.

Actually, the National Park Service did build one structure in the grove long ago—a log cabin. The Russell Cabin—or Merced Grove Cabin, as it's sometimes called—served as a ranger station and as an occasional retreat for the park superintendent. The cabin is in fine shape but it's boarded-up and not currently used.

DIRECTIONS TO TRAILHEAD From the junction or Highway 120 Tioga Road and Big Oak Flat Road (also Highway 120) proceed west on the latter road 3.7 miles (that's 3.5 miles past Crane Flat Campground) to the signed turnout for Merced Grove on the left (south) side of the road. The signed trail departs from the small parking area.

THE HIKE The fairly level road travels through a mixed forest. At first, tree-lovers are apt to cringe a bit when they look to the west of the road and see so many fire-destroyed trees.

However, the tree vistas soon improve. At the half-mile mark, you'll reach a signed junction, fork left, and begin a steep descent among an inspiring mixture of ponderosa pine, sugar pine, incense cedar and white fir.

After a mile's descent from the junction, you'll reach the first sequoias—a half-dozen fine specimens located to the right of the road. A tiny creek trickles between two of the giants.

Walk a few more minutes down the road to the old ranger cabin and more inspiring tall trees. Sketchy trails lead down to the creek and more sequoias, but most hikers will be content to linger by the cabin, then retrace their steps back to the trailhead.

■ HETCH HETCHY
Hetch Hetchy Trail
To Wapama Falls is 4 miles round trip; to Rancheria Falls is 13 miles round trip with 800-foot elevation gain

Almost no one living now remembers how Hetch Hetchy Valley looked before it was flooded with water in 1915. It certainly looks beautiful in the old photographs and paintings we can view today. Travel books of that early era, and descriptions by conservationists, including John Muir, who struggled mightily to save Hetch Hetchy, say that it was second only to Yosemite Valley in grandeur.

When O'Shaughnessy Dam was completed and the waters of the Tuolumne River impounded, the valley became an 8-mile-long reservoir, providing water for the city of San Francisco. Today, the reservoir continues to serve its original function, although periodically proposals are circulated to drain the reservoir

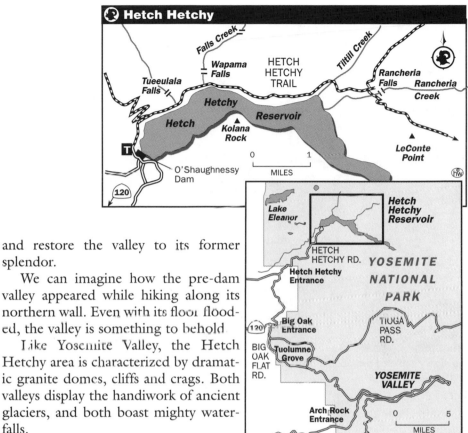

and restore the valley to its former splendor.

We can imagine how the pre-dam valley appeared while hiking along its northern wall. Even with its floor flooded, the valley is something to behold.

Like Yosemite Valley, the Hetch Hetchy area is characterized by dramatic granite domes, cliffs and crags. Both valleys display the handiwork of ancient glaciers, and both boast mighty waterfalls.

Hetch Hetchy's Wapama Falls spills 1,200 feet over a granite precipice. The falls are spawned by Falls Creek, a tributary of the Tuolumne River. At the end of the hike is tiny Rancheria Falls, providing a little water music for an inspiringly situated trail camp.

Linking the waterfalls is a path along the north side of Hetch Hetchy Reservoir. It's a fairly low elevation pathway, and therefore makes an enticing early-in-the-season Sierra jaunt. In the spring, Hetch Hetchy's falls are at their most vigorous.

DIRECTIONS TO TRAILHEAD From Highway 120, a mile west of Big Oak Flat entrance station, take the Hetch Hetchy turn-off and follow Evergreen Road, then Hetch Hetchy Road 16 miles to its end at the parking lot above O'Shaughnessy Dam and Hetch Hetchy Reservoir.

THE HIKE Proceed across the dam, reading en route the interpretive plaques detailing the dam's and reservoir's dimensions. Look to the north side of the canyon to view Hetch Hetchy Dome and Wapama Falls.

Alas, historic photos provide our only view of exquisite Hetch Hetchy Valley before it was dammed.

Travel through a 500-foot-long tunnel, emerging to join an old road that in turn leads over gray pine-dotted slopes.

A mile out, you'll reach a junction and head right (east) as the road gives way to a footpath. In another 0.5 mile, pass by seasonal Tueeulala Falls, and in another 0.5 mile, spot Wapama Falls, soon reached by winding trail. With the falls roaring in your ears. you'll cross a couple of branches of Fall Creek on a series of wood-and-steel bridges, then carefully climb oak- and poison oak-covered slopes.

The trail levels about 4 miles out, crosses a footbridge over a creek at 5 miles, then climbs past some inviting swimming holes and water slides along the creek. At the 6-mile mark, reach a junction with a connector trail that leads to a Ponderosa pine- and incense cedar-shaded campsite located below Rancheria Falls.

Stick with the main trail for another half-mile to reach a bridge over Rancheria Creek just above the falls. Enjoy the inspiring vista before retracing your steps to the trailhead.

■ LUKENS LAKE

Lukens Lake Trail

From Tioga Road to Lukens Lake is 1.6 miles round trip; from White Wolf Campground to Lukens Lake is 4.6 miles round trip

Were Lukens Lake located anywhere but in the middle of Yosemite National Park, it would surely be an even more compelling destination. You see, all it offers is a beautiful lake bordered by a red-fir forest and a lovely meadow. Oh, and the opportunity for picnicking, swimming and trout fishing, too.

Two family-style trails lead to Lukens. From Tioga Road an easy 0.5 mile ascent to a saddle and a 0.3 mile descent deliver you to the lake. A longer route travels to the lake from White Wolf Campground. Either way to go is a winner and offers hikers of all sizes the feeling of entering the remote Yosemite high country.

Lukens Lake gets its fair share of snow—and more—and it tends to linger into late spring and early summer. Don't be surprised if you find snow patches en route and the lake's meadow under water.

DIRECTIONS TO TRAILHEAD From the intersection of Big Oak Flat Road and Tioga Road, drive 17 miles on Tioga Road to a turnout on the right. Park here and cross the road to the trailhead.

The departure point for the longer hike is across from White Wolf Lodge. The turn-off for White Wolf is located 2 miles west of the shorter-walk trailhead off Tioga Road.

Explore idyllic Lukens Lake on a couple of easy trails; ideal for a family outing.

THE HIKE Carefully cross Tioga Road and pick up the signed trail to Lukens Lake. After a mellow ascent over a pine-forested ridge, the path drops to a meadow on the south end of the lake, then the trail bends east and north around the lake.

If you're bound for Lukens Lake the long way, you'll join the signed trail right across from the lodge and meander 0.75 mile through lodgepole pine forest. Cross the Middle Fork of the Tuolumne River on logs and in 0.25 mile intersect a trail that leads left to the Grand Canyon of the Tuolumne River. Your route is south, then east, through mellow (and sometimes mushy and mosquito-filled) meadows to a junction with Ten Lakes Trail. Here you fork right, cross the Tuolumne River, then ascend a final 0.25 mile to the lake.

■ **TEN LAKES BASIN**
Ten Lakes Trail
To first lakes is 12.8 miles round trip with 2,100-foot elevation gain; many side trips possible

John Muir named this alpine basin in the center of Yosemite National Park "Ten Lakes."

Scenically, some hikers rate the basin a "10." Numerically, ten lakes may be a bit of an exaggeration. More like seven lakes are worthy of the name; however, numerous tarns dot the ice-sculpted landscape and they could swell the count to more than ten.

The walk leads to two of the lakes; the balance can be reached by use trails or cross-country routes. It's a popular weekend backpacking trip, located at mid-level elevation (7,500 to 9,500 feet or so), meaning the trail can be hiked a bit earlier and a bit later in the seasons than higher trails on the Sierra Crest.

DIRECTIONS TO TRAILHEAD From Highway 120 (Tioga Road), drive 20 miles east of Crane Flat, 27 miles west of Tioga Pass, to the signed trailhead for Ten Lakes. Park on either side of the highway.

THE HIKE A half-minute's walk brings you to a trail junction. The left-forking path leads to Yosemite Valley while our Ten Lakes-bound trail heads right (north).

Ascend through Sierra juniper and Jeffrey pine forest toward the headwaters of Yosemite Creek. Emerging from the forest, the path climbs granite slopes and reaches a junction at the two-mile mark with a westbound trail leading to White Wolf Campground.

Continue your climb over forested slopes another 2 miles to Half Moon Meadow, seasonally sprinkled with corn lily, monkeyflower, aster and other wildflowers. Switchbacking steeply up from the meadow, you'll climb another mile, passing a junction with a right-forking connector trail that leads to Grant Lakes just before cresting a ridge—the divide between Tuolumne and Merced rivers.

Ridgetop (9,690 feet) views are of Ten Lakes Basin, Sierra Crest peaks and, as you begin descending, of Grand Canyon of the Tuolumne.

A fairly steep 1-mile descent leads to Ten Lakes Basin's largest lake, another 0.5 mile to the second largest. If you have time and topo maps, strike out cross-country for the basin's more remote lakes and tarns.

■ NORTH DOME
Porcupine Creek, North Dome Trails
From Tioga Road to Indian Ridge Arch is 6.1 miles
round trip; North Dome summit is 9 miles round trip
with 600-foot elevation gain

Reaching the top of North Dome rewards the hiker with what is likely the most captivating and complete panorama of Yosemite Valley. Some Half Dome supporters say the Yosemite icon offers superior views, but North Dome devotees are quick to point out that North Dome offers something Half Dome can't provide: a view of Half Dome!

And not just any view of Half Dome—an in-your-face-available-only-to-the-hiker vista. From the top of North Dome unfolds a panorama of polished stone that includes Cloud's Rest, Glacier Point, Sentinel Dome and much more.

From a Yosemite Valley floor perspective, 7,542-foot North Dome dominates over the north wall of Tenaya Canyon opposite Half Dome. It appears impossible to ascend but, surprisingly, the rounded mass of granite can be traveled and topped by a moderately graded pathway.

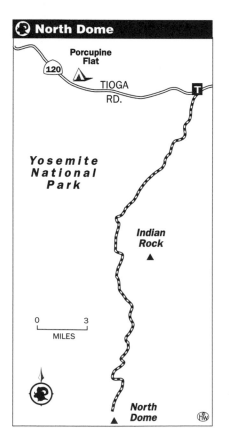

The path to the dome begins at Porcupine Flat (formerly a campground, closed in 1976 and relocated a mile down Tioga Road). Porcupine Flat is home to scores of the namesake animal, whose favorite food source is the inner bark of conifers—the area's lodgepole pines in particular.

In addition to the local lodgepoles, a generous selection of other Yosemite trees may be glimpsed en route: silver pine, Jeffrey pine, red fir and huckleberry oak. Several life zones overlap at this elevation (about 8,000 feet), creating this intriguing collection of trees. Those curious hikers who want to learn more about Yosemite's Conifer-Land can take Cones and Needles Trail, a short interpretive path that begins at a turnout on Tioga Road just west of the North Dome trailhead.

An intermediate destination—or extra added attraction—for this hike is Indian Rock, an unusual stone arch perched atop Indian Ridge. The delicate, 20-foot arch, scarcely one-foot thick at its thickest part, is not Yosemite's only arch (another is below the surface of the Tuolumne River in Tuolumne Meadows), but it is the only one accessible to hikers.

DIRECTIONS TO TRAILHEAD Signed North Dome trailhead is located off Tioga Road (Highway 120) some 24 miles east of Crane Flat and 1 mile east of Porcupine Flat Campground.

THE HIKE Follow the old campground road (first paved, then dirt) for 0.7 mile. The route narrows to signed Porcupine Creek Trail, crosses two branches of Porcupine Creek, and wanders through the forest for another 0.8 mile.

At the 1.5-mile mark, you'll intersect Snow Creek Trail. Walk right a dozen paces, then veer left almost immediately at a second junction.

The path begins a mellow ascent of Indian Ridge. Two miles out, the tree cover parts to permit a so-so view of Yosemite Valley. A switchbacking climb brings you to a saddle and to a signed side trail to Indian Rock.

Indian Rock Connector Trail (0.25 mile long) ascends rather steeply up rocky Indian Ridge, gains the ridgetop, and travels it north to the arch—or Indian Ridge Arch as it's sometimes called.

From the saddle, North Dome Trail descends along the forested crest of Indian Ridge for another 1.2 miles to meet the trail to Yosemite Falls at about 4 miles from the trailhead. Turn left and descend some tight switchbacks to the shoulder of North Dome, then across the top of the long, bald dome.

Savor the incomparable view of the Merced River flowing through Yosemite Valley far below and identify the waterfalls cascading from the valley walls. Along with El Capitan, Three Brothers and the other prominent landmarks, be sure to look out at Little Yosemite Valley and Mt. Starr King.

■ MAY LAKE
May Lake Trail
2.4 miles round trip with 500-foot elevation gain

Situated in the geographical center of the national park are Mt. Hoffman and May Lake, two picturesque high country destinations.

The path to May Lake is an easy one. Beyond the lake, the climb to the top of 10,850-foot Mt. Hoffman is steep (1,500-foot gain in 2 miles). The prominent peak honors Charles F. Hoffman, chief mapmaker of the Whitney Geological Survey of 1863 that explored the area.

Tucked at the base of Mt. Hoffman, May Lake entices anglers in search of rainbow and brook trout. By the lake is one of Yosemite's High Sierra Camps, which offer meals and tent-cabin accommodations. Such camps are sited a day's hike apart on a 50-mile loop around Tuolumne Meadows and are usually reserved (for a fee) well in advance. Not to despair if you lack a reservation for

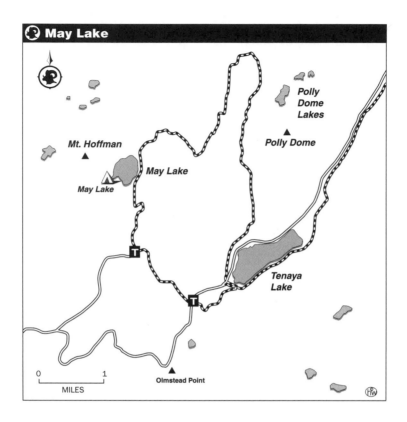

May Lake High Sierra Camp; a "regular" trail camp is located on the lake's south shore.

The walk to May Lake is short in distance but long on views: Cathedral Peak, Clouds Rest, Half Dome and of course Mt. Hoffman, thrusting, it seems, right out of the lake.

DIRECTIONS TO TRAILHEAD   From Tenaya Lake, head west on Tioga Road (Highway 120) 4 miles to the turn-off for May Lake. Turn north and drive 1.8 miles to road's end at the parking area.

THE HIKE   The hike passes through a forest of lodgepole pine and red fir that soon thins as the route climbs into rockier terrain. A half-mile out, enjoy the views of Half Dome and the castellated Cathedral Peaks.

The trail divides at May Lake: High Sierra Camp to the right, backpacker's camp to the left. Walk the lakeshore all the way around the lake if you'd like.

If the summit of Mt. Hoffman calls to you, know that it's a difficult 2-mile climb to the top. There's a sketchy use trail, a footpath that is neither officially established nor maintained. Head west, pass the campground and begin the ascent above the lake's south shore. The route traverses a meadow, then climbs northwest up to Hoffman's fairly flat summit ridge. Easiest (least difficult would be a better way to put it) of Hoffman's peaklets to scale is the west summit. Enjoy the view and return the way you came.

■ CLOUDS REST
Sunrise Lakes, Clouds Rest Trails
From Tenaya Lake to Sunrise Lakes is 10 miles
round trip; to Clouds Rest is 14 miles round trip
with 2,300-foot elevation gain

Climb to where the clouds rest, 9,926 feet high in the sky. Clouds Rest is higher than Half Dome, but safer and easier to climb.

In addition, Clouds Rest offers better views (some hikers say the best in the national park) than the famed Yosemite icon. From atop Clouds Rest, Yosemite's largest granite face, savor a panorama of rounded domes and sharp ridges.

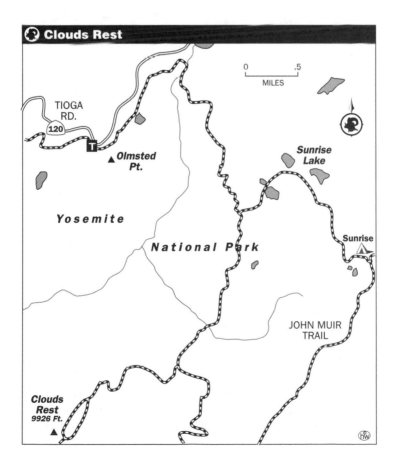

It's no secret how this peak got its appropriate name, Clouds Rest.

While an easier hike than the one up Half Dome, Clouds Rest Trail is far from easy. The final part of the climb is very steep, an ascent over a narrow ridge with a steep drop-off on either side.

DIRECTIONS TO TRAILHEAD From Highway 120 (Tioga Pass Road) 9 miles west of the Tuolumne Meadows Visitor Center and some 16 miles east of White Wolf, take the turn-off for the Tenaya Lake Walk-in Campground (at the southwest end of the lake). Leave your car in the large lot and begin your hike at the signs for Sunrise.

THE HIKE Follow the signs for Sunrise High Sierra Camp, soon crossing Tenaya Creek and making your way across meadowland and among stands of lodgepole pine.

A mile-and-a-half out, the ascent steepens, cresting a ridge at 3 miles, where there's a junction. Sunrise High Sierra Camp Trail heads left, while you continue straight (south), dropping from the ridgetop. All too soon you climb again, reaching another junction at the 5-mile mark. The left-branching trail is a connector leading to Sunrise Creek and a junction with the John Muir Trail. You continue straight through thinning forest toward a rocky ridge.

A quarter-mile from your goal, you crest this ridge, then carefully climb stacked layers of granite to the summit.

■ TENAYA LAKE
Tenaya Lake Trail
2.4 miles round trip

Tenaya makes everybody's Top Ten High Sierra Lakes list. Tucked in a basin of polished granite, the lake sparkles in the Sierra sun. No wonder they call this the Range of Light!

Tenaya is not only a real looker, it's hard to overlook. It's that big beauty you see right by Tioga Pass Road as you motor to Tuolumne Meadows. While you can see Tenaya from the highway, and can survey the lake from Olmsted Point, you'll appreciate it even more while walking Tenaya Trail.

Most visitors to the lake named for the chief of the native Awahneeche head for the picnic area or the white-sand strand and seem pretty oblivious that a trail follows the lakeshore.

DIRECTIONS TO TRAILHEAD   From its junction with Big Oak Flat Road, follow Highway 120 (Tioga Road) 32 miles to the east end of Tenaya Lake and a parking lot.

THE HIKE   Walk along the sandy beach, then join the path along the lake's southeast shore, contouring through pine forest. Watch for rock-climbers

The light plays prettily on Yosemite's high-country peaks—early morning and late afternoon are prime times for pure drama.

practicing their craft on 9,810-foot Polly Dome to the north. The path continues to Olmsted Point, but you can turn back whenever you feel so inclined.

Another option is to continue on the trail past its junction with the trail to Sunrise Lakes and back up to the parking area by Tioga Road. Loop-lovers can complete a loop around the lake by walking along the northwest shore; however, much of this not-very-tranquil path travels right next to Tioga Road.

■ CATHEDRAL LAKES
John Muir Trail
To Lower Cathedral Lake is 7.5 miles round trip with 1,000-foot elevation gain.

Standing watch over the Cathedral Lakes are the lofty spires of Cathedral Peak. Many of John Muir's effusive descriptions of the High Sierra have a spiritual tone, and refer to landscapes as sanctuaries, temples and cathedrals.

The John Muir Trail extends from Happy Isles in Yosemite Valley some 210 miles through what some backpackers consider the most scenic high country in the U.S.

The larger and lower Cathedral Lake is a popular weekend backpacker destination. A little too popular, perhaps. Unless you're continuing to higher and farther destinations on the John Muir Trail, Cathedral Lake is best enjoyed as a day-hike destination.

Around the lake, geologic history is written in the rocks. In the shadow of craggy Cathedral Peak are lakeside granite slabs that offer flat spots for sunning

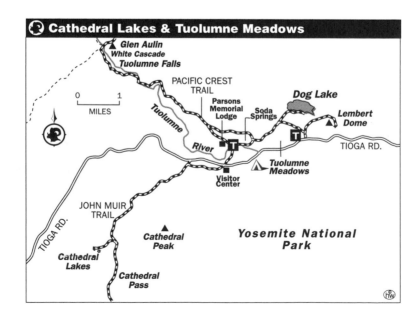

and picnicking. Near the lake are curious erratics: ice-transported boulders that were left here when the glaciers melted.

Hikers opting for a 13-mile hike can ascend to Sunrise High Sierra Camp, then loop over to Tenaya Lake. The park's shuttle-bus service links the two trailheads.

DIRECTIONS TO TRAIL-HEAD The small Cathedral Lakes trailhead is just off Highway 120 (Tioga Pass Road) 1.5 miles west of Tuolumne Campground entrance or some 24 miles east of White Wolf.

In summer, you can ride the free shuttle bus by leaving your car at the Tuolumne Meadows Wilderness Permit station or Tenaya Lake, if your prefer adding some miles to the Cathedral Lakes hike.

Sanctuary to remember: Cathedral Peaks.

THE HIKE From the parking area, walk 0.1 mile through the forest to a four-way junction. Proceed straight on steep John Muir Trail. It's dusty (the path is heavily used by stock) and steep going for the first 0.7 mile. The trail mellows for a time, passing among lodgepole pines before climbing again.

A bit more than 2 miles of ascent brings you to a forested saddle. Begin descending. Cathedral Peak appears on the skyline to your left. Three miles out, the trail divides. JMT leads another half mile to upper Cathedral Lake and some shoreline campsites. The right fork descends 0.5 mile to lower Cathedral Lake.

See Map
on Page
178

■ TUOLUMNE MEADOWS

Tuolumne Meadows Trail
From Tioga Road to Parsons Lodge
and Soda Springs is 1.5 miles round trip

Lush and lovely Tuolumne Meadow is likely the national park's best known site outside of Yosemite Valley, and for good reason. Easily accessible by short trails, the High Sierra's largest sub-alpine meadow is a glorious, wildflower-splashed basin ringed by forested slopes, roundish domes and sharp summits.

John Muir's first summer in the Sierra was spent as a shepherd, tending a flock of some 2,000 sheep pastured in Tuolumne Meadows. Muir's journals of that time are filled with the wonders of nature he observed along with his first thoughts about the preservation of Yosemite. Muir soon realized that sheep, which he later characterized as "hoofed locusts," and other grazing animals could destroy an alpine meadow.

Today a length of the John Muir Trail crosses the great naturalist's beloved Tuolumne Meadows. Other paths lead to Parsons Memorial Lodge, named for Edward Parsons, who fought alongside John Muir to preserve the park, Hetch Hetchy Valley and other wildlands during the early days of the Sierra Club. After Parsons, an accomplished photographer, outings leader and early Sierra Club President, died in 1915, the Club constructed this lodge in his honor.

Parsons Lodge, long ago deeded to the National Park Service, has served as a reading room/library for generations of visitors. Many a hiker has found a

Spend a memorable day exploring the bends of the Tuolumne River.

cool retreat on a hot summer's day or taken refuge from an afternoon thunderstorm.

Interpretive signs posted sporadically along Tuolumne Meadows paths offer insights about Parsons, Muir, the old Tioga Road and the Native American tribes who visited the meadows for so many centuries. For more information about the meadows, visit Tuolumne Meadows Visitor Center (open summer only), located about 0.1 mile west of the trailhead on Tioga Road.

DIRECTIONS TO THE TRAILHEAD I like to begin this ramble from the north side of Tioga Road, just 0.1 mile east of Tuolumne Meadows Visitor Center. Parking is along both sides of Tioga Road.

Some hikers prefer to access the Tuolumne Meadows trail system from the Lembert Dome/Glen Aulin/Soda Springs trailhead located a little farther east.

THE HIKE The wide path extends north across the meadows. Families linger along the bends of the Tuolumne River to fish or to enjoy one of the best picnic spots on the planet.

Cross the wooden bridge over the Tuolumne River, bend left along the river and take the signed trail forking right to Parsons Memorial Lodge. From the lodge, follow the signed path very briefly east to Soda Springs, a muddy area where carbonated water percolates up from the ground.

The trail loops past some interpretive plaques, then angles back toward the bridge over the Tuolumne River. From here you retrace your steps back to the trailhead.

See Map on Page 178

■ TUOLUMNE FALLS
AND GLEN AULIN
Pacific Crest Trail
To Tuolumne Falls is 9 miles round trip
with 400-foot elevation gain

In a national park that boasts Yosemite Falls and some of the world's best waterfalls, a relatively modest cascade such as Tuolumne Falls is apt to be overlooked. And not only is it a fraction of the size of the park's famed falls, it's located far from Waterfall Central, the Yosemite Valley.

Tuolumne Falls' allure arises at least as much from the footpath that reaches it as the falls itself. It's a classic Yosemite backcountry hike along a sterling stretch of the Pacific Crest Trail. A highlight is passage along the Tuolumne River, which mesmerizes with its glistening stones, shimmering pools and dancing rapids.

In one way this is an atypical Yosemite high-country hike; the trail doesn't climb a peak or pass, but instead descends quite modestly to the falls. Hikers missing the usual elevation change, and wishing to view three more waterfalls, can continue down the trail from Glen Aulin Camp.

At Glen Aulin, you can part company with the northbound Pacific Crest Trail and continue along the banks of the Tuolumne River. Visit California Falls with a 13-mile round trip, LeConte Falls with a 15-mile round trip, and the unusual Waterwheel Falls with a 16-mile round trip; it's a 2,000-foot elevation gain to return to the trailhead.

DIRECTIONS TO TRAILHEAD From the Tioga Road, at the east end of Tuolumne Meadows, take the turn-off for Lembert Dome. Park at the base of the dome or, better yet, drive 0.3 mile down the dirt road to a locked gate and the signed trail for Glen Aulin. Park alongside the road near the gate.

You can also start this hike at the trailhead 0.1 mile east of Tuolumne Meadows Visitor Center.

THE HIKE Tramp the Old Tioga Road, a wagon road of 1883 vintage, as it edges along Tuolumne Meadows. Fork right after 0.4 mile and join the trail toward Soda Springs and Parsons Memorial Lodge. The John Muir Trail heads off southbound over the Tuolumne River bridge, while your route visits Soda Springs, where rust-tinted carbonated water bubbles up.

From the springs, follow the signs for Glen Aulin and begin a mellow meander northwest that passes a junction with a trail from the stable after 0.8 mile, soon thereafter crosses a branch of Delaney Creek, and passes a junction with the trail to Young Lakes after another 0.4 mile.

Now you begin a traverse among great granite slabs and lodgepole pine. Where the trees give way, vistas include Unicorn and Cathedral peaks.

After crossing Dingley Creek, you'll reach the Tuolumne River about 2.5 miles from the trailhead. The PCT offers a 0.75 mile level contour along the river, then works its way up a granite outcropping which presents views of the river gorge below and Little Devils Postpile on the opposite bank. This basalt pillar was named for its volcanic kinship to rock formations in the National Park Service's Devils Postpile National Monument.

The path soon descends via rock stairs, crosses the Tuolumne River on a bridge, and heads down-river alongside the frisky Tuolumne's cascades to reach the top of Tuolumne Falls. Continue descending with the trail to the base of the falls, then past a lower Tuolumne Falls tumbler often called White Cascade.

PCT passes a junction with a trail leading to McGee Lake, then bends north to cross another bridge over the Tuolumne. The trail meets a short side path that leads over the Conness Creek bridge to Glen Aulin High Sierra Camp.

See Map on Page 178

■ LEMBERT DOME
Lembert Dome Trail
To Lembert Dome is 2.8 miles round trip

One way to characterize the hike up 9,450-foot Lembert Dome is "a lot of view for relatively little effort," yet the dome looks absolutely impossible to scale when regarding it from the trailhead.

For the time-short (but not stamina-short) traveler, able to do only one quick hike in the Tuolumne Meadows area, this is the one to do. You'll have Tuolumne Meadows at your feet, and a parade of peaks from Cathedral Peak all the way to Mt. Dana at Tioga Pass.

Geologists say Lembert Dome, located at the east end of Tuolumne Meadows, is not a true dome (such as Sentinel Dome) but a roche moutonée; the French phrase "rock sheep" describes a glacier-carved formation recognized by its sheer front and sloping back.

The roche moutonée was named for shepherd-naturalist Jean Baptiste Lembert who worked for a decade in Tuolumne Meadows, beginning in 1885. An unsolved mystery to this day is who shot him dead in his cabin—and why—in 1896. Another pleasant path beginning from the Lembert Dome trailhead is the one leading to Dog Lake. The shallow lake, one of Yosemite's warmest, attracts swimmers and picnickers.

DIRECTIONS TO TRAILHEAD Beside Tioga Road (Highway 120) at the east end of Tuolumne Meadows.

Hold onto your hat and watch your step when you gain the summit of Lembert Dome.

Despite the high altitude, the hike to Lembert Dome is a popular one.

THE HIKE Head north 0.1 mile to a junction. Dog Lake Trail forks left, while Lembert Dome Trail leads right, ascending through lodgepole-pine forest to a saddle.

Once you leave the sandy, dusty trail behind and begin traveling over bare granite, ducks mark the route.

Choose among a couple of routes over the bare rock to gain the summit, which can be very windy. Hold onto your hat and stay back from the edge!

■ MONO PASS

Mono Trail
From Dana Meadows to Mono Pass is 8 miles
round trip with a 900-foot elevation gain

A historic trail leading to a historic pass, as well as stirring views from the Sierra crest, are some of the highlights of a hike to Mono Pass.

Mono Pass is located on Yosemite's eastern boundary, where the national park meets Inyo National Forest and Ansel Adams Wilderness. From the often-wind-whipped pass, the view encompasses Mono Lake and surrounding arid lands, as well as the White Mountains on the California-Nevada border.

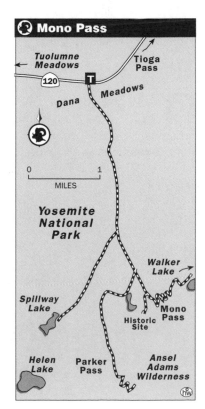

This hike—a modest effort by Sierra standards—yields big rewards: alpine lakes, mountains, meadows and panoramic views; for these reasons, Mono is a fairly popular trail.

Long before Yosemite became a national park, Native Americans traveled Mono Trail, which extended from the slopes above the west end of Yosemite Valley up to Porcupine Flat and then along a route much like that of today's Tioga Road. Mono Trail then surmounted Mono Pass and descended infamous Bloody Canyon, so-named by early prospectors and explorers for the sharp rocks that bloodied—and often killed—their horses and mules.

En route, you'll pass several prospectors' cabins, habitation for miners working the Golden Crown Mine in the 1880s. Some of the dwellings, constructed of material at hand—local whitebark pine—are in better shape than you might imagine considering the long and severe winters that occur here at 2 miles high.

DIRECTIONS TO TRAILHEAD Mono Pass Trailhead is located at a pullout off Tioga Road (Highway 120) at Dana Meadows, 1.5 miles west of the national park's Tioga Pass entry station on the south side of the road.

THE HIKE You'll begin in the company of lodgepole pines but soon leave them behind as the trail crosses Dana Meadows. At 0.5 mile, boulder-hop across the Tuolumne River and start a moderate ascent over a glacial moraine.

A bit more than a mile out, you'll pass a collapsing log cabin, and soon enter a sweet-smelling land of pine and sage, populated by legions of ground squirrels. About 2.2 miles out, Mono Trail junctions Spillway Lake Trail (a 2-mile pathway that leads to a little lake.)

Now Mono Trail begins climbing in earnest, passing the remains of another miners' cabin at the 3-mile mark and climbing to a junction with the spur trail leading (0.25 mile) to several more silver miners' cabins.

Continue to the top of 10,604-foot Mono Pass, which marks the boundary of Yosemite National Park. For the best views, press on a short 0.5 mile into Inyo National Forest to a point overlooking the head of Bloody Canyon. Savor views of Mono Lake and dry terrain, both flat and mountainous, to the east.

■ GAYLOR LAKES
Gaylor Lakes Trail
From Tioga Pass to Gaylor Lakes is 4 miles round trip with 900-foot elevation gain

O n the hike to Gaylor Lakes you're guaranteed to feel the "high" in the High Sierra. The climb begins in the shadow of Yosemite National Park's Tioga Pass Entrance Station at nearly 10,000 feet in elevation. It's the highest trailhead in the park.

This crumbling cabin is a remnant of boomtown days.

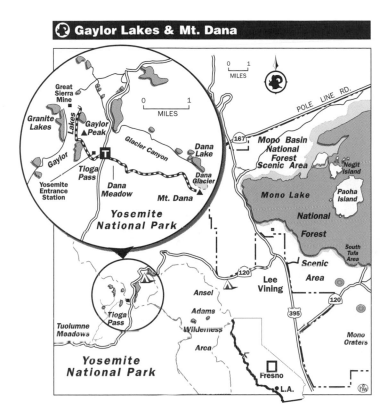

Gaylor Lakes & Mt. Dana

The path climbs through the rarefied air, delivering views of snow-capped peaks, to Gaylor Lakes, two cobalt gems rimmed by dramatic crags. Wildflower connoisseurs will marvel at hillsides known to bloom with lupine, columbine and corn lily. Daisy, Sierra wallflower, penstemon and spreading phlox add to the trailside bouquet.

And if lovely lakes, wildflowers and wonderful views aren't sufficiently enticing, this hike offers something else: a walk into history. Near trail's end is the site of the Great Sierra Mine, raison d'être for the predecessor of Tioga Road, and an ambitious undertaking even by the standards of gold-fever-crazed 19th-century prospectors.

In 1881 the Great Sierra Mining Company hauled tons of machinery to Gaylor Lakes Basin and beyond and proceeded to drill and blast a 1,784-foot-long main tunnel into the mountains back of upper Gaylor Lake.

For a few years the boomtown of Dana, complete with its own post office, thrived. Just north of Dana stood an even more remote town—Bennettville—headquarters of the mining company. After four futile years of digging, the miners abandoned efforts to uncover the rich vein of silver believed to lie buried deep in this rugged country.

Cone-shaped Gaylor Peak lies at trail's end.

A bit beyond upper Gaylor Lake, hikers will discover an old stone cabin, a rather well built structure with two-foot-thick rock walls that dates from the 1880s. Other mine ruins are located near the cabin.

With so much scenery packed into a short hike, this trail is fairly popular (at least for a park pathway so far removed from Yosemite Valley). Get an early start to avoid the crowds.

DIRECTIONS TO TRAILHEAD Head for Yosemite National Park's eastside entry station on Tioga Pass Road. Park in the lot west of the station. You'll share trailhead parking with hikers bound for Mt. Dana.

THE HIKE Begin with a very steep westward ascent switchbacking over slopes seasonally sprinkled with wildflowers. As you catch your breath, enjoy the in-your-face views of Mt. Dana to the east.

The path climbs past scattered, stunted whitebark pine and lodgepole pine. After a 0.75 mile ascent that seems much longer, you'll crest a rocky ridge and behold Gaylor Lakes and commanding Gaylor Peak to the east and a collection of Cathedral Peaks to the west.

Soon the path descends rapidly, losing some of that hard-won elevation, to the first (Middle) Gaylor Lake, located 1 mile from the trailhead. From the lake, the path follows the inlet creek on a mellow eastern ascent. A mile of walking through meadows brings you to Upper Gaylor Lake, situated at about 10,500 feet in elevation.

Admire the lake's stirring backdrop—cone-shaped Gaylor Peak. Follow the trail around the left (north) side of the lake. A steep 0.1 mile ascent takes you to the old stone cabin and the site of the Great Sierra Mine. A bit farther up the trail lie several mine shafts. (Keep away.)

See Map
on Page
187

■ MT. DANA

Mt. Dana Trail

From Tioga Pass to Mt. Dana summit is 6 miles round trip with 3,100-foot elevation gain

Mt. Dana, 13,050 feet high in the sky, is Yosemite's second highest peak, and a climb to remember. Only Mt. Lyell is higher (by 61 feet), and it requires mountaineering skills to gain its summit.

The path ascending Mt. Dana is not a regularly maintained route, but a use trail, one established a long time ago. The route is essentially the same one taken by Whitney Survey Party members William Brewer and Charles Hoffman, who first climbed the peak in 1863. Yosemite botanist extraordinaire, the late Dr. Carl Sharsmith, who worked more than a half-century in the park, helped design the modern route to reduce impact on the mountain's considerable alpine flora.

Dana Meadows and the boggy areas around two ponds offer abundant wild-flower displays, as do the higher, drier slopes. The seasonal sprinkling includes Indian paintbrush, alpine goldenrod, columbine, spreading phlox and lots of lupine. Those clusters of blue you'll spot above 12,000 feet in elevation are sky pilot, which blooms in July and August.

At 9,941 feet, Tioga Pass gives the hiker quite a headstart toward the summit. Ordinarily, to reach such a high High Sierra summit, a much longer approach, with a greater elevation gain, is required. Because of the peak's relatively short approach, Dana is one of the national park's most popular peaks to climb.

You'll need a map—and perhaps a scorecard—to identify and record all the peaks you'll see from atop Mt. Dana.

From the peaks on the park's boundary—Mt. Lyell, Mt. Gibbs, Mt. Conness and more—to peaks in the heart of Yosemite—Mt. Hoffman, Tuolumne Peak—this is a panorama to remember. The view also encompasses Saddlebag and Ellery lakes, just outside the park and Mono Lake and the high desert far to the east.

DIRECTIONS TO TRAILHEAD Drive to Yosemite National Park's east entrance station on Highway 120 (Tioga Pass Road), some 12 miles west of Highway 395. Park in the lot south of the entrance station on the west side of the road. The trail begins on the east side.

THE HIKE Begin with a moderate ascent through Dana Meadows, often wild-flower-strewn in summer and a short cruise through lodgepole-pine forest. After 0.5 mile, the real work begins. The going gets steeper and rockier with switchback after switchback. Trail markers help you stay on the right route.

Past timberline, you climb to a large rock cairn, about 2 miles from the trail-head and 11,500 feet in elevation. Here at the towering cairn, you get a good view of Mt. Dana's summit and say good-bye to the trail.

Choose from a variety of use trails/routes to ascend that last long mile (gaining 1,400 feet) to the summit.

From Dana's lovely meadow, you'll soon ascend numerous switchbacks to reach the peak.

CHAPTER 11

DEVILS POSTPILE
NATIONAL MONUMENT

No doubt at all how this national monument was named. It's easy to imagine that the collection of dark rock columns could be a pile of posts pushed up from the depths of the earth by the old devil himself.

Geologists have another explanation: An ancient lava flow helped create a formation of columnar basalt, as it's known. Such columnar-joined basalt outcroppings occur elsewhere in the world—Ireland's Giant Causeway and Scotland's Fingal's Cave in particular—but the postpile is one of the most perfect examples.

Subsequent glaciers excavated one side of the postpile, revealing a precipitous wall of columns 60 feet high. Glaciers also smoothed and polished the top of the posts, leaving behind a surface that resembles the tiled floor of an ancient Greek temple.

The postpile measures some 900 feet long and 200 feet high, about the same size as the Acropolis of Athens. Most of the columns are hexagonal, though these 6-sided creations are joined by 3-, 4-, 5- and 7-sided postpiles.

Along with its famed rock, the national monument's other natural attraction is the river—the Middle Fork of the San Joaquin. At one point the rushing river leaps 101 feet off the basalt cliffs, creating lovely Rainbow Falls. Stretches of the river are a fly-fishing paradise for brook trout, brown trout and rainbow trout.

Much of the national monument was severely burned by a 1992 fire, and the fire's effects are obvious to the hiker, whether bound for Rainbow Falls or most any other destination. Wildfire experts determined that the blaze began during a thunderstorm when lightning struck a snag. Embers smoldered for days, then a sudden breeze sent sparks into the dry brush. Firefighters responded to the blaze immediately, but winds up to 60 miles per hour whipped through the Middle Fork of the San Joaquin River canyon, fanning the flames and starting spot fires as far away as 7 miles from the center of the conflagration. It took 1,200 firefighters 10 days to control the blaze, which blackened 8,765 acres.

Because of the national monument's small size, a walk to Devils Postpile, a stroll along the river and a visit to Rainbow Falls just about exhaust the hiking possibilities in the national monument. Actually, it is a better place to walk to and from than through.

Among the planet's most perfect post piles (formations of columnar basalt), these dark outcroppings are a wonder to behold.

However, this little island of national park land is a great jump-off place for more ambitious hikes into the nearby Inyo National Forest's Ansel Adams Wilderness. Both the Pacific Crest Trail and John Muir Trail (traveling in tandem) cross the national monument. Fern Lake (13 miles round trip) and Minaret Lake (15 miles round trip) are two splendid all-day journeys that begin from Devils Postpile.

Getting to the national monument is easy enough but requires some advance planning. Some years ago the U.S. Forest Service restricted private vehicle access on the narrow entry road leading to Devils Postpile and instituted a shuttle-bus service. The idea was to reduce the impact on the area and its steep, narrow roadway during the busy summer months. For a modest fee, the hiker can ride the shuttle to Devils Postpile, Agnew Meadows, Reds Meadow Resort and other trailheads and destinations.

■ RAINBOW FALLS
Devils Postpile Trail, Fish Creek Trail
From Ranger Station to Devils Postpile is
0.8 mile round trip; to Rainbow Falls is 5 miles round trip

Somewhere over the rainbow is the Middle Fork of the San Joaquin River, which drops 101 feet over a rock ledge. Rainbow Falls is the happy result of this plummet and is the destination for a very popular walk. (Solitude seekers should hike elsewhere.)

Rainbow Falls is not only a popular walk, but an easy one. From the trailhead, the path descends to its destination, unlike most High Sierra hikes.

Geologists tell us that once upon a time, part of the San Joaquin River temporarily left its bed—migrating a quarter mile west—and carved a swatch through the cliffs. Later the river abandoned this detour and returned to its first course, dropping into its original bed over Rainbow Falls.

If you want to get right to Rainbow Falls, begin at the signed trailhead on the road just outside Reds Meadow.

Or you can join Fish Creek Trail, soon passing a junction with John Muir Trail and intersecting the path for Reds Meadow at 0.4 mile. Keep cruising downhill amidst towering conifers past the junction with the main Devils Postpile Trail at 0.7 mile. At the one-mile mark, you'll reach another junction and angle right for Rainbow Falls and a viewpoint. Another 0.25 mile walk leads to a second viewpoint and soon thereafter to a stairway that descends to the river.

Because the road into the national monument is so twisting and narrow, most private auto trips are prohibited from 7:30 a.m. to 5:30 p.m. You can drive if you reach the monument before 7:30 a.m. A better bet is to take the shuttle, which drops hikers off at the park, as well as several other trailheads and stops in the scenic vicinity.

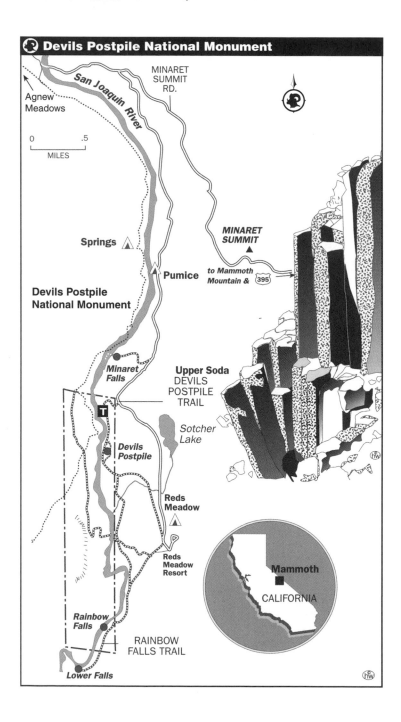

Devils Postpile National Monument

MINARET SUMMIT RD.

San Joaquin River

Agnew Meadows

0 .5
MILES

Springs

Pumice

MINARET SUMMIT

to Mammoth Mountain & 395

Devils Postpile National Monument

Minaret Falls

Upper Soda DEVILS POSTPILE TRAIL

Sotcher Lake

T

Devils Postpile

Reds Meadow

Reds Meadow Resort

Mammoth

CALIFORNIA

Rainbow Falls

RAINBOW FALLS TRAIL

Lower Falls

DIRECTIONS TO TRAILHEAD From Highway 395, some 25 miles south of Lee Vining and 35 miles north of Bishop, take the Mammoth Lakes/Highway 203 exit and head west 4 miles through the town of Mammoth Lakes. Turn right on Minaret Road (a continuation of Highway 203) and proceed another 4.5 miles to Reds Meadow Recreation Area. Early birds (before 7:30 a.m.) may drive another steep and winding 7.8 miles to a signed turn-off, then another 0.25 mile to the national monument parking lot.

Most hikers enjoy boarding the shuttle bus. Tickets are available for a reasonable cost for adults and for children 5 to 12. Children under five are free. Disembark the shuttle bus at the Devils Postpile parking lot. The footpath for this walk begins just past the ranger station.

THE HIKE Tramp the well-traveled pathway from the meadow near the ranger station along a mellow forest trail to the Devils Postpile. After exploring the basalt columns, join the way-marked Rainbow Falls trail at the base of the formation.

Wander past some singed lodgepole pines (the result of the 1992 blaze) along the San Joaquin River. The path meanders into Inyo National Forest for a time, then back into National Park Service domain. Keep straight at a junction, where a path branches left to Reds Meadow Resort.

After crossing a log bridge, the path drops to the falls. When the light is right, enjoy the waterfall's characteristic rainbows projected above the cascade. A second viewpoint is located at the base of the falls, a steep descent with many steps.

■ SAN JOAQUIN RIVER
River/Pacific Crest Trail
From Agnew Meadows Campground to
Reds Meadow is 7.5 miles one way

Beauty knows no boundaries. Devils Postpile is certainly a compelling destination, but it's a very small part of the surrounding high country, which includes Inyo National Forest and its John Muir and Ansel Adams wilderness areas. The famed Pacific Crest Trail offers a great way to the national monument, and a convenient shuttle bus offers an easy way back.

San Joaquin River Trail (PCT) offers something for everybody: sparkling pools for swimming, granite shores for sunbathing, clear tumbling water for trout anglers. And don't forget your camera for views of Minaret Falls, Pumice Flat, Mammoth Mountain and the surrounding wilderness.

This walk begins at Agnew Meadows Campground, visits the Devils Postpile, then travels to Reds Meadow Resort, which boasts cabins, a small cafe and a pack station. The trail travels in the shade of such trees as Jeffrey and lodgepole pine, red fir, Sierra juniper and mountain hemlock. Pumice-lined Minaret

Creek, as well as a white volcanic-rock outcropping known as Pumice Flat testify to the fiery geologic history of the Devils Postpile area.

DIRECTIONS TO TRAILHEAD From Highway 395, some 25 miles south of Lee Vining and 35 miles north of Bishop, take the Mammoth Lakes/Highway 203 exit and head west 4 miles through the town of Mammoth Lakes. Turn right on Minaret Road (a continuation of Highway 203) and proceed another 4.5 miles to Reds Meadow Recreation Area. Early birds (before 7:30 a.m.) may drive another steep and winding 7.8 miles to a signed turn-off, then another 0.25 mile to the national monument parking lot. From the Devils Postpile National Monument entry kiosk, continue another 2.7 miles and take the turn-off for Agnew Meadows Campground. Follow the camp road 0.3 mile to signed trailhead parking. If you take the intra-valley shuttle, get off at the Agnew Meadows Campground stop and walk along the camp road 0.3 mile to the trailhead. The footpath for this hike begins just past the ranger station.

THE HIKE From the trailhead (signed for Shadow Lake) the path makes a kind of false start—a 300-yard traverse to a second trailhead and parking lot next to fenced Agnew Meadows. Skirting Agnew Meadows, walk in the shade of Jeffrey pine and mountain hemlock to a junction just under a mile out, Bear left and make an easy half-mile descent to a second junction, where you intersect Pacific Crest Trail and head south toward Reds Meadow.

About 2 miles out, the River Trail really begins to feel like its name as the path meanders just above the San Joaquin. Inviting swimming holes and sunny rocks beckon the hiker to cool off and/or warm up. About 4 miles along, cross the river on a bridge to the outskirts of Upper Soda Springs Campground. (The shuttle bus stops at the campground, if you're thinking of calling it a day here.)

Past the camp, the path strays from the river and passes Pumice Flat and Pumice Campground. Then it's back to the riverside route at the 5-mile mark and an intersection with the short connector trail leading to the base of Minaret Falls. Enjoy a close-up view of the cascade, then travel another 0.5 mile to the north boundary of Devils Postpile National Monument and a trail junction.

Bid farewell to the PCT and instead fork left and drop to the San Joaquin River, crossing the river on a footbridge and continuing straight at another junction to the actual Devils Postpile. From the famed basalt columns, follow the main trail 0.5 mile through stands of Jeffrey pine to the national monument boundary and a junction with the path leading to Reds Meadow at 7 miles. You'll stay to the left of Reds Meadow Camp and connect to the main road, where you'll turn left and walk a final couple of hundred yards to the shuttle-bus stop.

12

SEQUOIA AND KINGS CANYON NATIONAL PARKS

I f you only drive through you'll be disappointed: Sequoia and Kings Canyon have the superlative scenery and postcard views found in other national parks, but you have to hike to see them.

Naturally the groves of sequoia are the primary draw to both namesake Sequoia and to Kings Canyon national park. Preserving these trees, the biggest on earth, was the prime reason for the formation of the park. The General Sherman, standing 274 feet tall and measuring 36.5 feet in diameter at the base of its massive trunk, is the largest of the large trees.

To begin a park visit with a walk among the big trees is sublime; to end your visit after a stop in the sequoias with the belief you've seen the parks, is a notion bordering on the ridiculous. Auto travel is restricted to lower and middle elevations, so if you want to fully experience the park you need to hike into the Sierra Nevada high country.

Sequoia, the nation's second national park, has expanded considerably over the years.

Trails explore a remarkable range of elevations from 1,600 to 14,000 feet, and a range of environments from Mediterranean to alpine. Kings Canyon is one of the continent's deepest canyons and 14,491-foot Mt. Whitney is the highest peak in the continental U.S.

These national parks, which now boast such big attractions, started out rather small. Sequoia, the nation's second national park, totaled 50,000 acres when it was established in 1890. General Grant National Park, forerunner of Kings Canyon, was established a week after Sequoia and initially included only 2,560 acres.

But in 1860, people came to saw the big trees, not see them. Grove upon grove of giant sequoias were toppled and milled into lumber. John Muir's nature writing and newspaperman George Stewart, editor of the *Visalia Delta*, marshaled public opinion to form Sequoia and General Grant national parks.

Mt. Whitney and adjacent high country were added to Sequoia National Park in 1926. Mineral King's valley, peaks, and alpine lakes became part of the park in 1978 after a lengthy battle between ski-resort developers and conservationists led by the Sierra Club.

A greatly expanded Kings Canyon National Park, incorporating the old General Grant National Park, was established in 1940. Sequoia and Kings Canyon national parks share a boundary and are administered as one park by the National Park Service.

The sequoias, reduced in number over millions of years by ecological and climatic changes, and further reduced by logging, survive today only in isolated groves on the Sierra Nevada's western slope. The most extensive sequoia groves, as well as the largest individual trees, are found in the national parks.

Some of the finest specimens of giant sequoia stand mightily in Sequoia National Park. Reach the small areas where they flourish from a number of trails.

Sequoias are survivors. Some live 3,000 years or more, and many mature park specimens are 1,500 years old. A very thick (up to 2 feet) bark resists insects, disease and fire.

The sequoias are not an endangered species, but other plants and animals in the park are threatened with extinction; for them, the park provides a haven.

One summer I followed a scientist studying the mountain yellow-legged frog, the highest-dwelling amphibian in the United States. The frog dwells along the headwaters of the Kaweah River in Sequoia National Park.

What can studying the precipitous decline in population of this obscure frog species, one that hibernates nine to ten months of the year, possibly tell us? Can learning about temperature regulation in the mountain yellow-legged frog contribute to an understanding of how humans thermo-regulate? Could the slightly acidic Kaweah River be exerting stress on the frog population due to acid rain? These are the kind of questions scientists ask in Sequoia National Park, which, like other national parks, is a living laboratory for researchers studying everything from avalanches to air pollution.

Park planners are committed to protecting the parks' invaluable resources. The John Muir-named Giant Forest, which holds the greatest concentration of sequoias also for many years held the park's greatest cluster of campgrounds, lodging and commercial structures. All commercial activity is being relocated to a new site west of Lodgepole just off Generals Highway.

Where the road ends, an extensive trail system begins. Almost half of one of the great trails of the world—the 225-mile long John Muir—extends through Sequoia and Kings Canyon national parks. The trail ends (or begins, for a majority of long-distance hikers) at Mt. Whitney. The famed High Sierra Trail extends east-west across Sequoia National Park.

Chase away this varmint—the marmot—before it takes a taste of vital engine parts.

The hiking season is a fairly short one. The middle elevations—4,000 to 8,000 feet—are often snow-covered from November through May. In Mineral King, and higher in the High Sierra, the summer hiking season is even shorter.

The parks offer memorable family walks among the big trees, pleasant excursions to lakes and waterfalls, and some challenging hikes high into the Sierra Nevada. Kings Canyon, where the mighty Kings River thunders down an extremely deep canyon, is a popular departure point for high-country hikes. Mineral King, a gorgeous, avalanche-scoured valley ringed by rugged 12,000-foot peaks, is another area irresistible to hikers. Views from atop the Great Western Divide and the many lakes hidden in glacial cirques compel hikers to return summer after summer.

■ EAGLE LAKE
Eagle Lake Trail
7 miles round trip with 2,200-foot elevation gain

Eagle Lake, a popular weekend backpacker destination, is reached by one of Mineral King's easier trails. Relatively easier, that is. A 2,200-foot gain at high altitude in 3.5 miles is a good workout to say the least.

When the light is right, the lake mirrors some of its scenic surroundings: weathered foxtail pines and polished granite walls, their shaded cracks and crevices patched by long-lingering snow.

Eagle, like many a Sierra lake, was "improved" to render it more reservoir-like. The Mt. Whitney Power Company built a rock dam to better control waters flowing down to their hydroelectric plant near Three Rivers.

En route to Eagle Lake, you'll encounter two strange waterways. The path crosses Spring Creek, which emerges as if from nowhere. Geologists speculate that it's of subterranean origin.

If the sudden appearance of Spring Creek isn't strange enough for Eagle Lake Trail hikers, they'll also witness the disappearance of Eagle Creek into a large sinkhole. The creek reappears down the hillside, leading to speculation that is channeled through a network of underground passageways in the marble rock below ground and emerges as . . . Spring Creek.

Very mysterious.

Experienced hikers, familiar with cross-country travel, can make a loop of this hike: climb a ridge from Eagle Lake then descend into Mosquito Lakes Basin. You'll arrive at Mosquito Lake #4 and follow the lake chain north until you join Mosquito Lakes Trail, which returns you to Mineral King.

DIRECTIONS TO TRAILHEAD From Highway 198, 3 miles northeast of the town of Three Rivers, turn right (east) on Mineral King Road and drive 25 miles to Cold Springs Campground. Beyond the camp, continue east on Mineral King Road another 1.5 miles past the ranger station to the trailhead parking area.

Warning: Rangers and fellow hikers report that for reasons unknown the local marmots have developed a taste for rubber, and during spring and early summer sometimes gnaw on vehicle belts and hoses. Pray the critters leave your car alone or park farther down the valley, where the marmots are less numerous, and walk up to the trailhead. Check your engine before departing.

THE HIKE The path leads south above the East Fork of the Kaweah River and soon crosses the strange Spring Creek on a wooden footbridge. About 0.75

mile out, the path crosses Eagle Creek, and then continues another 0.25 mile to a junction with White Chief Trail.

Stay right, tackling steep switchbacks that climb 0.5 mile over fir-clad mountainside. Observe Eagle Creek's disappearing act into a sinkhole, then continue across a meadow to the junction with Mosquito Lakes Trail, 2 miles out. (See Mosquito Lakes hike.)

Continue southwest toward Eagle Lake. Staying west of Eagle Creek, the trail switchbacks steeply, climbing white granite slopes and finally reaching the outlet of Eagle Lake.

■ MOSQUITO LAKES
Eagle Lake, Mosquito Lakes Trails
To first Mosquito Lake is 7.2 miles round trip;
to fifth Mosquito Lake is 10.2 miles round trip

Tucked in a little valley at the base of Hengst Peak, five Mosquito Lakes beckon the day hiker and backpacker. Each glacier-carved lake fills a rocky bowl and seems to have its own special quality.

Mosquito Lakes Trail ascends in stair-step fashion from one lake to another. Actually, only the first lake (where no camping is allowed) is reached by maintained trail. Beyond Mosquito Lake #1 you'll follow sketchy paths, cairns and blazes to reach the upper lakes.

In season, expect hordes of the mosquitoes that gave the lakes their name. Take precautions and plenty of insect repellent to fully enjoy this hike.

DIRECTIONS TO TRAILHEAD From Highway 198, 3 miles northeast of the town of Three Rivers, turn right (east) on Mineral King Road and drive 25 miles to Cold Springs Campground. Beyond the camp, continue east on Mineral King Road another 1.5 miles past the ranger station to the trailhead parking area.

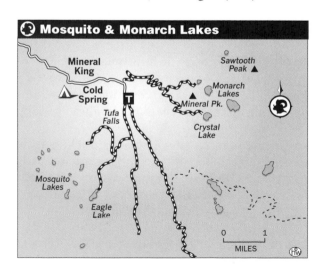

THE HIKE The path leads south above the East Fork of the Kaweah River and soon crosses the strange Spring Creek on a wooden footbridge. About 0.75 mile out, the path crosses Eagle Creek, and then continues another 0.25 mile to a junction with White Chief Trail.

Stay right, tackling steep switchbacks that climb 0.5 mile over fir-clad mountainside. Observe Eagle Creek's disappearing act into a sinkhole, then continue across a meadow to the junction with Mosquito Lakes Trail, 2 miles out.

At the 2-mile junction stay right, traversing a lodgepole-pine-fringed meadow. Soon, you begin some serious climbing, tackling a ridge with some steep switchbacks and getting some good views of Sawtooth Peak. You make your way to a saddle, nearly 3 miles out.

Now the path descends through dense red-fir forest before reaching the boulder-strewn shore of Lower Mosquito Lake.

Head right along the lakeshore, cross Mosquito Creek, and follow the use trail up a narrow forested valley, then over a rocky section to the second Mosquito Lake. Cross the lake's outlet creek and begin following ducks up the forested mountainside to the next "stairstep."

Continue up-valley, hiking east of Mosquito #3 and west of Mosquito #4, considered to have the best campsites. Mosquito #5, largest of the lot, has the most dramatic scenery.

See Map on Page 202

■ MONARCH LAKES
Monarch Lakes, Crystal Lakes Trails
To Monarch Lakes is 9 miles round trip with 2,600-foot elevation gain; to Crystal Lake is 9.8 miles round trip with 3,000-foot elevation gain

Monarch Lakes and Crystal Lakes are two more superb sets of high-country lakes. "High" is the operative word here; lung-popping ascents through thin air are required to reach the lakes.

The hikes to both lakes share a common trailhead and the first 3.5 miles of trail. A majority of backpackers head for Monarch—bound for Sawtooth Pass and the backcountry beyond. First-timers too, enjoy Monarch Lakes and their memorable trail. Looming over "Little" Monarch Lake is 11,615-foot Mineral Peak. Some rock-scrambling leads to the larger Monarch lake.

Lower Crystal Lake, nestled in a rocky bowl below some awesome peaks, beckons fishermen and day hikers. It's yet another Sierra Lake made more reservoir-like by the Mt. Whitney Power Company. From the lake's dam, built in 1903, enjoy excellent Mineral King vistas.

One reason Mineral King trails are so steep is they follow routes used by miners in the 1870s to reach the silver mines. Miner paths, like those of their Native American predecessors, opted for beeline connections from Point A to Point B without switchbacks. Mineral King miners left behind their hillside diggings and some steep trails in their (vain) search for silver.

Snow often lingers on the park's high peaks and passes well into summer.

The trail to Monarch Lakes is definitely an old mining route; the path to Crystal Lake, while more modern, is plenty steep, too. White Chief Peak and other stone ramparts are part of the fine views from the trail.

Experienced hikers with map and compass skills can make loop trips from Monarch Lakes to Crystal Lake. From upper Monarch Lake, a rocky ravine leads to a saddle, the rocky ridge between Mineral Peak and Great Western Divide. From atop the ridge, you descend to upper Crystal Lake and the Crystal Lake Trail.

This jaunt begins with a visit to Groundhog Meadow, named for the abundant furry marmots—relatives of the woodchucks on the East Coast. Miners, not exactly finicky eaters, frequently ate them. Marmots, not exactly finicky eaters themselves, may be exacting revenge: they frequently eat the rubber hoses and fan belts of cars parked at the trailhead.

DIRECTIONS TO TRAILHEAD   From Mineral King Road, 1 mile east of Mineral King Ranger Station, turn into the Sawtooth Parking area.

THE HIKE   The no-nonsense trail begins its steady ascent. A few hundred yards up the trail look for a small waterfall on Monarch Creek. A side trail leads southeast to the base of the falls.

A quarter-mile out, you pass a junction with Timber Gap Trail and, after a mile, reach Groundhog Meadow. Marmots frolic in the meadow that's seasonally brightened by such wildflowers as Indian paintbrush, corn lily, and shooting star.

Cross Monarch Creek and begin a steep ascent over slopes spiked with red fir and juniper. Three-and-a-half miles out, you reach the Monarch Lakes/ Crystal Lakes junction.

To Monarch Lakes: The ascent mellows somewhat as you probe Monarch Canyon, where snow often lingers into summer. Look up ahead to towering, toothsome Sawtooth Peak (12,343 feet) and the notch on its shoulder—Sawtooth Pass. After negotiating some shifting shale, cross Monarch Creek and arrive at the smaller of the two Monarch lakes. A bit of rock scrambling brings you to the larger Monarch Lake.

To Crystal Lake: Ascend the rugged path a severe 0.25 mile to rocky Chihuahua Bowl, where you'll find piled tailings, stone foundations and the sealed entrance to Chihuahua Mine. The mine, a difficult-to-work operation (no water supply) failed to produce the silver and gold its investors had hoped.

More climbing brings you to the foxtail-pine-dotted ridgetop, about 0.75 mile from the trail junction. Note diminutive Cobalt Lake below; after a short descent, you'll see an unsigned trail dropping down to it.

Crystal Lake Trail contours along rocky slopes for a short while, then begins climbing again via some tight switchbacks to a junction with the short side trail that leads to Upper Crystal Lake. Continue straight for Lower Crystal Lake.

■ MORO ROCK
Moro Rock Trail
0.6 mile round trip with 300-foot elevation gain

The top of Moro Rock is by far Sequoia's most popular vista point. "I climbed Moro Rock" T-shirts have been an enduring souvenir for more than three decades.

The view from on high is one reason for the rock's fame and acclaim. From the 6,736-foot granite summit, the hiker savors magnificent vistas of the Middle Fork of the Kaweah River, located some 4,000 feet below. The panorama also includes the Great Western Divide and its near-14,000-footers, and one-third or so of Sequoia National Park. On especially clear days, view the San Joaquin Valley and glimpse the Coast Range on the distant horizon, more than 100 miles away

The trail itself—more of a stairway, really—is a stunning example of the trail builder's art (circa 1931) and another reason for Moro Rock's popularity as a sight-to-see. Park Service interpretation at the trailhead details how the path was hewn from the granite. One wonders how early park visitors braved the rock without ramps and railings.

Perhaps such improvements have made Moro Rock a bit too popular, because summer auto traffic around the rock is dispiriting, to say the least. Park planners have considered closing the access road to autos and making it accessible only to hikers and shuttle buses.

Hikers can at least avoid the trailhead jam by hiking to Moro Rock (a 3-mile walk or so) from the central Giant Forest area. An early start, a sunset hike or an autumn excursion can also help beat the crowds.

DIRECTIONS TO TRAILHEAD
From Giant Forest Village, follow Crescent Meadow Road 1.5 miles to the Moro Rock parking area.

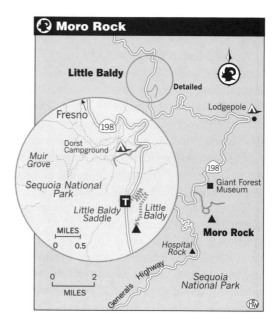

THE HIKE   Start marching up the trail—a series of switchbacks and 353 granite steps. No need to wait to start enjoying the grand views because they unfold as you ascend, but the summit panorama is the most glorious of all.

■ GENERAL SHERMAN TREE
Congress Trail
2-mile loop

I think that I shall never see, a politician as lovely as a tree.

With all due respect to poet Joyce Kilmer, I can't help wondering why so many magnificent trees in Sequoia National Park are stuck with the names of politicos and obscure presidents. Okay, the Washington Tree I can see, but the McKinley Tree? The Cleveland Tree?

Don't look for the John F. Kennedy Tree or the George Bush Tree. The National Park Service abandoned the practice of naming big trees after World War II.

Politics aside, if you want to forget about campaign trails and take a real one, I suggest a walk, short or long, through the magnificent Giant Forest. Congress Trail, which visits groups of trees named for the House and Senate, as well as trees named for presidents and assorted famous personages, is an interpreted nature trail that loops through the Giant Forest, where four of the five largest trees dwell. Despite the crowds, the park's most popular path is an enjoyable and educational walk for the whole family.

Sure it's a tourist attraction, reached by the masses via a paved trail, but no visit to Sequoia National Park would be complete without a look at the General Sherman Tree, the world's largest living thing.

The tree's vital statistics: 275 feet high, 2,300 to 2,700 years old. General Sherman is some 52,500 cubic feet in volume and weighs an estimated 2.8 million pounds.

The tree was named for Civil War General William Sherman, then renamed the Karl Marx Tree for a time by the Kaweah Colonists, who founded what they hoped would be a socialist utopia here in the forest.

DIRECTIONS TO TRAILHEAD From Giant Forest Village, follow Generals Highway 2 miles east to the turn-off for General Sherman Tree and park in the gargantuan lot. Be patient in summer; gridlock is not uncommon.

THE HIKE Pay your respects to the General Sherman Tree, pick up an interpretive brochure from the dispenser, and join the paved Congress Trail. Cross Sherman Creek on a wooden bridge and begin your tour of the giant sequoias, including aptly named Leaning Tree and some fire-scarred old veterans.

About a mile out, you'll pass a junction with Alta Trail (See Alta Meadow/Peak hike) and soon reach an inspiring group known as The Senate. A short descent along the fern-filled forest path brings you to The House, another wondrous group. The path visits McKinley Tree, then continues a final 0.5 mile back to the trailhead.

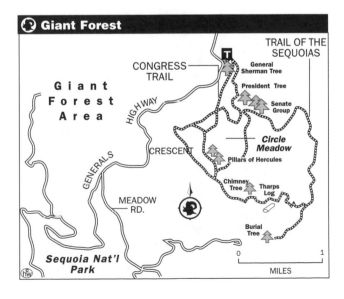

See Map on Page 207

■ GIANT FOREST
Trail of the Sequoias
6-mile loop with 500-foot elevation gain

Some 50 miles of trail wander through the Giant Forest, offering the hiker bountiful options for exploration. Forest temperatures are comfortable—neither too hot nor too cold—and the terrain is nowhere near as steep and rugged as it is in other areas of the park.

Trail of the Sequoias is a memorable half-day ramble through the Giant Forest. You'll begin with much-traveled Congress Trail before joining Trail of the Sequoias for a grand, clockwise tour of the tall trees.

Ancient the trees are, but they're not frozen in time and they display their individuality: some lightning-struck sequoias have lost their crowns, others have been blackened by fire. Some long-dead specimens still stand.

The National Park Service has made a couple of major changes in its Giant Forest management policy. After many decades of fire suppression efforts, the agency has instituted a program of controlled burns designed to improve the forest's health, and to reduce the risk by removing accumulated brush and thinning vegetation. (It's a bit disconcerting to some visitors when they see blackened tree trunks and don't realize that fire is a necessary element of forest ecology.)

Another worthy park project is the removal of most buildings from the Giant Forest. Tourist facilities and services are being relocated a few miles north to Wuksachi Village.

DIRECTIONS TO TRAILHEAD Trail of the Sequoias begins near the General Sherman Tree at the northeast side of the parking lot.

Meander easy, family-friendly paths among the giant sequoias.

THE HIKE Accompanied by visitors from around the world, march along paved Congress Trail a short mile to a junction with Trail of the Sequoias. Join this path for a half-mile ascent to this hike's high point, then descend gradually 1.5 miles among more sequoias to Long Meadow.

At the upper end of this meadow is Tharps Log, a cabin used for 30 summers until 1890 by cattle rancher Hale Tharp. From the cabin, you'll join Crescent Meadows Trail, passing the severely scarred but still standing Chimney Tree.

Four miles out, join Huckleberry Trail for a brief climb, then follow signs to Circle Meadow, very shortly arriving at another trail junction.

Trail of the Sequoias forks right (northeast), traveling a mile to the Senate Group, then rejoining Congress Trail for the return to the General Sherman Tree trailhead.

You could also fork left (northwest) and return via Black Arch and Cattle Cabin, rejoining Congress Trail at McKinley Tree and returning to the trailhead.

■ ALTA MEADOW AND ALTA PEAK
Lakes, Panther Gap, Alta Trails
To Panther Gap is 5.5 miles round trip with 1,100-foot elevation gain; to Alta Meadow is 11.5 miles round trip with 2,000-foot elevation gain; to Alta Peak is 13.75 miles with 3,900-foot elevation gain

Two memorable destinations beckon the day hiker from the Wolverton trailhead. Alta Meadow, a fine camping area, and Alta Peak, offering inspiring High Sierra views.

The route to the top of 11,204-foot Alta Peak is via a very steep trail. Alta Peak and mighty Mt. Whitney are the only major Sequoia National Park peaks reached by maintained trail. Efforts are rewarded by a panorama of peaks: Mt. Goddard and company to the north, the summits about Mineral King to the south, mighty Mt. Whitney to the east, and, beyond the sometimes foggy, sometimes smoggy San Joaquin Valley, the Coast Range to the west.

DIRECTIONS TO TRAILHEAD From Generals Highway, 3 miles past Giant Forest Village, turn into the Wolverton area parking. The Wolverton turn-off is 1.5 miles southeast of Lodgepole Village.

THE HIKE The trail soon turns east, tracing the ridge between Lodgepole and Wolverton. Soon you follow Wolverton Creek.

Join Panther Gap Trail after another 0.75 mile and reach Panther Gap (elevation 8,400 feet) after yet another mile's climb. Enjoy the good views (of Great Western Divide and the Kaweah River's Middle Fork), then continue east

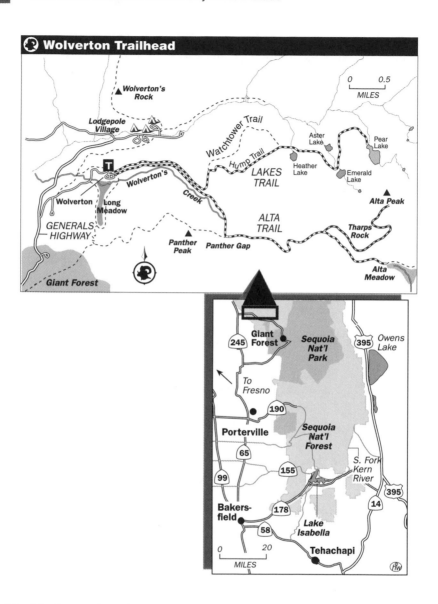

on Alta Trail, traveling from red-fir forest into a brushier environs of manzanita and chinquapin.

Shortly after passing a junction with Seven-Mile Hill Trail (which leads south to the High Sierra Trail), you'll reach Mehrten Meadow. The meadow, tucked in a bowl, has a small creek and some campsites. Another 0.75 mile ascent takes you over the 9,000-foot elevation to a trail junction. The left fork leads to Alta Peak, the right fork to Alta Meadow.

To Alta Peak: Ascend very steeply north on the trail. Thin air, and a nearly 2000-foot climb in the next 2 miles mean very slow progress for even the well-conditioned hiker. Looming above is the granite dome of Tharps Rock. A thousand-foot elevation gain over rocky, pine-dotted slopes takes you to timberline. Near the summit, the trail fades to oblivion and you make your way over lichen-decorated slabs of granite to the very top. Savor the far-reaching panoramas as well as views of nearer terrain below to the north—Pear and Emerald lakes.

To Alta Meadow: The lower trail travels a mellow mile (with only a modest elevation gain) to the large, enchanting ridgeline meadow.

See Map on Page 210

■ HEATHER AND PEAR LAKES
Lakes, Watchtower, Hump Trails
From Wolverton to Heather Lake is 8.4 miles round trip; to Emerald Lake is 10.5 miles round trip; to Pear Lake is 12.5 miles round trip with 2,200-foot elevation gain

Lakes Trail delivers the promise in its name: Heather, Emerald, Aster and Pear lakes. Named for the red heather growing nearby, Heather Lake, first along the way, is a worthy goal. With an early start, the ambitious hiker could visit all four lakes and return in a day.

The little lakes called tarns rest in rock bowls that were scoured by glaciers long ago. The path to the lakes is the most popular in the Wolverton area—so popular that there is a quota on backcountry camping. No such restrictions are placed on day hiking, however.

Even without the lakes, Lakes Trail would be a compelling path. Hiking over the Watchtower, an awesome granite formation, is a walk along the edge of the world—or at least along the edge of a precipitous cliff. Watchtower Trail was dynamited out of the rock by the Civilian Conservation Corps back in the 1930s and remains a stunning example of the trail builder's art. The path is dangerous when icy or covered with snow.

A less nerve-wracking alternative to the Watchtower is Hump Trail, which rises every bit as steeply as its name suggests. Both Watchtower and Hump Trail lead to the lakes.

DIRECTIONS TO TRAILHEAD From Generals Highway, 3 miles north of Giant Forest Village, take the Wolverton turn-off and proceed 1.5 miles to the large parking area and signed Lakes Trail.

THE HIKE The trail soon turns east, traveling up a ridge amidst red-fir forest. A mile out, the route climbs above Wolverton Creek. After another 0.75 mile you'll pass a junction with Panther Gap Trail and soon come to a junction with Watchtower and Hump trails. Remember, both trails lead to Heather Lake and beyond.

Watchtower Trail: The path ascends moderately for a mile to the Watchtower, then climbs out on the granite ledge. Beyond the Watchtower, the dizzying path traces the cliff face, far, far, above Tokopah Valley. Great views are below if you dare take your eyes off the precipitous trail, which rejoins Hump Trail in another 0.75 mile.

Hump Trail: Begin a 1.25-mile grind, soon discovering what a hump this is to get over. You gain more than a thousand feet in elevation in the first mile, ascending through red-fir forest to a more rocky landscape. At the top of the hump, enjoy the views, then switchback down to meet Watchtower Trail.

An easy 0.25 mile of travel brings you to Heather Lake. The trail then ascends and descends the foxtail-pine-spiked ridge 1.25 miles to Aster and Emerald lakes. Like Heather, Emerald Lake is situated at about 9,200 feet in elevation. Towering above the lake and its ten campsites is Alta Peak (See Alta Peak/Alta Meadow Hike.)

The path turns north and climbs another ridge, this one separating Emerald Lake from Pear Lake, and continues to a junction. A quarter-mile-long side trail leads to the Pear Lake Ranger Station (staffed in summer). Stay with the right fork and ascend a short 0.5 mile to Pear Lake. Enjoy the grandeur of the lake and its backdrop of granite peaks.

■ TWIN LAKES
Twin Lakes Trail
To Cahoon Meadow is 5 miles round trip with 1,000-foot elevation gain; to Clover Creek Trail Camp is 10 miles round trip with 2,000-foot gain; to Twin Lakes is 13.6 miles round trip with 2,700-foot gain

Some veteran Sierra hikers find Pear Lake a bit too populated for their tastes and take the trail to Twin Lakes instead. While backpackers journey to Twin Lakes, the destination is out-of-range for most day hikers.

Twin Lakes, perched in a basin below Silliman Crest, are not a matched set, but do offer an inviting destination. The smaller twin is fringed with marshy meadows, the larger lake's shoreline is a combination of forest and big boulders.

If you're not quite up for the all-day jaunt to Twin Lakes and back, Clover Creek Camp, 5 miles out, beckons with good fishing and fine picnic areas.

If you're a fast walker and a fast talker (convince a friend or relative to pick you up at another trailhead) you could make this a one-way hike. You'd continue over JO Pass to Rowell Meadow in Sequoia National Forest, then on to the Sunset Meadow Trailhead. Figure an 11-mile, one-way trek—perhaps easier to manage if you begin at Sunset Meadow and return to "civilization" at Lodgepole.

DIRECTIONS TO TRAILHEAD At the east end of Lodgepole, at Log Bridge over the Marble Fork of the Kaweah River, park in the lot on the south side of

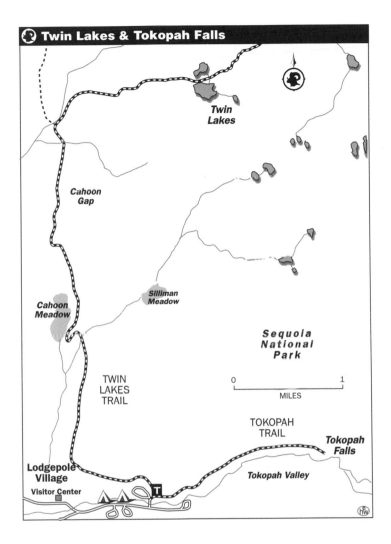

the river. Cross the bridge on foot to the signed trailhead, located a short distance past the Tokopah Falls trailhead.

THE HIKE Skirt Lodgepole Campground, then ascend briskly west up wooded slopes, then north above Silliman Creek. Climbing through a thick forest of lodgepole pine and fir, you cross Silliman Creek at the two-mile mark, then reach the campsites at lush Cahoon Meadow after another 0.5 mile of travel.

Another 2 miles of climbing bring you to fir-forested Cahoon Gap. The path then descends 0.75 mile to Clover Creek Camp.

Leveling out, the trail follows Clover Creek Valley to a junction with JO Pass Trail. Keep right and begin another 2-mile climb through thinning forest, along the Twin Lakes outlet creek, and over granite slopes. The path deposits you on the north shore of the larger lake. Take a short spur trail leftward to the smaller of the Twin Lakes.

See Map on Page 213

■ TOKOPAH FALLS
Tokopah Valley Trail
3.5 miles round trip with 500-foot elevation gain

Lodgepole Campground, Sequoia National Park's major recreation hub, lies at the bottom of a dramatic canyon cut by the Marble Fork of the Kaweah River. For the hiker, this hub's canyon-bottom location means it's all uphill from here.

Tokopah is said to be a native Yokut word meaning "high mountain valley." Not high enough, you might think as you stand in the 6,700-foot-high valley, gaze way up at the surrounding backcountry and think of the ascent required to reach it.

Happily for the casual hiker there is a fairly easy trail that parallels the Marble Fork and delivers the hiker to 1,200-foot-high Tokopah Falls, often regarded as the finest in Sequoia and Kings Canyon national parks. The falls, most vigorous in the spring when windblown spray can soak you as you approach, cascade over the dramatic granite cliffs.

Equally inspiring is the hike to the falls, which offers close-up views of the Marble Fork, a glacially carved tributary of the Kaweah River, and the magnificent Watchtower looming above Tokopah Valley. Other highlights include the polished-granite canyon walls, the boulder-strewn river bed and a mixed forest of lodgepole pine, fir and incense cedar.

This is a popular hike, particularly with campers staying at Lodgepole Campground. Hit the trail early if it's solitude you crave.

DIRECTIONS TO TRAILHEAD Begin at Lodgepole's east end by Log Bridge over the Marble Fork of the Kaweah River. The trail begins just north of the bridge. Parking is on the south side of the river.

THE HIKE Follow the woodsy trail along the Kaweah River, emerging from the forest in 0.5 mile to get a pretty good view of the Tokopah Valley. You'll cross a meadow (stay on trail) and a bit more than a mile out, cross Horse Creek on a wooden footbridge.

As you near the falls, you'll cross bouldered terrain on an well-engineered length of trail, then lift your eyes to behold Tokopah Falls. The impressive path, which was dynamited right into the granite, leads to the edge of the falls.

■ MUIR GROVE
Muir Grove Trail
4 miles round trip

These sequoias are off the beaten track. No roads come near. No tour buses, no parking lots, no crowds.

Maybe this isolation makes Muir Grove as special as it is.

It's not that isolated, though; it's just an easy 2-mile walk from Dorst Creek Campground. Still, because it's a hike, not a highway, that visits the grove, few travelers take the time to walk to this magnificent stand of sequoias.

John Muir's nature writing and conservation efforts helped to sway public and political opinions to create Sequoia and General Grant (the forerunner of Kings Canyon) national parks; it's a proper tribute to the great naturalist that Muir Grove was named for him.

DIRECTIONS TO TRAILHEAD Locate the signed beginning of Muir Grove Trail near the Group Camp area of Dorst Creek Campground. Look for a log bridge on the right side of the road.

THE HIKE Begin a mild descent through sugar-pine and fir forest, soon following a tributary of Dorst Creek. The Dorst place names in these parts honor Captain Joseph Dorst, leader of the cavalry troop stationed here to protect Sequoia and General Grant national parks after they were set aside in 1890.

After meandering for 0.75 mile past ferns and wildflowers, the pleasant path then ascends a quarter-mile up a rocky ridge. You'll spot Muir Grove in the distance, then descend into and climb out of a canyon before reaching the grove of huge sequoias.

The trail appears to continue, but actually it disappears a short distance after the grove.

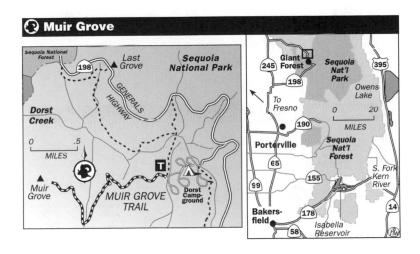

■ MIST FALLS
Mist Falls Trail
8 miles round trip with 600-foot elevation gain

If hikes had theme music, "Play Misty for Me" would be it for this wonderful walk to aptly named Mist Falls. Wind whisking water through the canyon of the South Fork of the Kings River makes the mist.

No waterfall connoisseur will mistake King Canyon's cascades for Yosemite's renowned falls, but some, like Mist Falls, are very special in their own way. Mist hovers around the lip of the falls and sprays the mossy rocks and trees downriver. Sometimes it's so misty that one can scarcely discern Mist Falls, which is not very high (50 feet or so) but puts on a great show.

Like other High Sierra waterfalls, Mist Falls is best in spring when the Kings River is at its most vigorous. Later in summer the waterfall is considerably diminished.

The path is fairly busy because the four-plus miles to the falls are fairly flat ones.

DIRECTIONS TO TRAILHEAD   Take Highway 180 to the park's Big Stump entrance and Grant Grove. Proceed 37 winding miles to a parking lot and information station at Road's End, some 6 miles past Cedar Grove Village.

THE HIKE   Cross Copper Creek on a wooden footbridge and set out over flat, sunny terrain with a scattering of incense cedar and ponderosa pine. A mile and half out, the path leads into thicker, wetter, fern-filled forest.

At the 2-mile (halfway) mark you reach a signed junction. The right fork leads over a bridge and along Bubbs Creek (this trip has alternate return-trip possibilities). Stay left for Mist Falls.

Continue low along the canyon wall above the Kings River. The path heads north, passing through both thick, shady forest and exposed, open areas of brush and boulders.

Four miles out, the trail reaches an overlook above the falls. A short trail takes you down to the river bank and the base of the falls.

On your return, back at the trail's halfway point, consider returning via the path that extends along the other (south) side of the Kings River.

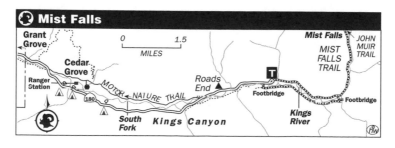

■ GRANT GROVE
North Grove Loop Trail
1.5 miles round trip

Geneeral Grant Tree is big in popularity. It was the showpiece of General Grant National Park, forerunner of Kings Canyon, set aside in 1890. Designated "the Nation's Christmas Tree" in 1926, Christmas services are still held beneath its boughs. Congress proclaimed the tree a National Shrine in 1956, a living memorial to the nation's war dead.

General Grant Tree is just plain big: 267.4 feet high, the third largest tree in the world, and an estimated 2,000 years old. While third in size, it's Number One in base diameter—more than 40 feet!

Admiration for the General has in no way diminished over the years. The parking lot is often full of tour buses, the perimeter around the tree enveloped by a sea of humanity.

Still, the tree is something to behold and no visit to General Grant...er, Kings Canyon National Park would be complete without it. While you're in the General's neighborhood, take the 0.5-mile interpretive loop past a sequoia named for Grant's Civil War-rival—Robert E. Lee—and the awesome Fallen Monarch. Split rail fences around the mighty sequoias keep tree-lovers from trampling the giants' fragile roots.

Not far from the madding crowd—in fact just across the vast parking lot— tranquility, in the form of North Grove, awaits. Wander through a peaceful forest of sugar pine, white fir and sequoia, the latter seeming all the more grand

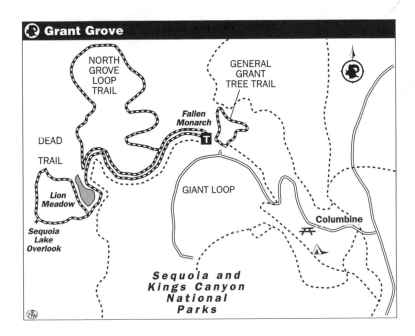

Grant Grove

in the company of trees of lesser girth and stature.

If you happen to be staying at adjacent Azalea Campground you can avoid the zoo-like Grant Tree parking lot by taking a connector trail to the trailhead.

DIRECTIONS TO TRAILHEAD From Highway 180 at the Kings Canyon National Park Big Stump entrance, take the Azalea Campground/Grant Tree turn-off and proceed a mile to the large parking lot. North Grove Trail begins at the far side of the recreational vehicle/bus parking area.

THE HIKE Start with a brief descent on a paved road before veering right on signed North Grove Loop Trail. Your path, an old dirt road, descends 0.75 mile through a mixed forest of incense cedar, sugar pine and the occasional sequoia to the bottom of a hill and a junction with Old Millwood Road. This retiring road once extended to Millwood, an 1890s mill town from which sequoia logs were sent by flume down to the San Joaquin Valley town of Sanger, near Fresno.

North Grove Trail now ascends south and east to a more distinct junction, where you bear left for the return to the parking area.

The mighty General Grant Tree—more than 2,000 years old and still thriving.

If you'd like a 3-mile round trip, bear right at the above-mentioned junction and descend 0.25 mile to Lion Meadow, joining a narrower path that leads to the Dead Giant, a towering, hollow, but still standing sequoia. You'll pass a view point overlooking Sequoia Lake in Sequoia National Forest, then join a wide dirt road to ascend to the trailhead.

■ ZUMWALT MEADOW
AND ROARING RIVER FALLS
Zumwalt Meadow Loop, River Trails
Loop around Zumwalt Meadow is 1.5 miles round trip;
to Roaring River Falls is 3.6 miles round trip

The hike around Zumwalt Meadow and along the South Fork of the Kings River shows off a gentler, more subtle side of the park—a contrast to steep Sierra slopes and towering sequoias.

Lawyer jokes aside, few attorneys are honored with their names attached to lovely landscapes. So it's with some surprise that we hikers learn that Zumwalt Meadow was named for Daniel K. Zumwalt, whose client was the Southern Pacific Railroad. History is hazy about Zumwalt's behind-the-scenes role in aiding the formation of General Grant National Park, forerunner of Kings Canyon.

Zumwalt Meadow, like its namesake's role in history, is fading away. Trees surrounding the meadow are slowly engulfing the grassy meadow, a natural progression that occurs frequently in the park and elsewhere in the High Sierra.

A second scenic attraction en route—Roaring River Falls—is curiously named also. The falls are not named for their roar but rather from the Roaring River, which creates them. Some waterfall critics say the two falls (about 20 and 40 feet) resemble chutes more than cascades, though such distinctions seem irrelevant when eyeing the inspirational scene.

Sure you can visit Roaring River Falls by way of a paved, tourist-trafficked 0.2-mile path from Highway 180, but taking the long way via Zumwalt Meadow will add something very special to your park experience.

DIRECTIONS TO TRAILHEAD Follow Highway 180 nearly to its terminus at Roads End. Look for the signed parking area on the right side of the highway.

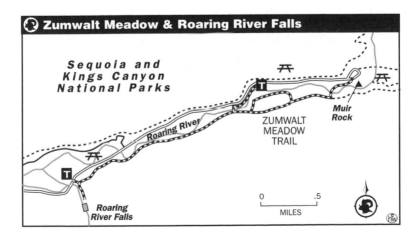

Suspended high above Kings River, the bridge takes hikers to memorable sights in Zumwalt Meadow.

THE HIKE Head down-river along the bank to a suspension bridge. Cross over the Kings River and head back up-river. Soon you junction the loop trail and a choice of directions.

Fork right to begin a saunter along the south leg, which soon crosses a rock slide, boulders that rolled down from mighty Grand Sentinel towering to your right. Savor changing vistas of the river and meadow, as well as Grand Sentinel and North Dome.

The return (north) leg heads along the river with the meadow on your left this time. After joining a wooden walkway over a boggy area, you close the loop. Retrace your steps back to the suspension bridge and the parking lot or keep walking down-river from the suspension bridge another 1.8 miles to Roaring River Falls.

■ MT. WHITNEY
Mt. Whitney Trail
From Whitney Portal to summit is 21.4 miles
round trip with 6,100-foot elevation gain

You can't get any higher than the 14,491-foot summit of Mt. Whitney, highest of all peaks in the continental U.S., and a once-in-a-lifetime (at least!) hiking experience.

The summit, on the eastern boundary of Sequoia National Park can be climbed by the most fit and least altitude-sickness-prone hikers in one day. A two-to-three-day trip through the Inyo National Forest to the summit is more enjoyable for most hikers. Many Whitney hikers prefer to backpack to Trail Camp, 6 miles from the trailhead at an elevation of 12,039 feet, then get a crack-of-dawn start for the 4.7-mile climb to the peak.

Hikers come from across the nation and from around the world to climb the fairly popular Mt. Whitney Trail, which climbs the mountain's most accessible slopes. Even Whitney's least steep side, means a vigorous ascent and a challenging trail; however, no technical mountaineering skills are needed to reach the top.

It's somewhat fitting, somewhat not, that this highest of the High Sierra was named for Yale-trained geologist Dwight Whitney. At Whitney's urging, the California legislature founded and funded the State Geological Survey and placed him in charge.

In 1871, Whitney sent Clarence King, mountaineer extraordinaire and Geological Survey researcher, to the High Sierra for his second attempt (bad weather had hampered the first) at finding the highest peak. King reached what he thought was the highest peak and named it "Whitney." Alas, it was discovered a few years later that King had climbed the wrong peak (Mt. Langley) located 6 miles south.

Before King could return to scale the right peak, some Lone Pine residents had scaled it and named it Fisherman's Peak.

The last couple of miles of trail to Whitney's summit is the climax of the John Muir Trail, which begins in Yosemite Valley; this meeting on the map of Muir and Whitney is ironic because Whitney really disliked the great naturalist.

Whitney had long insisted Yosemite Valley was the work of faulting. Upstart Muir advanced the then-revolutionary theory that Yosemite was carved by glaciers. "A mere sheepherder, an ignoramus," Whitney called Muir. "A more absurd theory was never advanced."

Unhappily for Whitney's place in geologic history, Muir's glaciation theory has proved to be correct. Still, Whitney's name remains on the top, elevation-wise anyway, a few hundred feet higher than 14,015-foot Mt. Muir, just south of Mt. Whitney.

Answering the call of science (astronomy, meteorology) and scientists, Lone Pine residents financed and constructed the Mt. Whitney Trail in 1904. In 1909 a stone summit hut (which still stands today) was built by the Smithsonian Institute to study planet Mars.

Over the years, the trail has been rehabilitated and realigned, and it stands today—graded switchbacks hewn out of granite walls—as one of the finest examples in America of the trail-builder's art.

To ensure a quality hiking experience on Mt. Whitney Trail, the Forest Service maintains a quota system from May 22 to October 15; permits are issued to

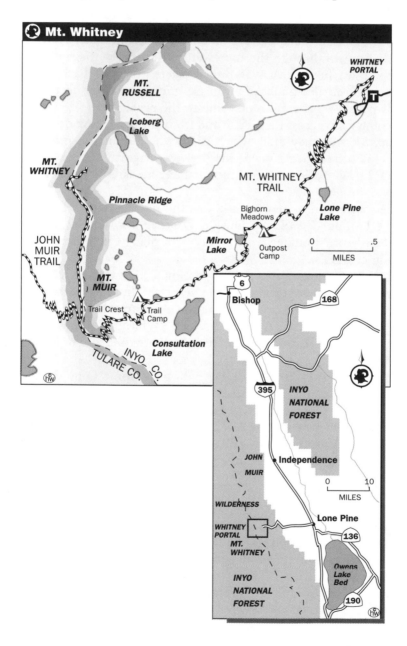

50 hikers a day. Since all 50 permits may be reserved by mail, your chances of getting one on a summer weekend by showing up in person are slim to none. A much better bet is a weekday hike after Labor Day. Reservations for it must be made from March 1 to May 31 and mail must be postmarked within this period.

Best months for a Whitney trek are July through September, when the trail is clear of snow and day time temperatures are in the 70s. Depending on the snowfall, experienced mountaineers stretch the season from June to October.

By some estimates, about half the people who make a reservation reach the summit. Do not exceed your ability and level of condition by forcing yourself to make the top. The trail is absolutely stunning the whole way; your day won't be wasted if you turn around short of the summit. The mountain will be waiting for you when you return to try again.

Take all the Forest Service's warnings about the climb and the climate very seriously. Every hiker wants to avoid altitude sickness.

DIRECTIONS TO TRAILHEAD From Highway 395 in Lone Pine, turn west on Whitney Portal Road and drive 12 miles to Whitney Portal. Here you'll find a large hikers parking lot, trailhead information board, toilets and drinking water, a walk-in campground, even an overflow parking area 0.25 mile short of the trailhead.

THE HIKE From Whitney Portal, the path climbs open slopes dotted with Jeffrey pine and white fir. A half mile out, the trail crosses the north fork of Lone Pine Creek and shortly thereafter enters the John Muir Wilderness.

The trail switchbacks up 2 more miles to Lone Pine Lake. The rock-walled lake itself is reached by a short (200 yards or so) side trail. The lake is perfect for a (cold) swim.

After another 0.5 mile of climbing, the path skirts the south side of Bighorn Meadows and 0.5 mile beyond reaches Outpost Camp, a pleasant enough camp but usually ignored by summit-bound hikers because it's too low and too far from the top.

A little farther up the trail, 4 miles from the trailhead, is tiny Mirror Lake (10,640 feet). Switchbacking above the lake, the trail passes the last foxtail pine and emerges above treeline. Six miles out, you climb to 12,000 feet and reach Trail Camp, the best place to camp on the mountain and the last reliable water before the summit.

Now you begin ascending nearly a hundred switchbacks as you climb 2.25 miles to Trailcrest, a pass, at 13,714 feet. Catch your breath and enjoy the grand westward vistas of Sequoia National Park.

The trail dips very briefly and meets the John Muir Trail joining our path from the west. The climb continues, as the path winds among large blocks of talus and between dramatic rock pinnacles.

A final rocky scramble brings you to the summit. Sign the summit register and enjoy the fabulous view.

Unmistakably, these are the Pinnacles; they are located far from easy view in Central California.

13

PINNACLES NATIONAL MONUMENT

Nothing prepares you for the sight of them.

The approach from the west offers a view of classic California cattle country—round, rolling, grassy hills. Suddenly, popping out of the land like a stage set, are the towering rock spires of the Pinnacles, a Bryce Canyon in miniature and a place like no other in California.

The Pinnacles crown the obscure Gabilan Range, which extends behind and south of the area from Salinas to King City, and which forms the boundary between Monterey and San Benito counties. The Pinnacles are located some 150 miles south of San Francisco, 300 miles north of Los Angeles, and about 25 miles from nowhere.

About the only one ever to sing the praises of the Gabilans is John Steinbeck, in his novel, *East of Eden:* "I remember that the Gabilan Mountains to the east of the valley were light gray mountains full of sun and loveliness and kind of invitation, so that you wanted to climb into their warm foothills almost as you want to climb into the lap of a beloved mother."

Steinbeck, however, meant the gentle Gabilans that line his beloved Salinas Valley, not the rugged volcanic anomaly that is the Pinnacles.

The Pinnacles are far from pastoral. The San Andreas fault is 4 miles east of the national monument's eastern boundary. You can see the infamous rift zone from the Pinnacles' high-country trails.

The fault's movement is responsible for devastating earthquakes, notably the great 1906 San Francisco earthquake. Scientists estimate that the Pacific plate, on the west

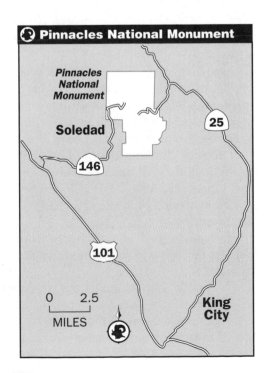

Pinnacles National Monument

Pinnacles National Monument

Soledad

25

146

101

0   2.5
MILES

King City

side of the San Andreas, is moving northward at a rate of about 1.5 inches a year.

As you hike the park's trails, you might contemplate that if present theory holds up, in a few million years Pinnacles will be located where San Francisco is. And a few million more years after that, Los Angeles will be located where the Pinnacles now stand.

The Pinnacles volcanic formation, as geologists call the sky-scraping rock, is about 23 million years old. Millions of years after the volcanoes fell silent and cold, wind, water and earthquake faulting sculpted the rock into the fantastic formations we see today.

Costanoan Indians roamed the Gabilans for 500 years, but occupied the Pinnacles area only sporadically. In the 1820s, the Spanish named the range for a raptor—*gabilan,* or sparrow hawk.

Giving the Pinnacles some press in the 19th century was the notorious bandit, Tiburcio Vasquez, who hid from the sheriff in the maze of rocks, plus many a tale of lost silver mines.

Pioneers moved into the valley surrounding the Pinnacles in the mid-19th century. These early settlers called the great rock backdrop to their homes and farms the "Palisades." During the 1890s, local ranchers began efforts to save the region from exploitation by miners. Local guide and tireless lobbyist Schuyler Hain, along with Stanford University President David Starr Jordan, sparked the preservation drive, which was successful in 1908 when President Theodore Roosevelt established Pinnacles National Monument. In 2000, President Bill Clinton signed a proclamation that enlarged the national monument to 24,000 acres, with a transfer of lands from the U.S. Bureau of Land Management.

As a young man, the great conservationist, Sierra Club Director and Friends of the Earth founder David Brower was an accomplished rock climber who made several first ascents of various pinnacles in the 1930s. Brower spoke fondly of his climbing adventures in the Pinnacles in his autobiography, *For Earth's Sake: The Life and Times of David Brower.*

The rock climbing boom of the 1980s brought greatly increased attention to the national monument—among climbers, anyway. Dragonfly Dome, Condor Crags, Swallow Crack, Toilet Seat and Spasm Block are some of the colorfully named rock faces reached by the monument's more than 500 climbing routes.

By national park standards, the Pinnacles are relatively small. But there's a lot of park packed in and around the pinnacles that gave the national monument its name.

Besides the high spires, there are slopes bristling with gray pine, dark caves, wildflower-strewn meadows, rolling grassland and a pretty canyon cut by Chalone Creek. Most of the monument's major features can only be visited on foot. Pinnacles is very much a hiker's park—a most memorable one.

■ NORTH WILDERNESS
North Wilderness Trail
From Chaparral Ranger Station, a 9.9-mile loop
with 1,000-foot elevation gain

Pinnacles pathways deliver on the promise of their names: High Peaks to the High Peaks, Balconies Trail to Balconies Cliffs. North Wilderness Trail is no exception; it travels to—you guessed it—the north wilderness part of the national monument.

In addition to high spires, hikers who accept the challenge of trekking the park's North Wilderness will also view slopes bristling with gray pine, dark caves and a pretty canyon cut by Chalone Creek.

Besides serving up some super scenery, North Wilderness Trail might be memorable for another reason: it's the hardest hike in the park. This trip will be most enjoyable for experienced hikers with good backcountry navigation skills.

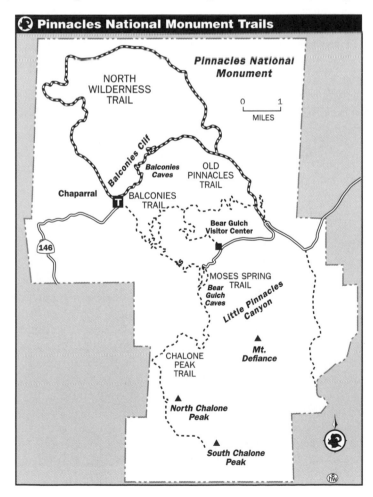

In keeping with the wilderness designation, the Park Service only minimally maintains North Wilderness Trail. Signs are sparse, though metal fence posts do mark the path. Expect a steep, brush-crowded, sketchy-in-spots trail, as well as a dozen creek crossings.

As described, this walk begins at Chaparral Ranger Station. You could also make a similar loop beginning from Chalone Creek Picnic Area. Add another 2 miles to the total distance.

DIRECTIONS TO TRAILHEAD   From Highway 101 in Soledad, take the Soledad/ Highway 146 exit eastbound. Drive 12 miles to the Chaparral Ranger Station and parking area. At the end of the parking lot, follow the trail to the walk-in campground. The path begin at a break in the fence.

THE HIKE   The path leads through grassland, then climbs a ridgeline, serving up good views of the monument.

Some 3.5 miles from the trailhead, North Wilderness Trail turns east and you begin a mellow descent along the north fork of Chalone Creek. You'll make several creek crossings, traveling from bank to bank amidst a riparian mixture of cottonwood, willow, oak and sycamore. Three-and-a-half more miles of hiking bring you to a junction with Old Pinnacles Trail.

Turn west up this wide path and begin a gentle 1.3-mile climb along the west fork of Chalone Creek to a junction. Balconies Cliff Trail (0.8 mile) offers good views of the Balconies while Balconies Cave Trail (0.4 mile) travels right through the caves.

The two paths meet, and a final 0.6 mile on Balconies Trail leads you back to the Chaparral trailhead.

See Map on Page 227

■ **BEAR GULCH CAVES**
Moses Spring Trail
2-miles round trip

Bear Gulch Cave is easily the national monument's most popular walk. The cave (caves, actually) formed long time ago when huge boulders slowly worked their way down from the walls above and wedged atop a narrow gulch.

You can reach the caves via Moses Spring Trail, a self-guided nature trail. Keyed to an interpretive pamphlet (available from the Visitor Center), this path introduces the monument's major ecological communities—Foothill Woodland, Riparian, Chaparral and Rock, and Scree.

Whether you can visit any, some, or all of Bear Gulch Cave is linked to Park Service management policies concerning the special residents of the caves—a colony of Townsend's big-eared bats. When the bats are not using the cave for hibernation or pupping, some access to the cave is permitted.

The Park Service has installed a new gate about halfway into the cave to protect the bats' habitat. A trail allows hikers to enter the cave and then continue
on to the reservoir without having to double back.

DIRECTIONS TO TRAILHEAD Most visitors begin this hike from Bear
Gulch Visitor Center and continue up to the reservoir. A limited amount of
parking is available just up the road from Bear Gulch Picnic Area.

THE HIKE Begin travel in an oak woodland, soon passing a junction with
High Peaks Trail. Walk through a short tunnel, constructed in the late 1930s
by those master trail-builders, the Civilian Conservation Corps.

Moses Spring Trail leads to the cave. After your passage through and around
the caves, you'll again meet Moses Spring Trail.

Enlivening Bear Gulch is Moses Spring, a seep in the rock. Water trickles
down into Fern Chamber and nourishes lush chain ferns.

Continue to Bear Gulch Reservoir, a handsome rock-rimmed lakelet. Don't
miss the reflections of the wondrous stone statuary in the water.

See Map
on Page
227

■ CONDOR GULCH AND HIGH PEAKS
Condor Gulch, High Peaks Trails
5.2 miles round trip loop with 1,400-foot elevation gain

The Civilian Conservation Corps built many miles of trails throughout
our western national parks and forests during the 1930s. Some of the
very best efforts of these young men can be enjoyed today in the High Peaks
area of Pinnacles National Monument.

The corps constructed "pigeon hole" steps in order to ascend the dramatic
escarpments and installed handrails (but didn't overdo it) along high ledges.
While walkers wary of heights might want to hike elsewhere, those not predis-
posed to acrophobia will relish the adventure of hiking into the High Peaks
area.

One of the Pinnacle's best hikes is a circuit through the High Peaks area that
begins from the Visitor Center in the east side of the national monument. By
combining a couple of different trails you can climb brushy ridges, penetrate
oak-dotted gulches, and get great views of—and from—the Pinnacles.

High point, both literally and figuratively, of the hike is the High Peaks, a
reddish-orange collection of cloud-piercing crags. Stair steps carved into stone
aid your ascent of the High Peaks.

Condor Gulch Trail, which leads to the High Peaks, is also the first half of
the 3.8-mile-long Pinnacles Geological Trail. Hikers interested in lava flows,
plate tectonics, the nearby San Andreas fault, and the 23-million-year-long geologic story of the Pinnacles should purchase a pamphlet keyed to the trail from

the park Visitor Center. (The second half of the Geological Trail drops down to Chalone Creek.)

DIRECTIONS TO THE TRAILHEAD   From Highway 101 in King City, take the First Street exit and travel a mile north through town to Highway G13. Head east on the highway (called Bitterwater Road in Monterey County and King City Road in San Benito County) 15 miles to a junction with Highway 25.

A series of stairsteps and handrails assist hikers heading to the High Peaks.

Turn left (north) and continue 14.2 miles to Pinnacles Highway (146). Turn left and drive 5 miles to the Pinnacles National Monument Bear Gulch Visitor Center.

THE HIKE Signed Condor Gulch Trail ascends 1 mile up a slope blanketed with manzanita, ceanothus and chamise to a viewpoint. Take in the view upward of the towering Pinnacles and the view downward of the park Visitor Center, then continue the stiff ascent on a series of switchbacks. A long 0.75 mile climb brings you to a ridgecrest junction with High Peaks Trail.

The trail's right fork heads east back down toward the Chalone Creek picnic area, but you turn left toward High Peaks, whose jagged spires frame views of Chalone Creek Valley and the Balconies Cliffs area of the west side of the national monument. After 0.6 mile of travel, the path splits; a right branch leads to a meeting with Jupiter Canyon Trail and passage to the west entrance of the park while our left branch enters the maze of Pinnacles.

Occasional hand rails and steps hewn into the stone help you negotiate the steepest sections of the High Peaks Trail. After surmounting two sharp ridgecrests, this thrill-a-minute, 0.6-mile section of trail delivers you to a saddle and a junction with Juniper Canyon Trail.

At the saddle is a restroom and a bench from which you can take in the spectacular view.

It's all downhill from here as High Peaks Trail rapidly descends a long, brush-covered ridge. Near the bottom, in Bear Gulch, you'll pass a couple of rock-climbers' access trails, then join Moses Spring Trail and continue through a long picnic area back to the Visitor Center.

See Map
on Page
227

■ JUNIPER CANYON AND HIGH PEAKS
Juniper Canyon, High Peaks,
Old Pinnacles, and Balconies Trails
8.5 mile loop with 1,500-foot elevation gain;
longer and much shorter loops possible

The west side of the national monument offers a range of loops from easy to more difficult. This tour from Chaparral Ranger Station visits several park highlights.

Before you hit the trail, pick up the Balconies Self-Guiding Trail brochure at the Chaparral Ranger Station. Check the batteries on your flashlight. You must have a light to walk through Balconies Caves.

DIRECTIONS TO TRAILHEAD From Highway 101 in Soledad, take the Soledad/Highway 146 exit eastbound. Drive 12 miles to road's end at a

A delightfully diverse day awaits the hiker who explores the west side of the monument.

parking lot at Pinnacles National Monument. The trail to High Peaks leaves from the east side of the park entry road.

THE HIKE Juniper Canyon Trail meanders along Oak Tree Spring Creek, which is frozen in winter. The path passes scattered oaks and begins a series of switchbacks among large rocks. After more than a mile of steep ascent, you can catch your breath at the junction with High Peaks Trail. There's a bench here, from which the resting hiker can get grand views of the surrounding high peaks.

The trail steepens, heading for the "Steep and Narrow," a sharp ridge crest in the heart of the High Peaks. Pipe handrails fastened to the stone help you negotiate the narrow trail. You'll head up and down staircases hewn into the rock by Civilian Conservation Corps workers of the 1930s. The half a mile or so of trail snaking among the peaks is terrific—unless of course you're afraid of heights.

Emerge from the high peaks with a great view eastward of the San Andreas fault zone and of nearby Chalone Creek Valley. Pass an intersection with Condor Gulch Trail, which leads down to Bear Gulch Visitor Center at the east-side entrance of the park. Stay with High Peaks Trail toward Chalone Creek Picnic Ground.

Leaving the rocky spires behind, descend through oak-dotted grassland. This stretch of trail displays a profusion of wildflowers in spring. The trail drops past some glassy-looking volcanic outcroppings and through chaparral to the bridge over Chalone Creek and the signed junction with Old Pinnacles Trail, which follows the west fork of Chalone Creek. The trail ascends very gently beneath the boughs of gray pine and occasionally crosses the creek.

Springtime wildflower displays are lovely near the creek. In mid-winter, the large pear-shaped pods of the California buckeye enlarge and split open to release large chestnut-like seeds; in May and June snowy-white flowers blossom on the long, erect spikes of the plant.

As the trail bends south, you'll come to a signed intersection. A trail on your right leads up to the Balconies Cliffs, while the one straight ahead leads to Balconies Caves. Head into the caves.

The caves were formed when boulders, loosened by erosion and earthquakes, slowly moved down into this very narrow canyon, forming a roof over it. Running water enlarged the caves.

Emerging from the caves, join the Balconies self-guided nature trail. If you have the Park Service pamphlet, you can learn about everything from volcanism to lichen, as you return to the trailhead.

■ NORTH CHALONE PEAK

Chalone Peak Trail

To North Chalone Peak is 8.4 miles
round trip with 2,000-foot elevation gain

The national monument's highest summit is 3,304-foot North Chalone Peak. From the peak's lookout, hikers are rewarded with a 360-degree panorama that includes most of the Pinnacles, the Salinas Valley, the Diablo Range to the east and the Santa Lucia Mountains and the Pacific Ocean to the west.

A wide, well-engineered pathway and a fire road (closed to all but official vehicles) take hikers to the top. The Civilian Conservation Corps, so instrumental in the construction of park trails, began work on a path linking North Chalone Peak to South Chalone Peak; World War II intervened, however, and the project was abandoned. For many years the path was blanketed by chaparral, but it has since been partially restored and is passable.

Hikers in top form with route-finding skills, might consider a long return via the South Wilderness Trail and South Chalone Creek Valley route. Ask rangers for more information.

DIRECTIONS TO TRAILHEAD Begin from the Pinnacles National Monument Visitor Center or continue another 0.3 mile to the end of the road.

THE HIKE Follow Moses Spring Trail to Bear Gulch Reservoir.From the east side of the reservoir's Bear Gulch Dam, the Chalone Peak Trail passes through coast live oak, then ascends brushy slopes blanketed with chamise, manzanita and toyon.

Rewarding your efforts well before the summit are views of the monument's High Peaks, as well as Mt. Defiance and Little Pinnacles.

Some 3.5 miles from the trailhead, the track briefly joins a fire road, then the peak's lookout road, which leads 0.5 mile along the summit ridge to North Chalone Peak.

Dominating the southern view is, of course, South Chalone Peak. To get there, descend 0.25 mile and pick up the trail. Descend 0.6 mile to a saddle between North and South Chalone peaks, then climb another 0.6 mile to the summit of South Chalone.

14

MANZANAR NATIONAL HISTORIC SITE

■ MANZANAR JAPANESE RELOCATION SITE

Manzanar Trail

0.5 to 2 miles round trip

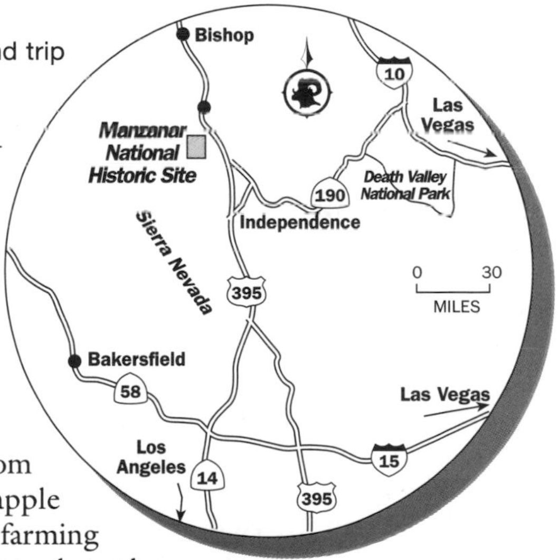

For some 60 years, stone guardhouses, cement foundation, a cemetery and remnant orchards located on the lonely bleak edge of the Owens Valley at the base of the eastern Sierra, were all that remained to remind passersby of Manzanar, a sad chapter in American history.

Manzanar, the land was called, from the Spanish word meaning "apple orchards." From 1910 to 1932 a farming community by that name grew apples and peaches—said to be among the sweetest in the state—before water rights were lost to Los Angeles and its aqueduct, and the orchards and hamlet were abandoned.

As a farming community, Manzanar was little noted; as a site of the first World War II Japanese-American Relocation Camp, it will be long remembered. Some 10,000 Americans of Japanese heritage (the majority of whom were U.S. citizens) were uprooted from their homes and businesses and confined here from 1942 to 1945.

Manzanar in modern times has become synonymous with America's darker impulses, with the country's highly emotional state after that "day of infamy," the Japanese bombing of Pearl Harbor, Hawaii, on December 7, 1941. As a plaque near the entrance to the historic site reads: "May the injustice and humiliation suffered here as a result of hysteria, racism and economic exploitation never emerge again."

Two months after the bombing, President Franklin Roosevelt signed Executive Order 90060, which required all those of Japanese descent living on the West Coast to be sent to relocation camps. The U.S. Supreme Court upheld the executive order with the rationale that in time of war, military judgment (concern about spies and saboteurs) superseded the civil rights of citizens.

During its three-plus years of operation, greater Manzanar spread over 6,000 acres, and included schools, housing, a sewage treatment plant, cultivated fields and an airport. A 550-acre core complex that contained housing and administrative offices was ringed by barbed wire and under surveillance by guards posted in eight 50-foot towers; it's this center section that's preserved today in the historic site.

Historians and National Park Service experts regard Manzanar as offering the best interpretive opportunity of the ten relocation sites scattered around the West. This is a primary reason why Manzanar National Historic Site was established in 1992.

As budget permits, the National Park Service intends to increase interpretation at Manzanar. Even with the passage of so much time, it remains an emotionally charged task. In addition, the Manzanar story would not be complete without mention of the farming community that preceded the relocation center and the centuries of use by native Paiute and Shoshone.

Begin your visit to Manzanar with a 3.3-mile auto tour that follows roads around the camp's perimeter. The tour is keyed to signs and a pamphlet that that identify where the camouflage netting factory, Buddhist temple, Catholic church, and many other structures once stood.

The historic Manzanar High School auditorium has been restored and adapted for use at the site's Visitor Center, which opened in 2004. At the Visitor Center there's a theater and some 8,000 feet of exhibit space. It's open from 8:30 a.m. until 5 p.m. daily.

The National Park Service is currently restoring a mess hall, relocated to Manzanar from the Bishop Airport. This mess hall is of the same type as the three dozen used by the Japanese who were interned here.

To learn more about Manzanar, visit the Eastern California Museum, which holds a significant collection of photographs and artifacts from the relocation camp era. The museum is located at 155 N. Grant Street in Independence.

DIRECTIONS TO TRAILHEAD Manzanar National Historic Site is located on the west side of Highway 395, 12 miles north of Lone Pine and 6 miles south of Independence.

THE HIKE The National Park Service encourages walking around the site. Don't miss the chicken farm, the gardens in block 22, and the orchards. Rangers frequently offer guided tours (30 to 90 minutes long).

As you walk the dusty lanes, most of what you'll see—rock gardens, traces of an irrigation aqueduct, concrete foundations—offer only small clues to what was, at the time, the Owens Valley's largest community. This is a ghost town where there are more ghosts than town.

Among Manzanar's most intriguing ruins are the twin sentry stations located near the turn-off from Highway 395. The stone creations are a unique pagoda style.

More than twenty (mostly non-native) trees shade the site, including cottonwood, silver maple, poplar, elm, black walnut and Tree of Heaven, as well as such fruit trees as apple, peach and plum. Grasses, cactus, dozens of shrubs and even some wetland plants cover this surprisingly botanically diverse land. More than a hundred species of birds have been counted around Manzanar.

Expect grand, sweeping views of a unique landscape when you visit Death Valley.

CHAPTER FIFTEEN 15

DEATH VALLEY NATIONAL PARK

Entering Death Valley National Park at Townes Pass, State Highway 190 crests the rolling Panamint Range and descends into Emigrant Wash. Along the road I spot the new sign: Welcome to Death Valley National Park.

Park? Death Valley National Park? The Forty-niners, whose suffering gave the valley its name, would have howled at the notion. "Death Valley National Park" seems a contradiction in terms, an oxymoron of the great outdoors.

Park? Other four-letter words are more often associated with Death Valley: gold, mine, heat, lost, dead. And the four-letter words shouted by teamsters

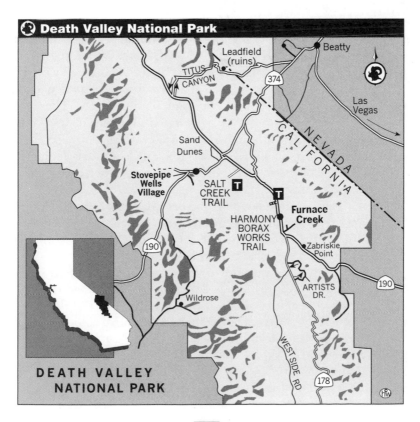

Colorfully festooned signs on the road to the Racetrack.

who drove the 20-mule-team borax wagons need not be repeated.

There is something about the desert, and especially this desert, that at first glance seems the antithesis of all that park-goers find desirable. To the needs of most park visitors—shade, water, and easy-to-follow self-guided nature trails—Death Valley answers with a resounding "no."

And the word "park" suggests a landscape under human control. In this great land of extremes, nothing could be farther from the truth. A bighorn sheep standing watch atop painted cliffs, sunlight and shadow playing atop the salt and soda floor, a blue-gray cascade of gravel pouring down a gorge to a land below the level of the sea—this territory is as ungovernable as its flaming sunsets.

In Death Valley, the forces of the earth are exposed to view with dramatic clarity: a sudden fault and a sink became a lake. The water evaporated, leaving behind borax and above all, fantastic scenery. Although Death Valley is called a valley, in actuality it is not. Valleys are carved by rivers. Death Valley is what geologists call a graben. Here a block of the earth's crust has dropped down along fault lines in relation to its mountain walls.

At Racetrack Playa, a dry lake bed, visitors puzzle over rocks that weigh as much as one-quarter ton and move mysteriously across the mud floor, leaving trails as a record of their movement. Research suggests that a combination of powerful winds and rain may skid the rocks over slick clay.

Looking west from Badwater, the lowest point in the Western Hemisphere at 282 feet below sea level, the eye is drawn to what appears to be a shallow stream of water flowing across the floor of the valley. But this flow is a *trompe l'oeil*, a mirage caused by the strange terrain and deceptive colorings. Light plays upon the valley floor and the mind spins as though caught in a color wheel, from the gray and gold of sunrise to the lavender and purple of sunset to the star-flecked ebony of night.

From the crest of the Black Mountains at Dante's View unfolds a panorama never to be forgotten. A vertical mile down lies the lowest spot on the continent. Opposite the overlook, across the valley, rise Telescope Peak and the snow-clad summits of the Panamints. Farther still, on the western horizon, loom the granite ramparts of the Sierra Nevada. North and south from Dante's view rises the Funeral Range. And from here, too, is the glimmer of that alkaline pool called Badwater—or is that just a mirage?

There's evidence all through the park of prehistoric hunters and gatherers. At least four separate American Indian cultures have existed over time. And when the first white men arrived in their covered wagons, the Panamint Indians inhabited the area.

The early gold-seekers, seeking a shortcut to the California goldfields in 1849, became lost and disoriented. Some perished along the way, and the land became known as Death Valley.

Many of Death Valley's topographical features are associated with hellish images—Funeral Mountains, Furnace Creek, Dante's View, Coffin Peak and Devils Golf Course—but the national park can be a place of serenity.

A multitude of living things have miraculously adapted to living in this land of little water, extreme heat and high winds. Two dozen Death Valley plant species grow nowhere else on earth, including Death Valley sandpaper plant, Panamint locoweed, and napkin-ring buckwheat.

In spring, even this most forbidding of deserts breaks into bloom. The deep blue pea shaped flowers of the indigo bush brighten Daylight Pass. Lupine, paintbrush and Panamint daisies grow on the lower slopes of the Panamint Mountains while Mojave wildrose and mariposa lily dot the higher slopes.

Two hundred species of birds are found in Death Valley. The brown whip-like stems of the creosote bush help shelter the movements of the kangaroo rat, desert tortoise and antelope ground squirrel. Night covers the movements of bobcat, fox and coyote. Small bands of bighorn sheep roam remote slopes and peaks. Three species of desert pupfish, survivors from the Ice Age, are found in the valley's saline creeks and pools.

Despite the outward harshness of this land, when you get to know the valley, you see it in a different light. As naturalist Joseph Wood Krutch put it: "Hardship looks attractive, scarcity becomes desirable, starkness takes on an unexpected beauty."

■ BADWATER
Badwater Trail
From Badwater Road across Salt Flats is 1 mile round trip

Badwater—and some of the nearby canyons off Badwater Road—offers object lessons of Death Valley geology in action, as well as shifting patterns of light and iridescent colors that make hikes in this part of the national park ones to remember.

A hike across the barren salt flats to Badwater and beyond may just be the definitive Death Valley experience. It's an excursion into extremes—the lowest land in North America and one of the hottest places on earth. Because temperature increases as elevation decreases, Badwater is no place to linger in the summer, when temperatures of 120 degrees F. are regularly recorded.

While Badwater is not the planet's lowest land (that distinction belongs to the Dead Sea, located some 1,290 feet below sea level in Israel), its proximity to adja-

Badwater (c. 1939): Styles may have changed, but little else has in this ancient and amazing land.

cent high country makes its lowness seem quite pronounced. National-park high point Telescope Peak (11,048 feet) is located fewer than 20 miles west of Badwater.

A "Sea Level" sign posted high on the cliffs above Badwater helps visitors imagine just what a depression 282 feet represents. These cliffs thrust skyward all the way up to Dante's View, 5,775 feet above sea level.

As the story goes, an early mapmaker named the briny pools "Badwater" when his mule refused to partake of the water. Badwater's water is indeed bad— as is most surface water in Death Valley—because of an extremely high concentration of salts; undrinkable it is, but not poisonous.

While Badwater's environmental conditions are hostile to life, some plants and animals manage to survive. Patches of grass and clumps of pickleweed edge the shallow pools, where water beetles and the larvae of insects can be observed.

DIRECTIONS TO TRAILHEAD From the junction of Highways 190 and 178, head south on the latter (Badwater Road) for 16.5 miles to the signed Badwater parking area on the west side of the road.

THE HIKE A causeway leads out onto the salt flats. To really get a feel for the enormity of the valley floor, continue past the well-beaten pathway farther out onto the salt flats.

■ GOLDEN CANYON, ZABRISKIE POINT
Golden Canyon Trail
To Red Cathedral is 2.5 miles round trip; to Zabriskie Point is 6 miles round trip with 700-foot elevation gain

Before sunrise, photographers set up their tripods at Zabriskie Point and point their cameras down at the pale mudstone hills of Golden Canyon and the great valley beyond. The panoramic view of Golden Canyon through a lens is magnificent, but don't miss getting right into the canyon itself— which is possible only by hitting the trail.

Until the rainy winter of 1976, Golden Canyon had a road running through it. A desert deluge washed away the road, and it's been a trail ever since.

The first mile of Golden Canyon Trail is a self-guided interpretive trail. Pick up a copy of the National Park Service's "Trail Guide to Golden Canyon" pamphlet, available at Visitor Centers. Stops in the guide are keyed to numbers along the trail, and will likely tell you more about Miocene volcanic activity, Jurassic granitic intrusion and Precambrian erosion than you ever wanted to know.

At the end of the nature trail, the path branches. One fork heads for Red Cathedral, also called Red Cliffs. The red color is essentially iron oxide—rust—produced by weathering of rocks with a high iron content.

A second trail branch climbs 2 miles through badlands to Zabriskie Point. While it's true that you can drive to Zabriskie Point, you'll appreciate the view much more by sweating up those switchbacks on foot.

DIRECTIONS TO TRAILHEAD From the Furnace Creek Visitor Center, drive south on Highway 190, forking right onto Highway 178. The signed Golden Canyon Trail is on your left, 3 miles from the Visitor Center.

THE HIKE From the parking lot, hike up the alluvial fan into the canyon. Marvel at the tilted, faulted rock walls of the canyon as they close in around you. Notice the ripple marks, created long ago by water lapping at the shore of an ancient lake.

Deeper and deeper into the badlands you go. Watch for white crystalline outcroppings of borax—the same stuff of 20-mule team fame.

At the end of the nature trail, you can continue up the main canyon a quarter-mile to the old Golden Canyon parking lot. The trail narrows and you continue by squeezing through boulders and ascending a short ladder to the base of Red Cathedral, a colorful natural amphitheater.

Returning to the trail fork, this time you'll follow the trail signed with the international hiker's symbol and begin climbing toward Manly Beacon, a pin-

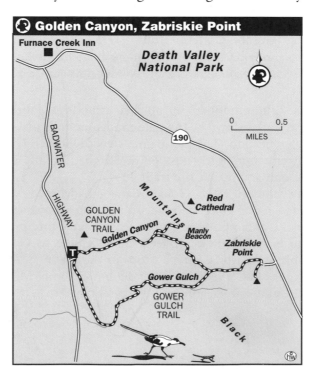

One of the most photographed sights in Death Valley is deeply furrowed Golden Canyon.

nacle of gold clay. The trail crests at the shoulder of the beacon, then descends into the badlands.

Watch for Park Service signs to stay on the trail, which is a bit difficult to follow as it leads up and down the severely eroded siltstone hills.

A final steep grade brings you to Zabriskie Point, named for Christian Brevoort Zabriskie, one of the early leaders of Death Valley borax operations. Enjoy the grand view of the valley, framed by the badlands just below and the Panamint Mountains to the west. Walk back the way you came.

■ HARMONY BORAX WORKS
Harmony Borax Works Trail
2.6 miles round trip; to Haystacks is 5 miles round trip

Death Valley National Park. It seems almost a contradiction in terms, particularly when you hike out to the old Harmony Borax Works—a rock salt landscape as tortured as you'll ever find.

A park?

Surely if the notion of a park was ever mentioned to one of the rough drivers of the twenty-mule-team borax wagons that crossed Death Valley, the response would be unprintable in a family guidebook.

But back to borax. In Death Valley, strangely enough, the borax story and the park story are almost inseparable. Borax super-salesman Stephen T. Mather became the first director of the National Park Service in 1916.

Enormous, creaking borax wagons once hauled "white gold" across Death Valley.

The relics of the boiling tanks used in the process to refine borax.

"White gold," Death Valley prospectors called it. Borax is not exactly a glamorous substance, but has proved to be a profitable one. From 1883 to 1888, more than 20 million pounds of borax were transported from the Harmony Borax Works.

Transport of the borax was the stuff of legends, too. The famous twenty-mule teams hauled the huge loaded wagons 165 miles to the rail station at Mojave.

Down-on-his-luck prospector Aaron Winters first discovered borax on the salt flats of Furnace Creek in 1881. He was ecstatic when San Francisco investor William Coleman purchased his rights to the borax field for $20,000. Coleman financed construction of the Harmony Borax Works, an endeavor that depended first and foremost on the labors of Chinese-Americans who gathered the fibrous clusters of borate called "cottonballs."

After purification at the borax works, the substance was loaded into custom 15-foot-long wagons to be hauled by ten pairs of mules. The animals were controlled by a long jerk line and legendary mule-skinner profanity.

To learn more about this colorful era, visit the Borax Museum at Furnace Creek Ranch and the park Visitor Center, also located in Furnace Creek.

DIRECTIONS TO TRAILHEAD Reach Harmony Borax Works from Furnace Creek by following Highway 190 for 1.5 miles to the signed turn-off on the west side of the highway.

THE HIKE A short trail with interpretive signs leads past the ruins of the old borax refinery and some outlying buildings.

The main trail leads 1.3 miles over the salt flats. You'll travel through a wash to trail's end at a wooden post. From here it's less than 200 yards to the edge of the salt marsh where borax was mined.

Adventurous hikers can make the trail-less trek across sometimes spongy terrain to the borax hay stacks, two-foot-high piles of sodium calcium borate balls stacked here in the 1880s by Chinese laborers to prove claim assessment work. The hike—and the photo opportunities—are particularly good early in the morning.

■ SALT CREEK
Salt Creek Interpretive Trail
1 to 2 miles round trip

Salt Creek is the home of the Salt Creek pupfish, found nowhere else on earth. A nature trail along a boardwalk tells its amazing story.

Many desert creatures display unusual adaptation to the rigors of life in arid lands and changes in their environment, but few have had to make more remarkable adjustments than the tiny Salt Creek pupfish.

Thousands of years ago a large freshwater lake covered the area. Gradually this lake shrunk smaller and smaller while the lake's salinity greatly increased. Many plants and animals failed to adapt to an environment radically different from the one in which their forebears had existed.

Death Valley coyotes are far from shy.

But the pupfish adapted—evolved the ability to filter salt water, remove the excess salt and excrete it through kidneys or gills. And the inch-long fish, used to a lot of water and a fairly constant temperature, adapted to life in a relatively tiny amount of water that varies in temperature from near freezing to nearly 100 degrees.

Once the pupfish were so numerous that the valley's native peoples harvested them for food. They were still numerous when the 1938 *WPA Guide to Death Valley* described them: "Prospectors amuse themselves by holding a pan full of crumbs just below the surface and watching the greedy fish crowd in to eat. They come so rapidly and in such numbers, that they sometimes make small waves."

Alas, by the 1970s, the pupfish was on the endangered species list. The pupfish population has since rebounded thanks to habitat improvement effort by wildlife biologists and a boardwalk built by the Park Service to reduce the impact of visitors on the soft creek banks.

Best months to see the fish are mid-April to September. In spring a million pupfish might be wriggling in the creek; by summer's end, a few thousand remain.

DIRECTIONS TO TRAILHEAD From State Highway 190, some 13 miles north of Furnace Creek, turn west onto a dirt road leading to the Salt Creek parking area.

THE HIKE Pick up a copy of the Park Service's Salt Creek Nature Trail pamphlet and begin your walk along the boardwalk. At the northern end of the loop, leave the boardwalk and take the footpath continuing north along the east side of the creek. Walk another 0.5 mile or so along the nearly 30-mile-long creek. You'll see more pupfish, as well as birds ranging from snipes to great blue herons.

■ TITUS CANYON
Titus Canyon Trail
Through narrow part of canyon is 4 to 5 miles round trip;
to Klare Spring is 12 miles round trip

In Titus Canyon, gray and white cliffs, red and green hills, and fractured and contorted rocks point to the tremendous geologic forces that shaped the land we call Death Valley National Park.

Titus Canyon offers the hiker—and the motorist (more about vehicles in a moment)—a chance to explore one of Death Valley's scenic gems. Hikers enter a twisting narrows, where a block of the earth's crust has dropped down along fault lines in relation to its mountain walls.

The canyon is named for Morris Titus, who in 1906 left the Nevada boom town of Rhyolite, near the California border (now a historic ghost town), with a prospecting party. When the prospector were camped in the canyon, water supplies dwindled. Titus left in search of water and help, but was never seen again.

Winding through the canyon is 28-mile-long Titus Canyon Road, a narrow, one-way dirt road. If you're doing the canyon by vehicle, the park suggests using four-wheel drive, though it is open to two-wheel-drive vehicles with good ground clearance. Check on road conditions at the park Visitor Center in Furnace Creek. Geology buffs will want to pick up a copy of the "Titus Canyon Road Guide" at the Visitor Center.

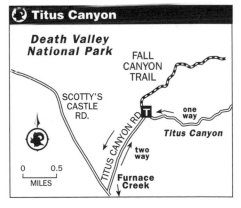

Plan on two to three hours for the drive, which takes you through a variety of environments. A historic highlight en route is a stop at the ghost town of Leadfield. The town boomed in 1925 due to the slick efforts of a promoter who controlled a very low grade deposit of lead ore. Soon a town was built in the narrow canyon; its population soon swelled to 300. A year later, the town was empty.

Today only a shack or two and some crumbling foundations mark Leadfield, but the road that serviced the mines and miners remains behind, beckoning to those who prospect for scenery.

While in theory, vehicles and hikers should not be sharing narrow through-fares, in practice, in Titus Canyon, the arrangement works fairly well. Those motorists who brave Titus Canyon are a courteous lot—and hikers can hear them coming from a long way off, thus avoiding potential mishaps.

DIRECTIONS TO TRAILHEAD To reach the start of one-way Titus Canyon Road: From Highway 190, a few miles from Stovepipe Wells, head northeast on Highway 374 toward Beatty, Nevada, some 25 miles away. About 4 miles short of Beatty is the signed turn-off for Titus Canyon.

You don't have to drive the 28-mile road to hike Titus Canyon. The lower part of Titus Canyon Road is two-way and takes you to the trailhead. From the junction of highways 374 and 190, you'll head north 14 miles on 190 to Titus Canyon Road.

Folded, faulted, and fractured rocks highlight the hike through Titus Canyon.

THE HIKE From the trailhead, it's moderate, uphill walking along the gravel floor of the canyon. As you hike along you'll marvel at the awesome folding and faulting of the canyon's rock walls. For a moderate walk through the rock show, continue a couple of miles up-canyon and turn around.

More gung-ho hikers will keep trekking up Titus Canyon, which widens a bit. Nearly 6 miles out is Klare Spring, a waterhole occasionally visited by a band of bighorn sheep.

Just beyond the spring is a wildly contorted section of canyon wall and a Park Service sign entitled "When Rocks Bend." Try to determine which end of the rock formation is up, then head back down Titus Canyon to the trailhead.

■ UBEHEBE CRATER
Little Hebe Crater Trail
From Ubehebe Crater to Little Hebe Crater
is 1 mile round trip with 200-foot elevation gain

Add volcanism to the list of cataclysms such as earthquakes and flash floods that caused high-speed changes to the Death Valley landscape.

Little Hebe and Ubehebe are sometimes called explosion craters. One look and you know why. Hot magma rose from the depths of the earth to meet the ground water, the resultant steam blasting out a crater and scattering cinders.

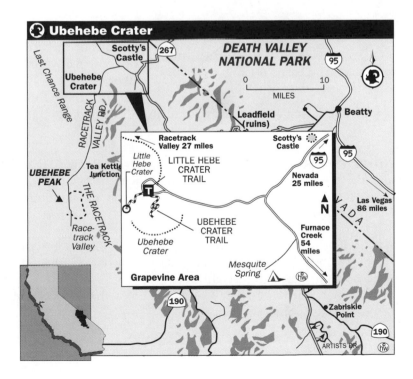

It's a steep hike down to the bottom of the Ubehebe Crater.

To the native Shoshone of Death Valley, the crater was known as Temp-pin-tta Wo' sah, "Basket in the Rock"—an apt description indeed. Half-mile in diameter Ubehebe is not the only "basket" around; to the south is Little Hebe Crater, and a cluster of smaller craters.

When measured by geological time, the craters are quite young—a few thousand years old. Most of the cinders covering the 6-mile area are from Ubehebe.

Although many visitors are drawn to the rim of Ubehebe, few descend to the bottom of the crater. If you do, watch your footing; the crater wall is a loose mixture of gravel and cinders. The mud flat at the bottom of the crater is the site of many short-lived lakes.

The more interesting walk is along the half-mile rim-to-rim route from Ubehebe to Little Hebe Crater.

DIRECTIONS TO TRAILHEAD   From the Grapevine Ranger Station at the north end of the park, continue north (don't take the right fork to Scotty's Castle) 2.8 miles to the signed turn-off for Ubehebe Crater and continue another 2.5 miles to the crater parking area.

THE HIKE   From the edge of 500-foot-deep Ubehebe Crater, join the south-trending path over loose cinders. The trail tops a couple of rises, then splits. You can either go down to Little Hebe or head farther south along the ridge.

Walk the perimeter of Little Hebe Crater and enjoy the views of the valley, and of the Last Chance Range to the west.

■ EUREKA DUNES
Eureka Dunes Trail
1 to 5 miles round trip

Between the Owens Valley and Death Valley, isolated and often over-looked Eureka Valley holds many surprises, chief among them the Eureka Dunes. The dunes, formerly known as the Eureka Dunes National Natural Landmark and administered by the BLM, were added to the expanded Death Valley National Park in 1994.

The dunes occupy the site of an ancient lakebed, whose shoreline can be identified northeast of the dunes. The one-time flat lakebed northwest of the dunes sometimes captures a little surface water; this happenstance delights photographers who focus their cameras on the water and capture the reflection of the Inyo Mountains.

The neighboring Last Chance Mountains get their fair share of the meager rains that fall in these parts—meaning the dunes are (relatively) well watered. Rain percolates downward, the water later nurturing some fifty different dune plants even in the driest of years.

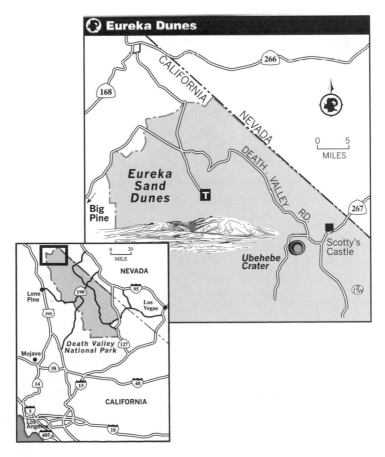

Three species of flora occur nowhere else: Eureka dunes milk vetch, Eureka dunes grass, and the showy, large white flowers of the Eureka dunes evening primrose.

Like their cousins, the Kelso Dunes in Mojave National Preserve, the Eureka Dunes "boom." Low vibrational sounds are created when the wind-polished, well-rounded grains of sand slip-slide underfoot. The booming, which has been compared to a low-altitude airplane and a Tibetan gong, is louder in the Kelso Dunes.

However, it's not the noise of Eureka Dunes, but their silence that impresses the hiker. The dunes, California's highest at nearly 700 feet high, are also impressive for their height and for their mass—0.5-mile wide and 3.5 miles long.

DIRECTIONS TO TRAILHEAD From the entrance station (fee) opposite Grapevine Campground, continue north on North Highway a short distance to a fork. The right fork leads to Scotty's Castle, but you continue toward Ubehebe Crater, 2.8 miles, then turn right onto dirt Death Valley Road. Drive some 21 miles northwest to Crankshaft Junction. Bear left, continuing on Death Valley Road which heads southwest up and over the Last Chance Range. (A few miles of the road through Hanging Rock Canyon are paved, the rest dirt.) After 12.3 miles, turn left (south) onto South Eureka Road and travel 10.7 miles to the north end of the dunes and a road fork.

An ungraded road goes east to the north side (near interpretive signs) and primitive campsites. You can safely drive straight ahead to the northwest corner of the dunes. Avoid getting stuck by staying on the established roads.

THE HIKE The trail-less walking is strictly free-form up—and across—the dunes. If you get to the top of the island of sand, you'll get a unique vista of Eureka Valley and the many mountains that surround it: the Last Chance Range to the northeast, the Saline Range to the west, the Inyo Mountains to the southwest.

■ TELESCOPE PEAK
Telescope Peak Trail
To Rogers and Bennett Peaks is 7 miles round trip
with 1,800 foot elevation gain; to Telescope Peak
is 14 miles round trip with 3,000-foot gain

Most park visitors are content to stop their cars at Badwater, 282 feet below sea level and look up at Telescope Peak, the greatest vertical rise in the lower 48 states. For the serious hiker, however, the challenge of climbing 11,049-foot Telescope Peak and looking down at Death Valley will prove irresistible. The views from Telescope Peak Trail include Badwater, low point

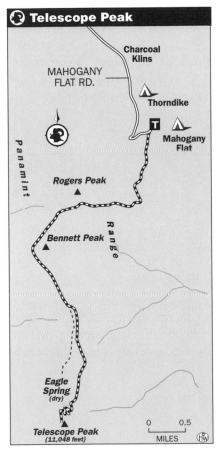

Telescope Peak

Charcoal Klins

MAHOGANY FLAT RD.

Thorndike

Mahogany Flat

Panamint

Rogers Peak

Bennett Peak

Range

Eagle Spring (dry)

Telescope Peak (11,048 feet)

0   0.5
MILES

of the continental U.S., and Mt. Whitney, the continental high point.

The trail starts where most trails end—a mile and a half in the sky—and climbs a sagebrush- and pinyon-pine-dotted hogback ridge to the pinnacle that is Telescope Peak. The well-maintained trails up Telescope and Wildrose peaks offer a distinctly different hiking experience than other park trails which, for the most part are of two types: nature/interpretive trails or cross-country routes through canyons or washes.

Magnificent vistas from the below sea-level salt pans to the snowy summits of the Sierra Nevada reward the hardy hiker who makes the ascent of Telescope Peak. The 360-degree panorama inspired one W.T. Henderson, first to ascend the great mountain in 1860, to declare: "You can see so far, it's just like looking through a telescope."

Best times to make the climb are from about mid-May to November. During the colder months, Telescope Peak and much of the trail are covered in snow. Check with the park for the latest trail conditions. Try to begin your hike at dawn, both to savor the sunrise and to allow sufficient time for the long journey.

DIRECTIONS TO TRAILHEAD From Highway 178, some 50 miles northeast of Highway 395 and Ridgecrest, turn right on Wildrose Canyon Road and follow it 9 miles to road's end at Mahogany Flat Campground. Park at the campground.

THE HIKE The path climbs over pinyon-pine-forested slopes and soon offers dramatic views of Death Valley and the Furnace Creek area. After 2 miles, the trail gains the spine of a ridge and soon a second valley comes into view: Panamint.

Three miles of moderate climbing bring you to a saddle between Rogers Peak and Bennett Peak. You can strike cross-country to reach the antennae-crowned summit, which stands about 400 feet higher than the trail. To reach Bennett Peak, continue on the main trail to a second saddle, then ascend cross-country past stands of limber pine to the top.

Telescope Peak Trail's final third is steep and remarkable. The path zigzags up the peak's steep east side, ascending through a stunted forest of limber and bristlecone pine.

From atop the peak, the far-reaching views include the White Mountains to the north, the High Sierra to the northwest. Off in those two patches of purple haze are Las Vegas far to the east and the San Gabriel Mountains above Los Angeles to the southwest.

16

JOSHUA TREE NATIONAL PARK

For many visitors, the Joshua trees are not the essence but the whole of their park experience. Joshua Tree National Park, however, is much more than a tableau of twisted yucca. It beckons the explorer with a diversity of desert environments, including sand dunes, native palm oases, cactus gardens and jumbles of jumbo granite.

The Joshua tree's distribution defines the very boundaries of the Mojave Desert. Here in its namesake national park, it reaches the southernmost limit of its range.

The park area is sometimes known as the "connecting" desert because of its location between the Mojave and the Colorado deserts, and because it shares characteristics of each. The Mojave, a desert of mountains, is (relatively) cooler-wetter-higher and forms the northern and western parts of the park. The southern and eastern sections of the park are part of the hotter-drier-lower Colorado Desert, characterized by a wide variety of desert flora, including ironwood, smoketree and native California fan palms. Cacti, especially cholla and ocotillo, thrive in the more southerly Colorado Desert (a part of the larger Sonoran Desert).

In 1994, under provisions of the federal California Desert Protection Act, Joshua Tree was "upgraded" to national-park status and expanded by about a quarter-million acres. The park attracts campers, hikers, and especially rock-climbers. From Hidden Valley to the Wonderland of Rocks, the park has emerged as one of the world's premiere rock-climbing destinations. The park

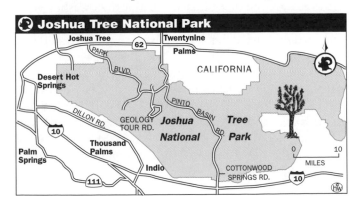

offers about 3,000 climbing routes, ranging from the easiest of bouldering to some of the sport's most difficult technical climbs.

The Visitor Center is located alongside one of JTNP's four palm oases—the Oasis of Mara, also known as Twentynine Palms. For many hundreds of years native Americans lived at "the place of little springs and much grass."

Two paved roads explore the heart of the park. The first loops through the high northwest section, visiting Queen and Lost Horse valleys, as well as the awesome boulder piles at Jumbo Rocks and Wonderland of Rocks. The second angles northwest-southeast across the park, and crosses both the Mojave Desert Joshua tree woodland and the cactus gardens of the Colorado Desert.

From Oasis Visitor Center, drive south to Jumbo Rocks, which is kind of a Joshua Tree National Park to the max: a vast array of rock formations, a Joshua-tree forest, the yucca-dotted desert open and wide. Check out Skull Rock (one of the many rocks in the area that appear to resemble humans, dinosaurs, monsters, cathedrals and castles) via a 1.5-mile-long nature trail that provides an introduction to the park's flora, wildlife and geology.

In Queen Valley, just west of Jumbo Rocks, is the signed beginning of Geology Tour Road, a rough dirt road (four-wheel drive recommended) extending 18 miles into the heart of the park. Motorists get close-up looks at the considerable erosive forces that shaped this land, forming the flattest of desert playas, or dry lake beds, as well as massive heaps of boulders that tower over the valley floor. Some good hikes begin off Geology Tour Road, which delivers a Joshua-tree woodland, a historic spring, abandoned mines and some fascinating native petroglyphs.

Farther west of Jumbo Rocks is Indian Cave, typical of the kind of shelter sought by the nomadic Cahuilla and Serrano Indian clans that traveled this desert land. A number of bedrock mortars found in the cave suggest its use as a work site by its aboriginal inhabitants. A 4-mile round trip trail climbs through a lunar landscape of rocks and Joshua trees to the top of 5,470-foot Ryan Mountain. Reward for the climb is one of the park's best views.

At Cap Rock Junction, the paved park road swings north toward the Wonderland of Rocks, twelve square miles of massive jumbled granite. This curious maze of stone hides groves of Joshua trees, trackless washes and several small pools of water.

Easiest, and certainly the safest way to explore the Wonderland, is to follow the 1.25-mile Barker Dam Loop Trail. The first part of the journey is on a nature trail that interprets botanical highlights; the second part visits some native petroglyphs and a little lake created a century ago by cattle ranchers.

Cottonwood Spring, near the south end of the park is a little palm- and cottonwood-shaded oasis that attracts desert birds and bird-watchers. From Cottonwood Campground a trail leads to the old Mastodon Gold Mine, then climbs behemoth-looking Mastodon Peak for a view stretching from Mt. San Jacinto above Palm Springs to the Salton Sea.

The national park holds two more of California's loveliest palm oases. Forty-nine Palms Oasis Trail winds up and over a hot, rocky crest to the dripping springs, pools, and the blessed shade of palms and cottonwoods. Lost Palms Oasis Trail visits the park's premier palm grove.

You'll see plenty of Joshua trees along the park's pathways, but there's much more for the hiker to discover. Two of my favorite footpaths are Black Rock Canyon Trail, which follows a classic desert wash, then ascends to the crest of the Little San Bernardino Mountains at Warren Peak. Desert and mountain views from the peak are stunning. Lost Horse Mine Trail visits one of the area's most successful gold mines, and offers a close-up look back into a colorful era, and some fine views into the heart of the park.

■ BLACK ROCK CANYON
Black Rock Canyon Trail
From Black Rock Campground to Warren Peak is 6 miles round trip with 1,000-foot elevation gain

A hike through Black Rock Canyon has just about everything a desert hike should have: plenty of cactus, pinyon-pine-dotted peaks, a sandy wash, dramatic rock formations, a hidden spring, grand vistas. And much more.

Tucked away in the northwest corner of the park, the Black Rock Canyon area also hosts forests of the shaggy Joshuas. *Yucca brevifolia* thrive at the higher elevations of this end of the national park.

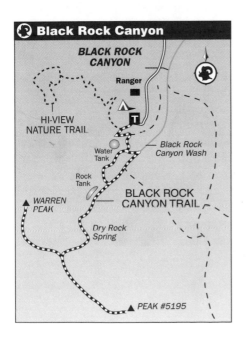

More than two hundred species of birds, including speedy road-runners, have been observed in and around Black Rock Canyon. Hikers frequently spot mule deer and rabbits—desert cottontails and black-tailed jack rabbits. Bighorn sheep are also sighted occasionally. A bit off the tourist track, Black Rock Canyon rarely makes the "must see" list of natural attractions at the national park. Ironically though, while Black Rock is often overlooked, it is one of the easiest places to reach. The canyon is close to Yucca Valley's commercial strip, very close to a residential neighborhood.

Maybe we nature-lovers practice a curious logic: If a beautiful place is near civilization it can't be that beautiful, right? In Black Rock Canyon's case, our logic would be faulty. The canyon matches the allure of much more remote regions of the national park.

Black Rock Canyon Trail follows a classic desert wash, then ascends to the crest of the Little San Bernardino Mountains at Warren Peak. Desert and mountain views from the peak are stunning.

DIRECTIONS TO TRAILHEAD From Highway 62 (Twentynine Palms Highway) in Yucca Valley, turn south on Joshua Lane and drive 5 miles through a residential area to Black Rock Ranger Station. Park at the station. The station has some interpretive displays and sells books and maps. Ask rangers for the latest trail information.

Walk uphill through the campground to campsite #30 and the trailhead.

THE HIKE From the upper end of the campground, the trail leads to a water tank, goes left a very short distance on a Park Service road, then angles right. After a few hundred yards, the trail splits. The main trail descends directly into Black Rock Canyon wash. (An upper trail crests a hill before it, too, descends into the wash.)

A quarter-mile from the trailhead, the path drops into the dry, sandy creekbed of Black Rock Canyon. You'll bear right and head up the wide canyon mouth, passing Joshua trees, desert willow and cholla.

A mile of wash walking leads you to the remains of some so-called "tanks," or rock basins that were built by early ranchers to hold water for their cattle.

Another quarter-mile up the wash is Black Rock Spring, sometimes dry, sometimes a trickle. Beyond the spring, the canyon narrows. You wend your way around beavertail cactus, pinyon pine and juniper.

(Near the head of the canyon, the trail splits. Turning left [east] cross-country will lead along a rough ridge to Peak 5195.)

If you follow the right fork of the rough trail, you'll climb to a dramatic ridge crest of the Little San Bernardino Mountains, then angle right (west) along the crest. A steep, 0.25 mile ascent past contorted, wind-blown juniper and pinyon pine brings you to the top of Warren Peak.

Oh what a grand clear-day view! North is the Mojave Desert. To the west is snowy Mt. San Gorgonio, Southern California's highest peak, as well as the San Bernardino Mountains and the deep trough of San Gorgonio Pass. Southwest lies mighty Mt. San Jacinto and to the south (this is often the murky part of the view) Palm Springs and the Coachella Valley. The peaks of the Little San Bernardino Mountains extend southeast, marching toward the Salton Sea.

■ FORTYNINE PALMS OASIS

Fortynine Palms Trail

To Fortynine Palms Oasis is 3 miles round trip
with 400-foot elevation gain

Fortynine Palms Oasis has retained a wonderful air of remoteness. From the parking area, an old Indian trail climbs a steep ridge and offers the hiker expansive views of the Sheephole and Bullion mountain ranges.

On the exposed ridge, barrel cacti, creosote, yucca, and brittlebush brave the heat. As the trail winds up and over a rocky crest, the restful green of the oasis comes into view.

At the oasis, nature's personality abruptly changes and the dry, sunbaked ridges give way to dripping springs, pools, and the blessed shade of palms and cottonwoods.

Unlike some oases, which are strung out for miles along a stream, Fortynine Palms is a close-knit palm family centered around a generous supply of surface water. Seeps and springs fill numerous basins set among the rocks at different levels. Other basins are supplied by "rain" drip drip-dripping from the upper levels. Mesquite and willow thrive alongside the palms. Singing house finches and croaking frogs provide a musical interlude.

Perched on a steep canyon wall, Fortynine Palms Oasis overlooks the town of Twentynine Palms, but its untouched beauty makes it seem a lot farther removed from civilization.

DIRECTIONS TO TRAILHEAD From Interstate 10, a few miles east of the Highway 111 turn-off going to Palm Springs, bear north on Highway 62. After passing the town of Yucca Valley, but before reaching the outskirts of Twentynine Palms, turn right on Canyon Road. (Hint: Look for

Noontime at the oasis—no camels, but plenty of smaller critters congregate here.

an animal hospital at the corner of Highway 62 and Canyon Road.) Follow Canyon Road 1.75 miles to its end at a National Park Service parking area and the trailhead.

THE HIKE The trail rises through a Spartan rockscape dotted with cacti and jojoba. After a brisk climb, catch your breath atop a ridgetop and enjoy the view of Twentynine Palms and the surrounding desert.

You may notice colorful patches of lichen adhering to the rocks. Lichen, which conducts the business of life as a limited partnership of algae and fungi, is very sensitive to air pollution; the health of this tiny plant is considered by some botanists to be related to air quality. Contemplate the abstract impressionist patterns of the lichen, inhale great draughts of fresh air, then follow the trail as it descends from the ridgetop.

The trail leads down slopes dotted with barrel cactus and mesquite. Soon the oasis comes into view. Lucky hikers may get a fleeting glimpse of bighorn sheep drinking from oasis pools or gamboling over nearby steep slopes.

As the path leads you to the palms, you'll notice many fire-blackened tree trunks. The grove has burned several times during the last 100 years. Fortunately, palms are among the most fireproof trees in existence, and fire—whether caused by man or lightning—seldom kills them. Fire may actually be beneficial for the palms because it serves to temporarily eliminate the competition of such trees as mesquite and cottonwood and bushes like arrowweed, all of them thirsty fellows and able to push their roots much deeper in search of water than palms. Burning also opens the oasis floor to sunlight, which seedling palms need.

Fortynine Palms Oasis celebrates life. Our native California fan palm clusters near handsome boulder-lined pools. Fuzzy cattails, ferns and grasses sway in the breeze. An oasis like this one gives the hiker a chance to view the desert in terms that are the exact opposite of its stereotypical dry hostility.

■ DESERT QUEEN MINE
Desert Queen Mine Trail
1.2 miles round trip

Perched atop cliffs north of Jumbo Rocks Campground are the considerable ruins of the Desert Queen Mine, one of the more profitable gold mines dug in the desert we now call Joshua Tree National Park. Shafts, stone building foundations, and rusting machinery are scattered about the slopes above Desert Queen Wash.

If murder and intrigue are what fascinate us about desert mines, then the Desert Queen is quite a story. The tale begins in 1894 when a prospector named Frank James discovered some rich gold ore in the hills north of Jumbo Rocks. Word of his discovery reached cattle rustler Jim McHaney, who, as the

Desert Queen Mine

Pine City (site)
Pine Spring (dry)
PINE CITY CANYON TRAIL
Pine City Canyon
DESERT QUEEN MINE TRAIL
Overlook
Desert Queen Mine
0 1 MILES
LUCK BOY VISTA TRAIL
Lucky Boy Vista

story goes, ordered his men to follow James to his claim and talk things over. One of McHaney's thugs, Charles Martin, shot him dead (though an inquest jury decided Martin acted in self-defense and did not need to stand trial). Jim McHaney and his more respectable brother Bill owned the Desert Queen for two years; however, the $30-40,000 yielded from a good-sized pocket of ore was squandered by high-living Jim (later to be convicted of counterfeiting) and the bank reclaimed the mine.

Hard-rock miner William Keys took control of the mine in 1915, Altadena jeweler Frederick Morton in 1931. Morton was convinced by a dubious "mining engineer" to acquire and to invest heavily in the Desert Queen. Against all odds, the miners under the supervision of "Mr. Hapwell" actually struck pay dirt. Hapwell set up a secret stamp mill nearby to process the ore and, of course, pocketed the profits. Meanwhile the fast-going-broke Morton sold stock in the Desert Queen without incorporating—a violation of securities law that soon got him convicted of fraud. The mysterious, and by some accounts wealthy, Mr. Hapwell dropped out of sight.

You can visit the ruins of the Desert Queen from a northern trailhead shared with the path to Pine City or from a southern trailhead at Split Rock Picnic Area.

DIRECTIONS TO TRAILHEAD From the park highway, opposite the geology tour road, turn right (north) for 1.25 miles to a parking area for the mine.

THE HIKE The path, an old mine road, heads east, past some building foundations. The trail forks. The right fork goes 2 miles south, past the site of the Eagle Cliff Mine to Split Rock Picnic Area.

Adventurous walkers can take the left fork and climb a bit through pinyon pine- and juniper-dotted Desert Queen Wash, passing a mining area called John's Camp and traveling 3 miles to the park road.

■ RYAN MOUNTAIN

Ryan Mountain Trail

From Sheep Pass to Ryan Mountain is
4 miles round trip with 700-foot elevation gain

This walk tours some Joshua trees, visits Indian Cave and ascends Ryan Mountain for a nice view of the rocky wonderland in this part of Joshua Tree National Park. Ryan Mountain is named for the Ryan brothers, Thomas and Jep, who had a homestead at the base of the mountain.

The view from atop Ryan Mountain is to be savored, and is one of the finest in the National Park.

DIRECTIONS TO TRAILHEAD From the Joshua Tree National Park Visitor Center at Twentynine Palms, drive 3 miles south on Utah Trail Road (the main park road), keeping right at Pinto Y junction and continuing another 8 miles to Sheep Pass Campground on your left. Park in the Ryan Mountain parking area. You can also begin this hike from the Indian Cave Turnout just up the road. Be sure to visit Indian Cave; a number of bedrock mortars found in the cave suggests its use as a work site by its aboriginal inhabitants.

THE HIKE From Sheep Pass Campground, the trail skirts the base of Ryan Mountain and passes through a lunar landscape of rocks and Joshua trees.

Soon you intersect a well-worn side trail coming up from your right. If you like, follow this brief trail down to Indian Cave, typical of the kind of shelter sought by nomadic Cahuilla and Serrano clans that traveled this desert land.

Continuing past the junction, Ryan Mountain Trail ascends moderately-to-steeply toward the peak. En route, you'll pass some very old rocks which make up the core of this mountain and the nearby Little San Bernardino range. For eons, these rocks have, since their creation, been metamorphosed by heat and pressure into completely new types, primarily gneiss and schist. No one knows their exact age, but geologists believe they're several hundred million years old.

⊙ Ryan Mountain & Lost Horse Mine

0   2
MILES

RYAN MOUNTAIN TRAIL

Sheep Pass

Ryan   Ryan Mountain

LOST HORSE MINE TRAIL   GEOLOGY TOUR RD.

Lost Horse Mine

Summit views are among the best in the park.

Atop Ryan Mountain (5,470 feet) you can sign the summit register, located in a tin can stuck in a pile of rocks that marks the top of the mountain. From the peak, you're treated to a panoramic view of Lost Horse, Queen, Hidden and Pleasant valleys. There's a lot of geologic history in the rocks shimmering on the ocean of sand below. Not all the rocks you see are as ancient as the ones on Ryan Mountain. Middle-aged rocks, predominately quartz monzonite, are found at Hidden Valley, Jumbo Rocks and White Tank. Younger rocks made of basaltic lava are mere infants at less than a million years old; they are found in Pleasant Valley.

See Map
on Page
264

■ LOST HORSE MINE
Lost Horse Mine Trail
To Lost Horse Mine is 3.5 miles round trip with
400-foot elevation gain

Lost Horse Mine was the most successful gold mining operation in this part of the Mojave. More than 9,000 ounces of gold were processed from ore dug here in the late 1890s. The mine's 10-stamp mill still stands, along with a couple of large cyanide settling tanks and a huge winch used on the main shaft. The trail to the mine offers a close-up look back into a colorful era and some fine views into the heart of the national park.

Many are the legends that swirl like the desert winds around the Lost Horse Mine. As the story goes, Johnny Lang in 1893 was camping in Pleasant Valley when his horse got loose. He tracked it out to the ranch belonging to Jim

McHaney, who told Lang his horse was "no longer lost" and threatened Lang's health and future.

Lang wandered over to the camp of fellow prospector Dutch Diebold, who told him that he, too, had been threatened by McHaney and his cowboys. A pity too, because he, Diebold, had discovered a promising gold prospect, but had been unable to mark his claim's boundaries. After sneaking in to inspect the claim, Johnny Lang and his father, George, purchased all rights from Diebold for $1,000.

At first it looked like a bad investment, because the Langs were prevented by McHaney's thugs from reaching their claim. Partners came and went, and by 1895, Johnny Lang owned the mine with the Ryan brothers, Thomas and Jep. Peak production years for the mine were 1896 through 1899. Gold ingots were hidden in a freight wagon and transported to Indio. The ruse fooled any would-be highwaymen.

But thievery of another sort plagued the Lost Horse Mine. The theft was of amalgam, lumps of quicksilver from which gold could later be separated. Seems in this matter of amalgam, the mill's day shift, supervised by Jep Ryan, far out-produced the night shift, supervised by Lang. One of Ryan's men espied Lang stealing amalgam. When Ryan gave Lang a choice—sell his share of the mine for $12,000 or go to the penitentiary—Lang sold.

Alas, Johnny Lang came to a sad end. Apparently, his stolen and buried amalgams supported him for quite some time, but by the end of 1924, he was old, weak and living in an isolated cabin. And hungry. He had shot and eaten his four burros and was forced to walk into town for food. He never made it.

Ruins—and colorful stories—are all that remain of Lost Horse Mine.

His partially mummified body wrapped in a canvas sleeping bag was found by prospector/rancher Bill Keys alongside present-day Keys View Road. He was buried where he fell.

DIRECTIONS TO TRAILHEAD From the central part of Joshua Tree National Park, turn south from Caprock Junction on Keys Road and drive 2.5 miles. Turn left on a short dirt road. Here you'll find a Park Service interpretive display about Johnny Lang's checkered career. (You can also visit Lang's grave, located a hundred feet north of the Lost Horse Mine turn-off on Keys Road.) The trail, a continuation of Lost Horse Mine Road, begins at a road barrier.

THE HIKE The trail, the old mine road, climbs above the left side of a wash.

An alternative route, for the first (or last) mile of this day hike, is to hike from the parking area directly up the wash. Pinyon pine and nolina (often mistaken for a yucca) dot the wash. Nolina leaves are more flexible than those of yucca, and its flowers smaller. The wash widens in about 0.75 mile and forks; bear left and a short ascent will take you to the mine road. Turn right on the road and follow it to the mine.

A few open shafts remain near the Lost Horse, so be careful when you explore the mine ruins. Note the stone foundations opposite the mill site. A little village for the mine workers was built here in the late 1890s. Scramble up to the top of the hill above the mine for a panoramic view of Queen Valley, Pleasant Valley and the desert ranges beyond.

■ WONDERLAND OF ROCKS
Barker Dam Loop Trail
From Parking Area to Barker Dam is 1.25 mile round trip

One of the many wonders of Joshua Tree National Park is the Wonderland of Rocks, 12 square miles of massive jumbled granite. This curious maze of stone hides groves of Joshua trees, trackless washes and several small pools of water.

Perhaps the easiest and certainly the safest way to explore the Wonderland is to follow the Barker Dam Loop Trail. The first part of the journey is on a nature trail that interprets the botanical highlights of the area. The last part of the loop trail visits some Indian petroglyphs.

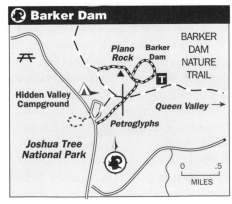

The little lake created by Barker Dam attracts many migratory bird species.

This hike's main destination is the small lake created by Barker Dam. A century ago, cowboys took advantage of the water catchment of this natural basin and brought their cattle to this corner of the Wonderland of Rocks. Barker and Shay Cattle Co. constructed the dam, which was later raised to its present height by Bill Keys and his family in the 1950s. Family members inscribed their names atop the dam's south wall and renamed it Bighorn Dam; however, Barker was the name that stuck.

The trail to Barker Dam, while interesting, is not likely to occupy much of a day for the intrepid hiker. One way to explore a little more of the Wonderland of Rocks is to pick up Wonderland Wash Ranch Trail to the Astrodomes. Departing from the next spur road and parking area past the Barker Dam trailhead, this path leads to the ruins of a pink house known as the Worth Bagley House. From the back corner of the house, you'll pick up a wash and follow an intermittent trail through boulder clusters. The trail is popular with rock climbers, who use this trail to reach the Astrodomes— steep, 300-foot-tall rocks that tower above the wash.

Myriad narrow canyons and washes lead into the Wonderland, but route-finding is extremely complex and recommended only for those with map and compass skills.

By Park Service regulation, the area is open only from 8 a.m. to 6 p.m.; this restriction is designed to allow the shy bighorn sheep a chance to reach water without human interference.

DIRECTIONS TO TRAILHEAD From I-10, a little east past the Highway 111 turn-off to Palm Springs, take Highway 62 northeast to the town of Joshua Tree. Continue 4 miles to the park entrance, then another 10 miles to Hidden Valley Campground. A dirt road leads 2 miles from Hidden Valley Campground to Barker Dam parking area.

THE HIKE From the north end of the parking area, join the signed trail that immediately penetrates the Wonderland of Rocks. You'll pass a special kind of oak, the turbinella, which has adjusted to the harsh conditions of desert life. The oaks are habitat for a multitude of birds and ground squirrels.

For the first 0.5 mile, interpretive signs point out the unique botany of this desert land. The path then squeezes through a narrow rock passageway and leads directly to the edge of the lake. Bird-watching is excellent here because many migratory species not normally associated with the desert are attracted to the lake. The morning and late afternoon hours are particularly tranquil times to visit the lake, and to contemplate the ever-changing reflections of the Wonderland of Rocks on the water.

The trail is a bit indistinct near Barker Dam, but resumes again in fine form near a strange-looking circular water trough, a holdover from the area's cattle-ranching days. A toilet-like float mechanism controlled the flow of water to the thirsty livestock.

The path turns south and soon passes a huge boulder known as Piano Rock. When this land was in private ownership, a piano was hauled atop this rock and played for the amusement of visitors and locals.

Beyond Piano Rock the trail enters a rock-rimmed valley. A brief leftward detour at a junction brings you to the Movie Petroglyphs, so named because in less-enlightened times, the native rock art was painted over by a film crew in order to make it more visible to the camera's eye.

Back on the main trail, you'll parallel some cliffs, perhaps get a glimpse of some Indian bedrock mortars, and loop back to the parking area.

■ MASTODON PEAK
Mastodon Peak Trail
3-mile loop trail with 400-foot elevation gain

Mastodon Peak Trail packs a lot of sight-seeing into a 3-mile walk: a cottonwood-shaded oasis, a gold mine and a grand desert view.

Mastodon Peak, named by early prospectors for its behemoth-like profile, was the site of the Mastodon Mine, a gold mine worked intermittently from 1919 to 1932. The ore was of high quality; however, the main ore body was cut off by a fault.

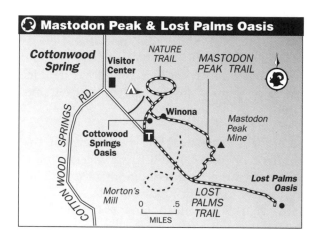

A mile down the trail from the mine is Winona, where some concrete foundations remain to mark the former mill and little town. Winona was home to workers at the Mastodon Mine, as well as workers at the mill, which processed ore from a number of nearby mines.

Views from elephantine-shaped Mastodon Peak include the Cottonwood Springs area and the Eagle Mountains. Clear-day panoramas extend from Mt. San Jacinto above Palm Springs to the Salton Sea.

DIRECTIONS TO TRAILHEAD Entering the national park from the south (via Interstate 10), travel 8 miles north of the park boundary to Cottonwood Spring Campground. Park at the Cottonwood Spring day-use area.

THE HIKE From the parking area, the path proceeds immediately to Cottonwood Spring, a collection of cottonwoods, California fan palms and cattails crowded around a trickling spring.

The path continues 0.5 mile, following a wash to a junction. Lost Palms Trail heads right, but you take the left fork to ascend Mastodon Peak. A short spur trail leads to the summit. Enjoy the views from Cottonwood Campground just below to the Coachella Valley beyond.

The main trail descends to the shafts and ruins of Mastodon Mine. Another mile of travel brings you to Winona. Some shady trees—including eucalyptus planted by miners—offer a pleasant rest stop. A last 0.25-mile brings you to a fork in the road. The right fork leads to the campground; the left fork returns to Cottonwood Spring parking lot.

■ LOST PALMS OASIS
Lost Palms Oasis Trail
From Cottonwood Spring Campground to Lost Palms
Oasis is 8 miles round trip with 300-foot elevation gain.

Lost Palms Oasis Trail passes through a cactus garden, crosses a number of desert washes, and takes you to the two southern oases in the National Park: Cottonwood and Lost Palms.

Largely manmade, Cottonwood Spring Oasis was once a popular overnight stop for freight-haulers and prospectors during the mining years of 1870 to 1910. Travelers and teamsters journeying from Banning to the Dale Goldfield east of Twentynine Palms rested at the oasis.

Lost Palms Oasis is a hidden gem. Nearly 100 palms are found in the deep canyon whose steep igneous walls sparkle in the desert sun.

DIRECTIONS TO TRAILHEAD From the south end of Joshua Tree National Park, follow the park road 8 miles to Cottonwood Spring Campground. Park your car at the campground. The trailhead is at the end of the campground.

THE HIKE Leaving Cottonwood Spring Campground, the trail ambles through a low desert environment of green-trunked palo verde, ironwood and cottonwood trees, spindly ocotillo plants and cholla cactus. Park Service identification plaques describe the area's flora and fauna.

The trail, a bit difficult to follow through the sandy wash, brings you to Cottonwood Spring Oasis in 0.5 mile. Cottonwood Spring is home to a wide variety of birds and a large number of bees.

From Cottonwood Spring, the trail marches over sandy hills, past heaps of huge rocks and along sandy draws and washes. A number of Park Service signs point the way at possibly confusing junctions. Finally, you rise above the washes and climb to a rocky outcropping overlooking the canyon harboring Lost Palms Oasis. From the overlook, descend the steep path around the boulders to the palms.

Little surface water is present at Lost Palms Oasis, but enough is underground for the palms to remain healthy. Lost Palms remained relatively untouched throughout the mining years, though some of its water was pumped to settlements 8 miles south at Chiriaco Summit. Adjacent to Lost Palms Canyon is a handsome upper canyon called Dike Springs.

Shy and reclusive desert bighorn sheep are often seen around this oasis—particularly in hot weather, when they need water more often.

Hole-in-the-Wall offers hikers a unique experience in a maze of rock.

CHAPTER SEVENTEEN

MOJAVE NATIONAL PRESERVE

As you hike up to the top of Kelso Dunes you might just find that the dunes sha-boom-sha-boom-sha-boom for you. Geologists speculate that the extreme dryness of the East Mojave Desert, combined with the wind-polished, rounded nature of the individual sand grains, has something to do with their musical ability.

Except for the sha-booming, the Kelso Dunes are absolutely quiet. Often hikers find they have a 45-square-mile formation of magnificently sculpted sand, the most extensive dune field in the West, all to themselves.

Two decades of park politicking finally ended in October 1994 when Congress passed a bill initiated by Sen. Alan Cranston, then shepherded by Sen. Dianne Feinstein once she took office. Called the California Desert Protection Act, it transferred the East Mojave National Scenic Area, administered by the U.S. Bureau of Land Management, to the National Park Service and established the Mojave National Preserve. The Mojave's elevated national profile has not yet attracted hordes of sightseers, though it's here that the Sonoran, Mojave, and Great Basin deserts converge.

To many travelers, the East Mojave is that vast, bleak, interminable stretch of desert to be crossed as quickly as possible while driving Interstate 15 from Barstow to Las Vegas. Few realize that I-15 is the northern boundary of what desert rats have long called "the Crown Jewel of the California Desert," and what is now called Mojave National Preserve. Some 17 million people live less than a 4-hour's drive from the East Mojave but few city dwellers can locate this desert land on the map, and even fewer visit.

Although virtually unknown, Mojave National Preserve is quite accessible; it's bounded north and south by two major Interstates, I-15 and I-40, and on the east by U.S. Highway 95. Just south of I-40 is one of the longest remaining stretches of old Route 66. Still, the area bounded by these three highways has long been dubbed "The Lonesome Triangle" and will probably keep this nickname for many years to come.

Mojave's 1.6. million acres include such wonders as canyons sculpted by the Mojave River, the vast caves of Mitchell Caverns, and the world's largest Joshua-tree forest. Mojave National Preserve offers the chance to relive history by hiking traditional paths to Fort Piute and Hole-in-the-Wall and by driving the old Mojave Road and fabled Route 66. In the preserve is a wonderful con-

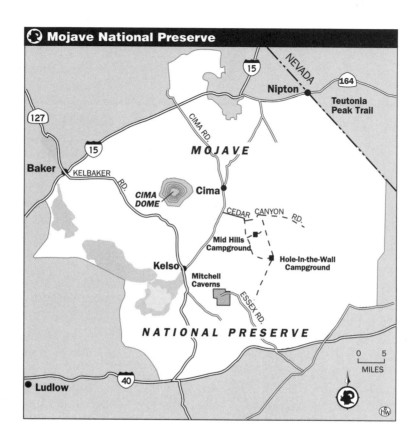

centration of mining history, back roads and footpaths, tabletop mesas, cinder cones, and a dozen mountain ranges. This diversity, everything that makes a desert a desert, draws us to experience its silent places. It's a call of the wild that can't be heard, only felt and experienced.

It's a grand view from atop the Kelso Dunes: the Kelso Mountains to the north, the Bristol Mountains to the southwest, the Granite Mountains to the south, and the Providence Mountains to the east. Everywhere are mountain ranges, small and large, from the jagged, red-colored spire-like Castle Peaks to flat-topped Table Mountain. In fact, despite evidence to the contrary—most notably the stunning Kelso Dunes—the East Mojave is really a desert of mountains not sand.

From the old Kelso Train Depot Visitor Center, lonesome backroads lead toward Cima Dome, a 75-square-mile chunk of uplifted volcanic rock. A geological rarity, Cima has been called the most symmetrical natural dome in the U.S. Another distinctive feature of the dome is its handsome rock outcroppings—the same type found in Joshua Tree National Park to the south. Rock-climbers, rock scramblers and hikers love Cima's rock show.

On and around Cima Dome is the world's largest and densest Joshua tree forest. Botanists say Cima's Joshuas are more symmetrical than their cousins elsewhere in the Mojave, though to me, every tree looks different, every one a rugged individualist with branches that seem like handfuls of daggers.

Hole-in-the-Wall and Mid Hills are the centerpieces of Mojave National Preserve. Both locales offer diverse desert scenery, fine campgrounds, and the feeling of being in the middle of nowhere though in fact located right in the middle of the preserve.

Linking Mid Hills to Hole-in-the-Wall is an 8-mile-long trail, my favorite pathway in the eastern Mojave; nearby is the preserve's best drive. In 1989, Wildhorse Canyon Road, which loops from Mid Hills Campground to Hole-in-the-Wall Campground, was declared the nation's first official "Back Country Byway," an honor bestowed upon America's most scenic backroads.

Hole-in-the-Wall is the kind of place Butch Cassidy and the Sundance Kid would choose as a hideout. Geologists call this twisted maze of red rock rhyolite, a kind of lava that existed as hot liquid far below the earth's surface, then crystallized. A series of iron rings aids descent into Hole-in-the-Wall; they're not particularly difficult for those who are reasonably agile and take their time.

Kelso Dunes, the Joshua trees, Hole-in-the-Wall and Mid Hills—the heart of the new preserve can be viewed in a weekend. But you'll need a week just to see all the major sights, and maybe a lifetime to really get to know Mojave National Preserve. Return for a meander through a "botanical island," the pinyon pine and juniper woodland in Caruthers Canyon; tour Ivanpah Valley, which supports the largest desert tortoise population in the California Desert, and see if you can spot one of the elusive, seldom seen creatures; climb atop enormous volcanic cinder cones, then with flashlights crawl through narrow lava tubes. Return to explore the ruins of Fort Piute, wonder about the lonely life of the soldiers stationed there, marvel at the ruts carved into rock by the wheels of pioneer wagon trains; and guess at the meaning of the petroglyphs left behind by the Native Americans, who roamed this land long ago.

Mojave National Preserve is a worthy addition to the national park system and a great place to take a hike.

■ KELBAKER HILLS
Kelbaker Hills Trail
2 miles round trip with 300-foot elevation gain

If Mojave National Preserve had a "Main Street," Kelbaker Road would be it. The road is the preserve's busiest, and provides access to several of its most popular attractions including the Kelso Depot and Kelso Dunes

The National Park Service recently installed a large Mojave National Preserve entry sign just outside of Baker on Kelbaker Road. The entry monument, one of those grand granite proclamations characteristic of other western national parks, emphasizes Kelbaker's status as the major Mojave road.

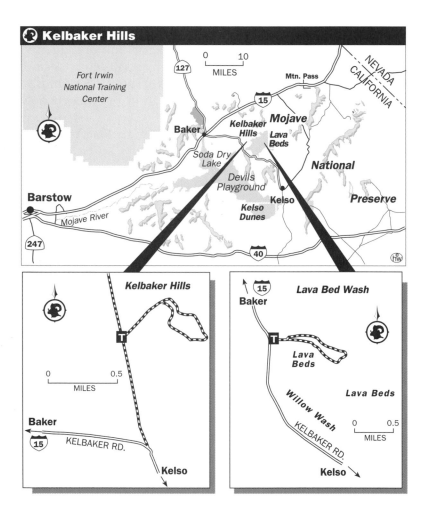

Most preserve visitors remain in their vehicles while driving Kelbaker Road from Baker to Kelso Depot and thus miss a couple of interesting sights en route. One of my favorite leg-stretcher jaunts is up into the Kelbaker Hills.

Here's your chance to name one of the preserve's geographic features. I call them the Kelbaker Hills because of their proximity to Kelbaker Road as well as for their location a dozen miles southeast of Baker and two-dozen miles northwest of Kelso; however, they don't really have a name on the map or one in common usage. Others have suggested the "Baker Hills" due to their close-to-town position or the "Rhyolite Hills" because of their volcanic composition.

By whatever name, these hills offer a close-to-the-paved-road wilderness experience, as well as a short (though moderately strenuous) hike.

DIRECTIONS TO TRAILHEAD   To access the Kelbaker Hills from Baker and I-15, drive 11 miles east on Kelbaker Road. Just as the road makes a pronounced bend right (south) turn left (north) on the unsigned dirt road. Drive

Out of-the-way sights In out-of-the-way places. A jack-o'-lantern greets a hiker in the Kelbaker Hills.

0.8 mile along the preserve's signed wilderness boundary. Look east of the road for a distinct gap in the Kelbaker Hills and scarce parking just east off the road where you can find it.

THE HIKE If you locate a sketchy old road extending east up the wash leading to the hills, take it; otherwise, simply walk up the wash toward the obvious gap in the hills. You route will angle toward the base of the tallest hills, and just to the left of them.

A bit more than 0.5 mile out, you'll observe a couple of narrow ravines (favorite burro routes, judging by the tracks) that lead to the top of the hills. Climb (careful, it's loose footing) any one of these ravines for good views of this part of the preserve.

Experienced rock-scramblers can make their way to the top of the highest hills. Those determined to make a loop hike out of this jaunt can do so by descending a ravine southeast and meeting the main wash that leads back to the gap in the hills, and then returning to the trailhead.

■ KELSO DUNES
Kelso Dunes Trail
To top of Kelso Dunes is 3 miles
round trip with 400-foot elevation gain

I n the heart of the heart of the preserve lie Kelso Dunes, one of the tallest dune systems in America.

And the dunes give off good vibrations, say many desert day hikers. The good vibrations that enthuse hikers are not the desert's spiritual emanations—which many visitors find considerable—but the Kelso Dunes' rare ability to make a low rumbling sound when sand slides down the steep slopes. This sound has been variously described as that of a kettle drum, low flying airplane or Tibetan gong.

The sand that forms Kelso Dunes blows in from the Mojave River basin. After traveling east 35 miles across a stark plain known as the Devils Playground, it's deposited in hills nearly 600 feet high. The westerlies carrying the sand rush headlong into winds from other directions, which is why the sand is dropped here, and why it stays here.

For further confirmation of the circular pattern of winds that formed the dunes, examine the bunches of grass on the lower slopes. You'll notice that the tips of the tall grasses have etched 360-degree circles on the sand.

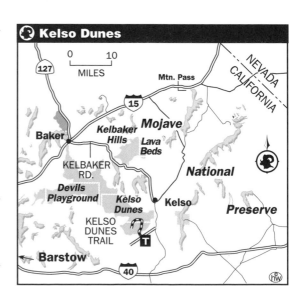

Other patterns on the sand are made by the desert's abundant, but rarely seen, wildlife. You might see the tracks of a coyote, kit fox, antelope ground squirrel, packrat, raven or sidewinder. Footprints of lizards and mice can be seen tacking this way and that over the sand. The dune's surface records the lightest pressure of the smallest feet.

DIRECTIONS TO TRAILHEAD From Interstate 15 in Baker, some 60 miles northeast of Barstow, turn south on Kelbaker Road and proceed about 35 miles to the town of Kelso. Pause to admire the classic neo-Spanish style Kelso Railroad Depot next to the Union Pacific tracks. The building is being restored as a major information center for Mojave National Preserve.

The view from the top is well worth the walk up Kelso Dunes.

From Kelso, continue on Kelbaker Road for another 7 miles to a signed dirt road and turn west (right). Drive slowly along this road (navigable for all but very low-slung passenger cars) 3 miles to a parking area. The trail to Kelso Dunes begins just up the dirt road from the parking area.

THE HIKE Only the first quarter-mile or so of the walk to the dunes is on established trail. Once the trail peters out, angle toward the low saddle atop the dunes, just to the right of the highest point.

Know the old saying "One step forward, two steps back"? This saying will take on new meaning if you attempt to take the most direct route to the top of the dunes by walking straight up the tallest sand hill.

As you cross the lower dunes, you'll pass some mesquite and creosote bushes. During spring of a good wildflower year, the lower dunes are bedecked with yellow and white desert primrose, pink sand verbena and yellow sunflowers.

When you reach the saddle located to the right of the high point, turn left and trek another hundred yards or so to the top. The black material crowning the top of the dunes is magnetite, an iron oxide, and one of about two dozen minerals found within the dune system.

Enjoy the view from the top: the Kelso Mountains to the north, the Bristol Mountains to the southwest, the Granite Mountains to the south, the Providence Mountains to the east. Everywhere you look there are mountain ranges, small and large.

In fact, despite evidence to the contrary—most notably the stunning dunes beneath your feet—the East Mojave is really a desert of mountains, not sand.

While atop the dunes, perhaps your footsteps will cause mini-avalanches and the dunes will sha-boom-sha-boom for you. There's speculation that the extreme dryness of the East Mojave, combined with the wind-polished, rounded nature of the individual sand grains, has something to do with their musical ability. After picking up good vibrations, descend the steep dune face (much easier on the way down!) and return to the trailhead.

■ CIMA DOME
Teutonia Peak Trail
To Teutonia Peak, is 4 miles round trip

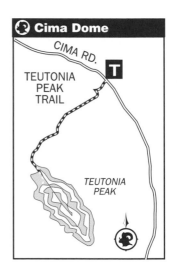

Cima Dome is certainly one of the easiest Mojave National Preserve sites to reach, but when you reach it, you may wonder why you did. It's not a geologic formation you can view close-up: the dome slopes so gently, it's best viewed from a distance. What Gertrude Stein said of Oakland comes to mind: "There's no there there."

Two places to get "the big picture" of Cima Dome are from Mid Hills Campground and from I-15 as you drive southeast of Baker and crest a low rise.

The dome is a mass of once-molten monzonite, a granite-like rock. Over thousands of years it's been extensively eroded, and it now sprawls over some 75 square miles. It's more than 10 miles in diameter.

Another distinctive feature of the dome is its handsome rock outcroppings—the same type found in Joshua Tree National Park to the south. Rock climbers, rock scramblers, and hikers love Cima's rock show.

The word to remember around Cima Dome is symmetry. A geological rarity, the almost perfectly symmetrical dome has been called the most symmetrical natural dome in the U.S. If you take a look at the area's USGS topographical map and study Cima's near-concentric contour lines, you'll probably agree with this symmetry claim.

Symmetry is also a word used in conjunction with the area's other natural attraction: the Joshua tree. Botanists say Cima's Joshuas are more symmetrical than their cousins elsewhere in the Mojave. Cima's Joshua trees are tall—some more than 25 feet tall—and several hundred years old. Collectively, they form the world's largest and densest Joshua-tree forest.

Here at an elevation of about 4,000 feet this distinct symbol of the Mojave desert truly thrives. Bring your camera!

This walk travels the famed Joshua-tree forest, then visits Cima Dome, which rises 1,500 feet above the surrounding desert playas.

DIRECTIONS TO TRAILHEAD   The beginning of the trail is just off Cima Road, a scenic byway that stretches 17 miles from the Cima Road exit on Interstate 15 south to Cima. The signed trailhead is about 9 miles from I-15.

The Cime Dome area hosts the world's largest Joshua tree forest.

THE HIKE The easy 2-mile Teutonia Peak Trail meanders through the Joshua tree forest and ascends to a lookout over Cima Dome. From the lookout, it's a 0.25 mile scramble over rocks to the top of Teutonia Peak (elevation 5,755 feet).

■ HOLE-IN-THE-WALL
Mid Hills to Hole-in-the-Wall Trail
From Mid Hills Campground to Hole-in-the-Wall Campground is 8 miles one-way with 1,000-foot elevation loss

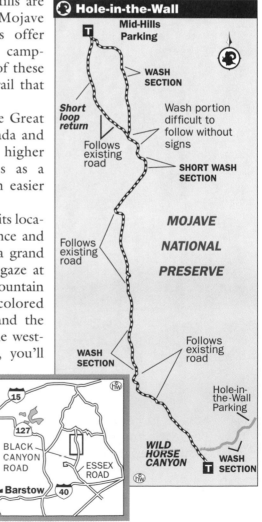

Hole-in-the-Wall and Mid Hills are the centerpieces of Mojave National Preserve. Both locales offer diverse desert scenery and fine campgrounds. Doubling the pleasure of these special places is an 8-mile-long trail that links them together.

Mile-high Mid Hills recalls the Great Basin Desert topography of Nevada and Utah. It's a thousand or so feet higher than Hole-in-the-Wall and thus as a starting point offers the hiker an easier way to go.

Mid Hills, so named because of its location halfway between the Providence and the New York Mountains, offers a grand observation point from which to gaze at the East Mojave's dominant mountain ranges: the coffee-with-cream-colored Pinto Mountains to the north, and the rolling Kelso Dunes shining on the western horizon. Looking northwest, you'll also get a superb view of Cima Dome, the 75-square-mile chunk of uplifted volcanic rock.

Hole-in-the-Wall is a second inviting locale, the kind of place Butch Cassidy and the Sundance Kid would choose as a hideout.

Hole-in-the-Wall is a twisted maze of red rock. Geologists call this rhyolite, a kind of lava that existed as hot liquid far below the earth's surface, then crystalized.

A series of iron rings aids descent into Banshee Canyon. They're not particularly difficult for those who are reasonably agile and take their time.

If you're not up for a long day hike, the 0.75-mile trip from Hole-in-the-Wall Campground to Banshee Canyon and the 5-mile jaunt to Wild Horse Canyon offer some easier alternatives.

A word about desert hiking in general and this desert hike in particular: You'll often travel in the bottoms of sandy washes instead of over more clearly defined trails found in forest locales. This means the hiker must rely on maps, a sense of direction, rock cairns and signs.

The hike is an adventurous excursion through a diverse desert environment. You'll see basin-and-range tabletop mesas, encounter large pinyon trees, and view an array of colorful cactus and lichen-covered granite rocks. East Mojave views—Table Mountain, Wild Horse Mesa, the Providence Range—are unparalleled.

DIRECTIONS TO TRAILHEAD From Interstate 40, approximately 42 miles west of Needles and nearly 100 miles east of Barstow, exit on Essex Road. Head north 9.5 miles to the junction of Essex Road and Black Canyon Road. Bear right on the latter road, which soon turns to dirt. (Well-graded Black Canyon Road is suitable for passenger cars.) After 8.5 miles of travel you'll spot Hole-in-the-Wall Campground on your left. Turn into the campground and park at the lip of Banshee Canyon on the upper loop of the camp road. The unsigned trail plunges right into the canyon.

Those wishing to park vehicles for day hikes on the trail are encouraged to use the new Wild Horse Canyon Trailhead on Wild Horse Canyon Road.

Another 9 or so miles of travel on Black Canyon Road brings you to the signed turn-off for Mid Hills Campground. You'll turn left and travel 2 miles to the campground. The Mid Hills trailhead is adjacent to a windmill immediately opposite the entrance road to the campground.

THE HIKE In a short distance, the path ascends to a saddle which offers splendid views of the Pinto Valley to the northeast. (The saddle is this hike's high point.)

From the saddle, the path angles south, descending into, then climbing out of a wash. (Keep a close eye on the trail; it's easy to lose here.)

The trail reaches a dirt road, follows it for a mere 100 feet, then turns sharply left to join a wash for a time, exits it, and crosses a road. You encounter another wash, enter it and exit it.

After a modest ascent, the trail joins a road, passes through a gate, and joins another road for a little more than a mile. This road serves up spectacular views to the south of the Providence Mountains and Wild Horse Mesa.

Adjacent to a group of large boulders, a road veers left but hikers bear right, soon turning sharp left with the road. The route passes through another gate, then works its way through a dense thicket of cholla cactus.

After following another wash, the trail crosses a dirt road, then soon joins a second road, which follows a wash to a dead-end at an abandoned dam. The trail ascends through some rocks, levels for a time, then descends. A quarter-mile before trail's end, you'll spy the Hole-in-the-Wall spur trail leading off to the left.

■ CARUTHERS CANYON

Caruthers Canyon Trail

From Caruthers Canyon to old Mine

is 3 miles round trip with 400-foot elevation gain

Botanists call them disjuncts. Bureaucrats call them UPAs (Unusual Plant Assemblages). The more lyrical naturalists among us call them islands on the land.

By whatever name, the isolated communities of pinyon pine and white fir in the New York Mountains of the East Mojave Desert are very special places. Nearly 300 plant species have been counted on the slopes of this range and in its colorfully named canyons—Cottonwood and Caruthers, Butcher Knife and Fourth of July.

Perhaps the most botanically unique area in the mountains, indeed in the whole Mojave National Preserve, is Caruthers Canyon. A cool, inviting pinyon-pine-juniper woodland stands in marked contrast to the sparsely vegetated sandscape common in other parts of the desert. The conifers are joined by oaks and a variety of coastal chaparral plants including manzanita, yerba santa, ceanothus and coffee berry.

What is a coastal ecosystem doing in the middle of a desert?

Botanists believe that during wetter times such coastal scrub vegetation was quite widespread. As the climate became more arid, coastal ecosystems were "stranded" atop high and moist slopes. The botanical islands high in the New York Mountains are outposts of Rocky Mountain and coastal California flora.

Caruthers Canyon is a treat for the hiker. An abandoned dirt road leads through a rocky basin and into a historic gold-mining region. Prospectors began digging in the New York Mountains

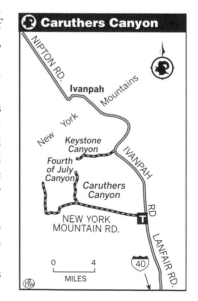

in the 1860s and continued well into the 20th century. At trail's end are a couple of gold-mine shafts.

The canyon's woodland offers great bird-watching. The western tanager, gray-headed junco, yellow-breasted chat and many more species are found here. Circling high in the sky are the raptors—golden eagles, prairie falcons and red-tailed hawks.

DIRECTIONS TO TRAILHEAD From I-40, 28 miles west of Needles, and some 117 miles east of Barstow, exit on Mt. Springs Road. You'll pass the tiny

Pinyon pines, great granite boulders, and clean fresh air.

town of Goffs (last chance for provisions) and head north 27.5 miles on the main road, known variously as Ivanpah-Goffs Road or Ivanpah Road, to New York Mountains Road. (Part of Ivanpah Road and New York Mountains Road are dirt; they are suitable for passenger cars with good ground clearance.) Turn left, west, on New York Mountains Road. A couple of OX Cattle Ranch buildings stand near this road's intersection with Ivanpah Road. Drive 5.5 miles to an unsigned junction with a dirt road and turn north. Proceed 2 miles to a woodland laced with turnouts that serve as unofficial campsites. Leave your car here; farther along, the road dips into a wash and gets very rough. From the Caruthers Canyon "Campground" follow the main dirt road up the canyon. As you ascend, look behind you for a great view of Table Mountain, the most dominant peak of the central part of Mojave.

THE HIKE   Handsome boulders line the trail and frame views of the tall peak before you, New York Mountain. The range's 7,532-foot signature peak is crowned with a botanical island of its own—a relict stand of Rocky Mountain white fir.

A half-mile farther, you'll come to a fork in the road. The right road climbs 0.25 mile to an old mining shack. Take the left fork, dipping in and out of a wash and gaining a great view of the canyon and its castellated walls.

If it's rained recently, you might find some water collected in pools on the rocky canyon bottom. Enjoy the tranquility of the gold mine area, but don't stray into the dark and dangerous shafts.

■ PIUTE CANYON
Piute Canyon Trail
To Fort Piute is 6.5 miles round trip
with 600-foot elevation gain

In 1865, Fort Piute was described by a visitor as "a Godforsaken place—the meanest I ever saw for a military station." It's doubtful that many would disagree; however, the ruins of the fort, along with pretty Piute Valley and Piute Creek, add up to an intriguing, way-off-the-beaten-path tour for the adventurous.

Fort Piute, located east of Lanfair Valley, at the southern end of the Piute Mountains, was established to provide a military presence in the desert, and to protect pioneer travelers on their westward journey.

Indians resisted the intrusion of settlers on tribal lands so there were frequent attacks on westbound sellers and mail wagons traveling the route from Prescott, Arizona to Los Angeles.

Subsequent military escorts protected travelers, but conditions at the outpost were intolerable for many soldiers stationed at Fort Piute. Desertion was a

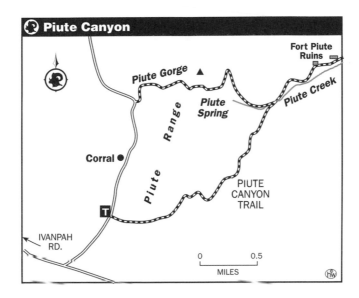

regular occurrence, and the outpost was officially staffed by just 18 men of the Company "D" 9th Infantry Division from 1867 to 1868.

Today the small, primitive installation lies in ruins; its thick rock-and-mortar walls have been weathered and crumbled to a height of just two or three feet. The stone outlines of the original buildings delineate three connecting rooms that served as a tiny living quarters, corral and cookhouse.

The walk along Piute Creek is of more than military interest. The only perennial stream in the preserve, Piute Creek is an oasis-like area where cottonwoods, willows and sedges flourish. Bighorn sheep frequently visit this watering site, as do a large number of birds. (This is a fragile ecosystem; not a recreation area. Please treat the creek gently.)

The hike to Fort Piute explores Piute Creek and gorge and gives you a chance to walk a portion of the historic Mojave Road. Following the Mojave Road Trail, as it's called, lets you walk back into time and get a glimpse of the hardships faced by early pioneers.

This is not a hike for the inexperienced or for first-time visitors to Mojave National Preserve; the roads and paths are unsigned and sometimes hard to follow. Experienced hikers and repeat visitors, however, will thoroughly enjoy their exploration of Fort Piute.

DIRECTIONS TO TRAILHEAD Head west on Interstate 40 and take the turn-off for the road leading to the hamlet of Goffs. Pass through Goffs and drive some 16 miles along Lanfair Road to a point about 100 feet beyond its junction with Cedar Canyon Road. Turn right (east) on a road that goes by four names: Cedar Canyon Road, the utility road, Cable Road and Pole Road. The latter three names arise from the fact that the road follows a buried telephone cable. Drive east, staying right at a junction 3.7 miles out, and sticking with the

The isolated ruins of Fort Piute.

cable road about 6 more miles to another junction where there's a cattle guard. Turn left before the cattleguard on another dirt road and proceed 0.5 mile to an abandoned section of the Mojave Road

From the intersection of Lanfair and Cedar Canyon roads, drive east on the utility road 9.5 miles. Turn north on the small dirt road that leads 0.5 mile to the old Mojave Road.

THE HIKE   Begin your trek at Piute Hill. Just over the crest of the hill, you meet old Mojave Road just over the crest of the hill. From atop the hill, pause to take in the view. Table Mountain can be seen directly to the west, and in the north are Castle Peaks.

Happily for hikers, the route leads down the difficult grade that challenged early pioneers. No doubt the volcanic rock on the road really rattled the settlers' wagons. On the 2 miles of travel on Mojave Road, you'll pass along loose, sandy trail near Piute Creek where there's nice picnicking. (The water is not safe to drink.) To avoid trampling the creekbed, try taking the trail on the north side of the creek.

About 0.5 mile from the fort, you'll cross the creek. The Mojave Road narrows. Look sharply for the Piute Canyon Trail coming in from the west. (This will be your optional return route.) Continue on a slight descent to the fort.

An interpretive marker provides some historic information about the history of "Fort Pah Ute, 1867-68." Don't sit on the walls or disturb the ruins; like all cultural resources in the desert, the fort is protected by federal law.

Head back along the Mojave Road 0.5 mile, bearing right on unsigned Piute Canyon Trail. This narrow path stays high on the canyon wall, heading west at first, then north. A half-mile along, you can see prominent Piute Gorge to the west; you'll be following this gorge back to the trailhead.

The trail is very faint; if you lose the path, keep heading west at first, then north. A half-mile along, you can see prominent Piute Gorge to the west; you'll be following this gorge back to the trailhead.

Keep heading west and descend to the floor of Piute Gorge. Expect a steep scramble to reach the bottom of the gorge.

At the bottom, you'll proceed west up Piute Gorge; stay on the gorge bottom. After 0.5 mile you'll come to an intersection where another canyon comes in from the left. Don't take this route, but continue up the gorge to the right.

At littler farther, a trail leading out of the gorge takes off to the left. (Keep a sharp eye out for this one.) Take this trail up to the rim of the gorge, where there's a scenic overlook. From here, follow the dirt road south past a corral back to the trailhead.

Intriguing rock formations offshore (top), and a lighthouse (below)
are part of Anacapa's allure.

18

CHANNEL ISLANDS NATIONAL PARK

Channel Islands National Park is a preserve for what some have called the "American Galapagos." Top priority was given to protecting sea lions and seals, endemic plants like the Santa Cruz pine, rich archaeological digs, and what may be the final resting place of Portuguese navigator Juan Rodríguez Cabrillo, who explored the California coast for the Spanish crown in the 16th century.

Would be adventurers enjoy the Visitor Center in Ventura Harbor as an exciting sneak preview of the splendid park out there in the Pacific, 12 to 60 miles away, a series of blue-tinged mountains floating on the horizon. The Visitor Center boasts excellent island history and ecology exhibits, and provides boat transportation information.

In 1980, five of the eight Channel Islands—Anacapa, San Miguel, Santa Barbara, Santa Cruz and Santa Rosa—became America's 40th national park. (The U.S. Navy practices maneuvers on San Nicholas and San Clemente. Farther south, Santa Catalina has pursued a destiny apart.) The waters surrounding the national park islands are protected as the Channel Islands National Marine Sanctuary.

On Anacapa, only 14 miles offshore from Ventura, you get the feeling that the Channel Islands may once have been connected to the mainland. Until recently, geologists had this same feeling, figuring that the Santa Monica Mountains, which bisect Los Angeles, marched out to sea and their peaks appeared offshore as the Channel Islands. This belief was based on the assumption that a land bridge was the only way terrestrial animals could have arrived. The discovery of fossil elephant bones on Santa Rosa and San Miguel changed their thinking. Scientists at first believed that the dwarf mammoth, a 6-foot cousin to the mainland behemoth, could not swim, so a land bridge was necessary. In truth, elephants

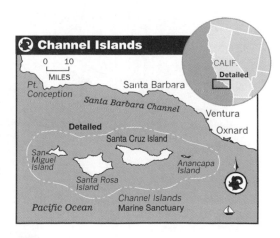

are excellent swimmers—their trunks are superb snorkels and air pockets in their skulls give the animals excellent buoyancy.

So the land-bridge theory is kaput, and it's now theorized that the islands rose out of the Pacific through volcanic action 14 million years ago, later sinking and rising many times as glaciation alternated with massive melting. The four northern islands were linked, until about 20,000 years ago, into a super-island called *Santaroasae,* only to part company during the final glacial melt into the wave-sculpted islands we see today.

The islands' even, sea-tempered climate and isolation from the mainland have benefited plants that either were altered through evolution on the mainland or have perished altogether. What you see on the islands is Southern California of a millennium ago.

Because of the fragile ecology, hiking on the islands is more regulated than it is in most places. You must always stay on the trail, and on some islands be accompanied by a national park ranger or a Nature Conservancy employee.

■ ANACAPA ISLAND
Anacapa Island Loop Trail
2 miles round trip

Anacapa, 12 miles southwest of Port Hueneme, is the most accessible Channel Island. It offers the hiker a sampling of the charms of the larger islands to the west. Below the tall wind-and-wave-cut cliffs, sea lions bark at the crashing breakers. Gulls, owls, and pelicans call the cliffs home.

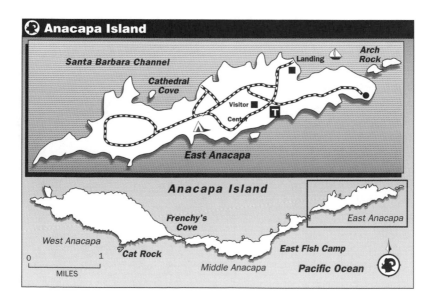

Anacapa is really three islets chained together with reefs that rise above the surface during low tide. West Anacapa is the largest segment, featuring great caves where the Chumash are said to have collected water dripping from the ceiling. The middle isle hosts a wind-battered eucalyptus grove.

In February and March, you may enjoy the sight of 30-ton gray whales passing south on their way to calving and mating waters off Baja California. In early spring, the giant coreopsis, one of the island's featured attractions, is something to behold. It is called the tree sunflower, an awkward thick-trunked perennial that grows as tall as ten feet.

The east isle, where the National Park maintains a Visitor Center, is the light of the Channel Islands; a Coast Guard lighthouse and foghorn warn ships of the dangerous channel.

Anacapa is small, but perfect-sized for the usual visit (2 to 3 hours). By the time you tour the lighthouse and Visitor Center, hike the self-guided trail and have lunch, it's time to board the boat for home.

DIRECTIONS TO TRAILHEAD   For the most up-to-date information about boat departures to Anacapa and to the other islands, contact Channel Islands National Park at (805) 658-5730 or the park concessionaire, Island Packers in Ventura Harbor at (805) 642-1393. The Channel Islands are also accessible from Santa Barbara; contact Sea Landing at (805) 963-3564.

THE HIKE   The nature trail leaves from the Visitor Center, where you can learn about island life, past and present. A helpful pamphlet is available describing the island's features. Remember to stay on the trail; the island's ground cover is easily damaged.

Along the trail, a campground and several inspiring cliff-edge nooks invite you to picnic. The trail loops in a figure-eight through the coreopsis and returns to the Visitor Center.

■ SANTA CRUZ ISLAND
Pelican Bay and Prisoners Harbor Trails
3 miles round trip around Pelican Bay;
6 miles round trip from Prisoners Harbor

Santa Cruz Island may not be celebrated in song like Santa Catalina (Ever hear The Four Preps' 1958 hit tune "Twenty-six Miles"?), but there are similarities. Like Catalina, Santa Cruz Island was, until recent years, a working cattle ranch. It's now managed by the Nature Conservancy and is part of Channel Island National Park.

Like Anacapa, Santa Cruz Island seems tantalizingly close to the mainland, dominating the seaward horizon of Santa Barbara. California's largest offshore island, it boasts the most varied coastline and topography, the highest peak, (2,434 feet) and safest harbors.

The island's anchorages hint at its history: Smugglers Cove, Prisoners Harbor (the island was once a Mexican penal colony), Coches Prietos ("Black Pigs," for the Mexican-introduced hogs). Chumash Indians had both permanent and summer villages on Santa Cruz until the early 1800s, when they were brought to the mainland and confined in Spanish missions.

In the 1800s, a colony of French and Italian immigrants led by Justinian Caire began a Mediterranean-style ranch, raising sheep and cattle, growing olives and almonds, even making wine. In 1937, Edwin Stanton of Los Angeles bought the western nine-tenths of the island from the Caire family. Edwin's son, Dr. Carey Stanton, ran the Santa Cruz Island Co. from 1957 until his death in 1987, when the era of family ownership of the island ended and the Nature Conservancy assumed management.

DIRECTIONS TO TRAILHEAD For the most up-to-date information about boat departures to the islands, contact Channel Islands National Park at (805) 658-5730 or the park concessionaire, Island Packers in Ventura Harbor at (805) 642-1393. The Channel Islands are also accessible from Santa Barbara; contact Sea Landing at (805) 963-3564.

Two of the most popular yet easily booked trips to Santa Cruz Island depart with Island Packers, the park's boat concession, from Ventura Harbor at 8 a.m. and return to the mainland between 5 and 6 p.m. Sometimes the boats pause to observe dolphins, whales, sea lions or seals. Plan on a 2-hour boat ride each way and about 5 hours on the island. You and three dozen others make up a good boatload.

THE HIKE The Main Ranch's main emphasis is on human history, while the Pelican Bay Trip stresses natural history.

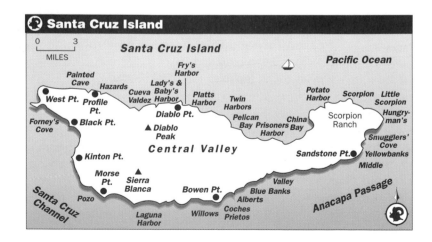

The lovely old ranch buildings evoke memories of days gone by.

Main Ranch Day Trip: From the landing at Prisoners Harbor, it's a 3-mile hike under old oaks and through eucalyptus groves along an old fennel-lined ranch road. Your party will be accompanied by a Nature Conservancy employee, who will point out some of the botanical and historical highlights encountered en route.

Upon arrival at the ranch, visitors eat lunch around a pool. (Bring a swimsuit so you can take a dip.) After lunch you can take a tour of the ranch buildings, including a tiny cabin converted into an anthropology museum, the main ranch house and some dilapidated winery buildings. A restored stone Catholic church celebrated its 100th anniversary in 1991 with a visit by Archbishop (now Cardinal) Roger Mahony. Next to the old church is a cemetery where both humans and ranch dogs rest in peace.

Pelican Bay Day Trip: After arrival at Pelican Bay, landing is by a small skiff onto a rocky ledge. You'll have to climb up a somewhat precipitous cliff trail to reach the picnic spot overlooking the bay.

A Nature Conservancy naturalist leads your group on an educational hike along the north shore. Two special botanical delights are a bishop-pine forest and a grove of Santa Cruz Island ironwood.

■ SANTA ROSA ISLAND
Lobo Canyon, East Point, Cherry Canyon Trails
5 miles round trip around Lobo Canyon; 1 mile around East Point; 3 miles around Cherry Canyon

Rolling grasslands cover much of Santa Rosa Island, which is cut by rugged oak- and ironwood-filled canyons. Torrey pines are found at Bechers Bay.

Santa Rosa had a considerable Chumash population when explorer Juan Rodríguez Cabrillo sailed by in 1542. Scientists who have examined the island's extensive archeological record believe the island was inhabited at least 10,000 years ago.

After the Chumash era, during Spain's rule over California, the island was land granted to Don Carlos and Don José Carrillo. For many years their families raised sheep on the island and were known on the mainland for hosting grand fiestas at shearing time.

In 1902, Walter Vail and J.W. Vickers bought the island and raised what many considered some of the finest cattle in California. The island became part of Channel Islands National Park in 1986.

The National Park Service offers a couple of ranger-guided walking tours of the island. Hikers are transported to the more remote trailheads by four-wheel-drive vehicles.

DIRECTIONS TO TRAILHEAD For the most up-to-date information about boat departures to the islands, contact Channel Islands National Park at (805) 658-5730 or the park concessionaire, Island Packers in Ventura Harbor at (805) 642-1393. The Channel Islands are also accessible from Santa Barbara; contact Sea Landing at (805) 963-3564.

THE HIKE Lobo Canyon (5 miles round trip): Hikers descend the sandstone-walled Canada Lobos, pausing to admire such native flora as island monkeyflower, dudleya and coreopsis. At the mouth of the canyon, near the ocean, is a Chumash village site. The hike continues, as the trail ascends the east wall of the canyon, then drops into Cow Canyon. At the mouth of Cow Canyon is an excellent tidepool area.

East Point Trail (1 mile round trip): Here's an opportunity for hikers to visit a rare stand of Torrey pines, and a large freshwater marsh where bird-watchers will enjoy viewing shorebirds and waterfowl. Trail's end is one of Santa Rosa's beautiful beaches.

The Torrey pines are an easy 3-mile-round-trip walk from the campground; the stand is located on a hillside. From the top of this hill are spectacular views of Bechers Bay.

Cherry Canyon Trail (3 miles round trip): Walking Cherry Canyon offers the opportunity to see some plants and animals that are found nowhere else. The trail heads 2 miles up the canyon to an oak grove. On the return trip, the trail offers far-reaching views of the interior, roaming deer and Roosevelt elk, and the dramatic sweep of Bechers Bay. Trail's end is the island's historic ranch complex.

■ SAN MIGUEL ISLAND
San Miguel Island Trail
From Cuyler Harbor to Lester Ranch is
3 miles round trip with 700-foot elevation gain

San Miguel is the westernmost of the Channel Islands. Eight miles long and 4 miles wide, it rises as a plateau, 400 to 800 feet above the sea. Wind-driven sands cover many of the hills which were severely overgrazed by sheep during the island's ranching days. Owned by the U.S. Navy, which once used it as a bombing site and missile-tracking station, San Miguel is now managed by the National Park Service.

Three species of cormorants, storm petrels, Cassin's auklets, and pigeon guillemot nest on the island. San Miguel is home to six pinniped species:

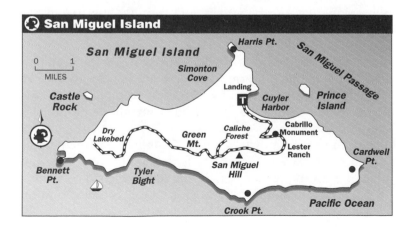

Hikers get commanding views from San Miguel Island high points.

California sea lion, northern elephant seal, steller sea lion, harbor seal, northern fur seal and Guadalupe fur seal. The island may host the largest elephant seal-population on earth. As many as 15,000 seals and sea lions can be seen basking on the rocks during mating season.

A trail runs most of the way from Cuyler Harbor to the west end of the island at Point Bennett, where the pinniped population is centered. The trail passes two round peaks, San Miguel and Green Mountain, and drops in and out of steep canyons to view the lunar landscape of the caliche forest. You must hike with the resident ranger and stay on established trails because the island's vegetation is fragile.

DIRECTIONS TO TRAILHEAD   For the most up-to-date information about boat departures to the islands, contact Channel Islands National Park at (805) 658-5730 or the park concessionaire, Island Packers in Ventura Harbor at (805) 642-1393. The Channel Islands are also accessible from Santa Barbara; contact Sea Landing at (805) 963-3564.

Plan a very long day—or better yet, an overnight trip to San Miguel. It's at least a 5-hour boat trip from Ventura.

THE HIKE   Follow the beach at Cuyler Harbor to the east. The harbor was named after the original government surveyor in the 1850s. The beach around the anchorage was formed by a bight of volcanic cliffs that extend to bold and precipitous Harris Point, the most prominent landmark on San Miguel's coast.

At the east end of the beach, about 0.75 mile from anchoring waters, a small footpath winds its way up the bluffs. It's a relatively steep trail following the edge of a stream-cut canyon. At the top of the canyon, the trail veers east and forks. The left fork leads a short distance to Cabrillo Monument.

You can anchor and come ashore at "The Palm Trees" during rough weather or under heavy swell conditions. In calm weather, however, come ashore at Gull Rock right in front of Nidever Canyon. You will be able to see the trail above the east side of the canyon. When you get to the top of the canyon the ranger station and pit toilet are straight ahead. Instead of going straight you can turn east, The trail ascends a short distance to the Cabrillo Monument. The Lester Ranch is a short distance beyond that.

Juan Rodríguez Cabrillo, Portuguese explorer, visited and wrote about San Miguel in October 1542. While on the island he fell and broke either an arm or a leg (historians are unsure about this). As a result of this injury he contracted gangrene and died on the island in January 1543. It's believed (historians disagree about this, too) he was buried here. In honor of Cabrillo, a monument was erected in 1937.

The right fork continues to the remains of a ranch house. Of the various ranchers and ranch managers to live on the island, the most well-known were the Lesters. They spent 12 years on the island, and their adventures were occasionally chronicled by the local press. When the Navy evicted the Lesters from the island in 1942, Mr. Lester went to a hill overlooking Harris Point, in his view the prettiest part of the island, and shot himself. Within a month his family moved back to the mainland. Not much is left of the ranch now. The buildings burned down in the 1960s and only a rubble of brick and scattered household items remains.

For a longer 14-mile round trip the hiker can continue on the trail past the ranch to the top of San Miguel Hill (861 feet), down, and then up again to the top of Green Mountain (850 feet). Ask rangers to tell you about the caliche forest, composed of fossil sand casts of ancient plants. Calcium carbonate reacted with the plants' organic acid, creating a ghostly forest.

■ SANTA BARBARA ISLAND
Signal Peak Loop Trail
Loop around isle is 2-5 miles round trip
with 500-foot elevation gain.

Only one square mile in area, Santa Barbara is the smallest Channel Island. It's located some 38 miles west of San Pedro—or quite a bit south of the other islands in the national park.

Geologically speaking, Santa Barbara arose a bit differently from the other isles. The island is a volcano, leftover from Miocene times, some 25 million years ago, and shares characteristics with Mexico's Guadalupe Islands.

From a distance, the triangular-shaped island looks barren—not a tree in sight. The tallest plant is the coreopsis, the giant sunflower that can grow 10 feet high.

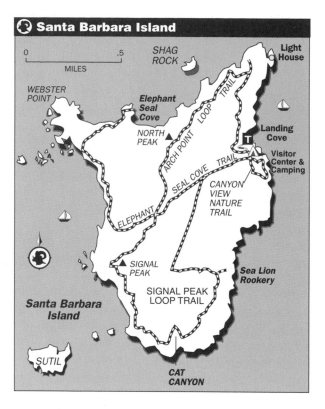

To bird-watchers, Santa Barbara means seabirds, lots of them—gulls, cormorants, pelicans and black oystercatchers. And the island boasts some rare birds, too: the black stormy petrel and the Xantus murrelet. Land birds commonly sighted include burrowing and barn owls, hummingbirds, horned larks and finches.

Besides the birds, another reason to bring binoculars to the island is to view sea lions and elephant seals. Webster Point on the western end of the isle is a favorite haul-out area for the pinnipeds.

Rich kelp beds surround the islands, habitat for a wide variety of fish. The subtidal waters harbor crabs, lobster, sea urchin and abalone, particularly the somewhat rare pink abalone.

Explorer Sebastian Vizcaíno sailed by on December 4, 1602. That day happened to be the day of remembrance for Saint Barbara, so the island was named for her. During the 1700s, the Spanish used the isle as a kind of navy base, from which they could set sail after the pirates plaguing their galleons.

Early in the 20th century, the isle's native flora was all but destroyed by burning, clearing, and planting nonnative grasses, followed by sheep grazing. Besides the grasses, iceplant, a South African import, began to spread over the island. Even when the hardy iceplant dies, it hurts the native plant community because it releases its salt-laden tissues into the soil, thus worsening the odds for the natives. Park service policy is to re-introduce native plants and eliminate non-natives.

DIRECTIONS TO TRAILHEAD Santa Barbara Island is infrequently serviced by boat, but it is possible to join a trip. Contact park headquarters.

THE HIKE Six miles of trail crisscross the island. A good place to start your exploration is Canyon View Nature Trail. Request an interpretive brochure from the resident ranger and enjoy learning about island ecology.

19

SANTA MONICA MOUNTAINS
NATIONAL RECREATION AREA

Bordered by two of the busiest freeways in the world—the Ventura and the San Diego—the Santa Monica Mountains remain a near-wilderness. Within easy reach of 16 million people, they nevertheless offer solitude and plenty of silent places.

The Santa Monica Mountains are the only relatively undeveloped mountain range in the U.S. that bisects a major metropolitan area. They stretch all the way from Griffith Park in the heart of Los Angeles to Point Mugu, 50 miles away. The range is 12 miles wide at its broadest point, and it reaches an elevation of a little over 3,000 feet.

One of the few east-west trending ranges in the country, the Santa Monica Mountains can cause a little geographic confusion to the first-time visitor. The Santa Monica Bay and Malibu coastline also extends east-west alongside the mountains, so that the mountain explorer actually looks south to view the ocean and heads west when traveling "up the coast."

The mountains are a Mediterranean ecosystem, the only one in the country under National Park Service protection. Large stretches are open and natural, covered with chaparral and oak trees, bright in spring with wildflowers. Oak woodland and fern glens shade gentle seasonal creeks.

Largest areas of open space are in the western part of the mountains. In the eastern part, open space is harder to come by, but those pockets that do exist are all the more valuable because they are so close to the metropolis. Canyons such as Los Lions, Caballero, Fryman and Franklin are precious resources.

Ancestors of the native Chumash lived in the mountains as early as 7,000 years ago. Abundant food sources helped the Chumash become the largest native population in California at the time of Juan Cabrillo's arrival in 1542.

Spanish missionaries, soldiers and settlers displaced the Chumash. During the 19th century, the Santa Monicas were controlled by a few large land holdings—including Rancho Topanga-Malibu-Sequit and Rancho Guadalasca—and used primarily for cattle raising. As the land holdings were broken up, the ranchers supplemented their modest livings by renting space to visiting equestrians and vacationers.

Conservationists proposed a Whitestone National Park in the 1930s and Toyon National Park in the 1960s, but it wasn't until Will Rogers, Topanga, Malibu Creek and Point Mugu state parks were set aside in the late 1960s that the mountains received any substantial government protection. In 1978 Santa Monica Mountains National Recreation was established. Several properties, small and large, have since been added to the park.

■ FRANKLIN CANYON
Hastain Loop Trail
2.5 miles round trip with 400-foot elevation gain

I t's appeared in your living room a hundred times, but you probably don't know its name.

The many faces of Franklin Canyon can be seen almost daily on television. Moviemakers consider the canyon a convincing substitute for a wide variety of locales ranging from High Sierra forest to jungle lagoon. Countless television shows have used the canyon as a stage.

Despite frequent invasions of Hollywood film crews, Franklin Canyon on most days offers hikers, birdwatchers and nature lovers a tranquil retreat. The canyon is protected by Franklin Canyon Ranch, a National Park Service preserve perched atop the hills above Beverly Hills.

Franklin Canyon and its visitors benefit enormously from interpretive efforts provided by the William O. Douglas Outdoor Classroom (WODOC), named for the Supreme Court justice and environmentalist whose eloquence on behalf of America's wildlands will long be remembered. WODOC offers a hike/nature experience for almost everyone. Each year, docents conduct thousands of schoolchildren through the canyon. Leading through the canyon are special trails for senior citizens, the disabled and the blind. Aerobic walks, moonlight hikes, bird walks and map-and-compass walks are offered regularly.

The upper part of the canyon centers around Upper Franklin Reservoir, which was constructed in 1910, then improved and expanded in the 1930s. After the 1971 San Fernando earthquake, the earthen dam was declared unsafe, so the reservoir is no longer part of the Southland's far-reaching waterworks system. Today the reservoir—now more lyrically referred to as Franklin Lake— is home to bass, catfish, ducks and coots. The 9-acre lake is an important stopover for migratory birds. More than 90 different species of birds have been sighted in the canyon.

Hastain Trail explores the lower part of Franklin Canyon. It ascends the eastern ridge of the canyon and offers fine views of both the San Fernando Valley and the west side of Los Angeles.

You can pick up a trail map at the Visitor Center-outdoor classroom headquarters.

DIRECTIONS TO TRAILHEAD From the San Fernando Valley: Exit the Ventura Freeway (101) on Coldwater Canyon Drive. Head south past Ventura Boulevard to the top of Coldwater Canyon Drive at Mulholland Drive. Cross Mulholland and proceed south on Franklin Canyon Drive. After a mile, the pavement ends. Continue 0.8 mile on a dirt road past Upper Franklin Reservoir to a junction and bear left onto Lake Drive. Parking is available on Lake Drive near the outdoor classroom headquarters.

From the westside of Los Angeles, proceed through the intersection of Beverly Drive and Coldwater Canyon Drive and follow Beverly Drive north for 1.2 miles. Turn right onto Franklin Canyon Drive and continue 0.8 mile to Lake

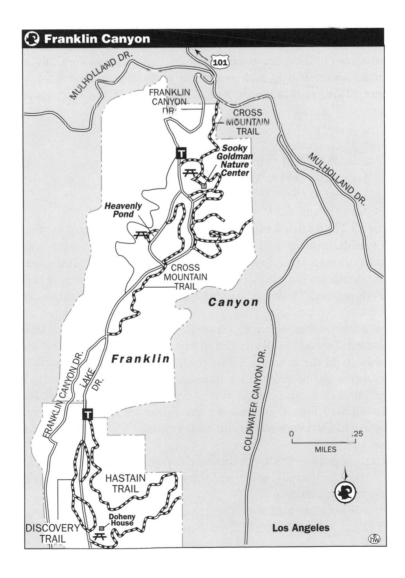

Drive. Make a sharp right for 0.7 mile to the outdoor classroom headquarters, Franklin Canyon Ranch House. Park along Lake Drive.

THE HIKE   From the Visitor Center, you may walk up Lake Drive to the start of Hastain Trail or cross Lake Drive to Canyon Trail, which winds beneath live oaks and sycamores and through a chaparral community on the west slope of the canyon. A rightward fork of Canyon Trail returns you to Lake Drive, which you'll follow a short distance to a fire road (Hastain Trail).

Hastain Trail ascends slopes covered with sage, bay laurel and chamise. Notice the outcroppings of Santa Monica slate, the oldest rock in the Hollywood Hills/Santa Monica Mountains. The slate is geological evidence that the mountains were once beneath the ocean.

A bit more than a mile's walk brings the hiker to an overlook where there's a good view of Beverly Hills and the Wilshire corridor. (The fire road—Hastain Trail—continues climbing to good views of Upper Franklin Canyon and the San Fernando Valley.) Turn right onto the distinct trail that descends to the nature center/outdoor classroom headquarters. Walk back up Lake Road to your car.

■ PARAMOUNT RANCH
Coyote Trail, Stream Terrace Trail
0.5-mile long nature trails

Even in 1921, Burbank was too busy a place for filming western movies on location, so Paramount Studios purchased a 4,000-acre spread in the then-remote Agoura area. Paramount Ranch had many a desirable location: mountains, meadows, creeks, canyons, oak and walnut groves. One dramatic mountain—Sugarloaf Peak—is said to have inspired the famous Paramount logo.

Besides innumerable westerns, such 1930s classics as *The Adventures of Marco Polo* and *Tom Sawyer* were filmed here.

Paramount sold the ranch in 1946 but a smaller part of it, including Western Town, continued to be used for filming. The ranch was particularly popular during the 1950s heyday of the TV western when *The Cisco Kid, Bat Masterson, Have Gun Will Travel,* and many more horse operas were filmed here. The ranch substituted for Colorado in the long-running TV series *Dr. Quinn, Medicine Woman.*

The National Park Service purchased the ranch in 1979. Today, filmmakers continue to use the Western town and the surrounding hills for features, television series and commercials.

The park doubled in size with the acquisition of the Historic Oaks portion of the old ranch by the Santa Monica Mountains Conservancy. Located adjacent to the existing Paramount Ranch property, this locale, too, was popular

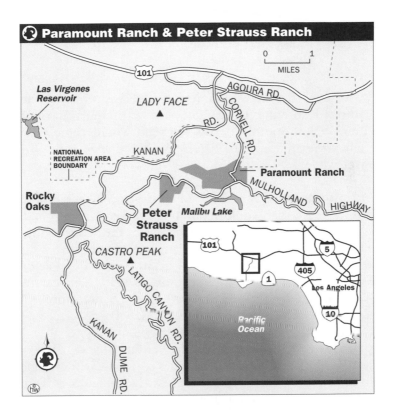

with moviemakers. And it was long cherished by the public as well, who knew it as the site of the Renaissance Pleasure Faire.

For the walker, Paramount Ranch offers a stroll through Western Town, a loop around what used to be a sports-car race track, and a couple of miles of hiking trail. Runners will note the ranch's 5-K route that links the race track and a couple of paths.

DIRECTIONS TO TRAILHEAD From the Ventura Freeway (101) in Agoura, exit on Kanan Road. Drive south 0.75 mile, forking left onto Cornell Road, then proceeding 2.5 miles to Paramount Ranch.

THE HIKE Coyote Canyon Nature Trail begins behind Western Town, heads up Medea Creek and meanders among some handsome oaks. Halfway along the trail, there's a good hilltop view back at Western Town and of Goat Buttes towering above nearby Malibu Creek State Park. Sometimes an interpretive brochure is available at the trailhead.

You can join Stream Terrace Trail south of the parking lot by the old racetrack. The path ascends a hill for vistas of Western Town, Malibu Lake and Sugarloaf Peak.

■ PETER STRAUSS RANCH
Peter Strauss Trail
0.6 mile round trip

Once boasted as "the largest swimming pool west of the Rockies," Lake Enchanto, a resort and amusement park, was popular in the 1930s and 40s. Sometimes 5,000 Southlanders a weekend would come to swim, fish, picnic and enjoy the amusement rides. A Big Band-style radio program was broadcast live, while L.A. notables and Hollywood stars danced the night away.

During the 1960s a plan was hatched to develop a theme park—Cornell World Famous Places—that would replicate Egyptian pyramids and Mt. Fuji. Meanwhile, Lake Enchanto itself disappeared when the dam backing up Triunfo Creek washed away in a flood. These plans never materialized, the property was sold for back taxes, and finally ended up in the hands of actor-producer Peter Strauss, who purchased the former resort in 1977. After Strauss restored and improved the property, it was acquired by the Santa Monica Mountains Conservancy, who deeded it to the National Park Service.

DIRECTIONS TO TRAILHEAD From the Ventura Freeway (101) in Agoura, exit on Kanan Road. Proceed south 2.75 miles to Troutdale Road and turn left. At Mulholland Highway, turn left again, cross the bridge over Triunfo Creek and turn into the Peter Strauss Ranch parking area. After parking, walk back to Mulholland, cross the bridge over Triunfo Creek, then join the signed trail behind the ranch house.

THE HIKE The trail begins near a eucalyptus grove and a former aviary, switchbacks up the hillside behind the ranch house, then loops back down the slope. Chaparral and some creekside oaks are the chief habitats.

■ CASTRO CREST
AND CORRAL CANYON
Backbone Trail
6-mile loop along Castro Crest and through
upper Solstice Canyon with 1,000-foot elevation gain

Stalk the rare Santa Susana tarweed—and some genuinely pretty flowering plants—on a nice loop trail along the Castro Crest area of the Santa Monica Mountains.

The tarweed is a humble enough plant, a low mass of woody stems and dull green herbage, clinging to life among the rocks. For most of the 20th century it was believed to exist only atop isolated sandstone outcroppings in its namesake Santa Susana Mountains. In 1977, the Santa Susana tarweed was

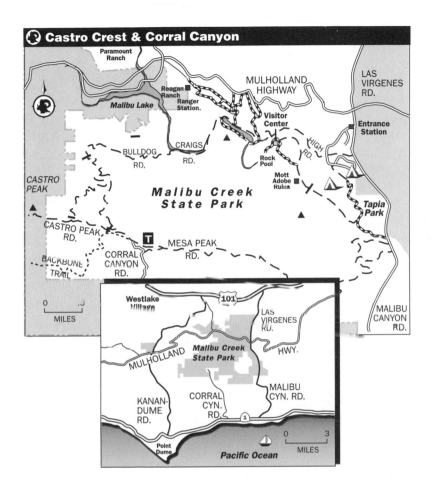

discovered high on the Castro Crest and in later years elsewhere around the Santa Monicas.

Geologically minded hikers will also enjoy tramping along Castro Crest. Towering above the parking area is the gray sandstone/mudstone Sespe Formation, formed 40 to 25 million years ago. Down in Solstice Canyon is the Coal Canyon Formation, of marine deposition, laid down 60 to 50 million years ago. Many mollusk fossils are visible in the long rock slabs.

Even those hikers without interest in botany or earth science will enjoy this outing. It samples both high and low segments of the Backbone Trail, provides great views and a good aerobic workout.

DIRECTIONS TO TRAILHEAD From Pacific Coast Highway, about 2 miles up-coast from Malibu Canyon Road, turn inland on Corral Canyon Road. Proceed 5.5 miles to road's end at a large dirt parking lot.

Castro Crest: Stalk the rare Santa Susana tarweed and enjoy the terrific views.

THE HIKE From the parking area, head past the locked gate up the wide dirt road, Castro Motorway. (You're walking the nearly complete Backbone Trail, which extends 65 miles across the spine of the range.) After a short climb, enjoy a fine clear-day view of Mt. Baldy and the San Gabriel Mountains, as well as of the Santa Susana Mountains—home of the elusive tarweed. A great place to look for the plant is about 0.75 mile from the trailhead on the north side of the dirt road near the junction of Castro Motorway with Bulldog Motorway.

Bulldog Motorway on your right leads to Malibu Creek State Park and its many miles of trail, but you continue climbing another 0.75 mile to a junction with Newton Canyon Motorway, which you'll join by bearing left. (Castro Motorway descends to a junction at a saddle. You could go straight (south) here and drop into Upper Solstice Canyon; this would cut off about 2 miles from the 6-mile round-trip distance of this hike.

Bear right on the stretch of Backbone Trail called Castro Trail and head west for a mile to paved Latigo Canyon Road. Walk along the road for a short while and join Newton Motorway on your left, which passes by a private residence, then descends to the saddle discussed above and the connector trail leading back toward Castro Motorway. Continue east, meandering along the monkeyflower- and paintbrush-sprinkled banks of Solstice Creek. Watch for a lovely meadow dotted with Johnny jump-ups and California poppies. The trail turns north with the creekbed, then climbs west for a time up a chaparral-covered slope back to the trailhead on Corral Canyon Road.

■ ZUMA CANYON
Zuma Loop, Zuma Ridge Trails
Around Zuma Canyon is 2-mile loop; via Zuma Ridge
Trail is 9.8-mile loop with 1,700-foot elevation

At first, when you turn inland off Pacific Coast Highway onto Bonsall Drive and enter Zuma Canyon, the canyon looks like many others in the Santa Monica Mountains: huge haciendas perched on precipitous slopes. But the road ends and only footpaths enter Zuma Canyon.

Malibu, Topanga, Temescal and Santa Ynez—perhaps these canyons and others in the Santa Monica Mountains looked like Zuma a century ago: a seasonal creek cascading over magnificent sandstone boulders, a jungle of willow and lush streamside flora, fern-fringed pools and towering rock walls.

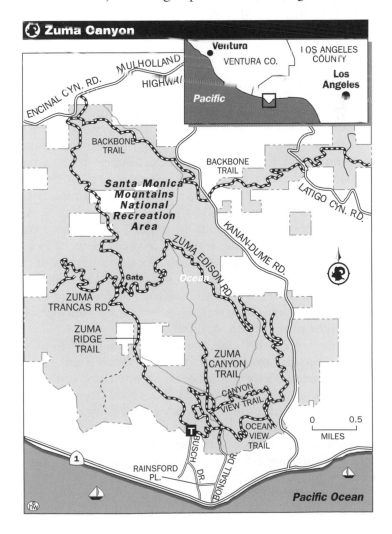

Zuma Canyon, which opened to public use in 1989, is one of the gems, if not the scenic gem, of the Santa Monica Mountains National Recreation Area. Over 15 years of National Park Service stewardship have brought improved trails, better access and signage to the canyon; however, the agency wisely left well enough alone, preserving the wild and remote flavor of this rugged country.

DIRECTIONS TO TRAILHEAD From Pacific Coast Highway in Malibu, head up-coast 1 mile past an intersection with Kanan-Dume Road and turn right on Bonsall Drive (this turn is just before the turn-off for Zuma Beach). Drive a mile (the last hundred yards on dirt road) to road's end at a parking lot.

Those hikers intending to start their excursion on the Zuma Ridge Trail, should continue very briefly up-coast past the Bonsall Drive turn-off on Pacific Coast Highway to the next major right turn—Busch Drive. Travel a bit over a mile to the small dirt parking lot and signed trail.

THE HIKE Hikers can partake of Zuma Canyon's grandeur via three routes: For an easy family walk join 2-mile Zuma Loop Trail, which explores the canyon mouth; hardy hikers will relish the challenge of the gorge—2 miles of trail-less creek-crossing and boulder-hopping—one of the most difficult hikes in the Santa Monicas; Zuma Ridge Trail lives up to the promise of its name. Hikers ascend Zuma Canyon's west ridge for grand ocean and mountain views, then follow a series of fire roads and footpaths to circle back to the trailhead. This loop around Zuma Canyon's walls is a great winter workout and conditioning hike. Two major ascents and descents en route are sure to burn off lots of calories.

Bring lots of water. Water is available at the Bonsall Drive trailhead but nowhere else on the hike. A water source is located about midway along the Zuma Ridge route, but it's for horses only. At the conclusion of this thirst-inducing trek, I like to reward myself with a giant healthy drink from the juice bar located just down the road from the trailhead at the corner of Busch Drive and Pacific Coast Highway. Those seeking a pre-hike caffeine lift will find a coffeehouse next to the juice bar. Ah, Malibu!

Just before you join Zuma Ridge Trail (a dirt road, gated to prevent vehicle entry) note the signed footpath (Ridge Canyon Access Trail) just to the east. This path will return you to the trailhead on the very last leg of your long loop.

Begin your shadeless ascent, following the dirt road below some water tanks. Up, up, up you go along the ridge between Zuma Canyon on your right and Trancas Canyon on your left. Pause frequently to catch your breath and to look behind you at the sparkling blue Pacific and the Malibu Riviera.

Three miles of vigorous ascent bring you to a junction with the right-forking Zuma Edison Road. What goes up must come down, and down east you go toward the floor of Zuma Canyon. After a mile's descent you'll pass a horse guzzler, then continue the steep descent another mile or so to the sycamore-shaded canyon bottom. By all means take a break here and marshal your energy for this hike's second major climb.

The road climbs southeast out of the canyon. Far below is Kanan-Dume Road, about a mile to the east. Zuma Edison Road bends north for 0.25 mile to intersect Zuma Canyon Connector Trail, a footpath that turns south to travel along a knife-edge ridge. This engaging path takes you 0.7 mile down to meet Kanan-Edison Road. Coast coastward as you descend this dirt fire road 1.3 miles to a junction with Canyon View Trail, a path that descends into the heart of Zuma Canyon. You could branch off on this pleasant trail, but in keeping with the ridge-route theme of this walk I prefer to continue on Kanan-Edison Road just 0.1 mile more to meet Ocean View Trail. This path descends westward 1.1 miles to the canyon bottom while serving up fine ocean views.

When you meet Zuma Canyon Trail, go left about 100 feet to meet Ridge-Canyon Access Trail. Join this 0.7-mile-long footpath on a climb from the canyon bottom up and over a low hill to return to the Busch Drive trailhead.

■ ROCKY OAKS
Rocky Oaks Trail
1 mile round trip

Until the late 1970s, Rocky Oaks was a working cattle ranch. The grassland (pasture) and pond (for cattle) are remnants of that era.

Rocky Oaks, acquired by the National Park Service in 1981, is one of those little places perfect for a picnic or a little leg-stretcher of a walk.

Saunter among the handsome old oaks.

DIRECTIONS TO TRAILHEAD From the Ventura Freeway (101) in Agoura, exit on Kanan Road and drive south. Turn right (west) onto Mulholland Drive, then turn right into the park.

THE HIKE From the parking area, a signed path leads to the oak-shaded picnic area; another path heads directly for the pond. Rainfall determines the depth—indeed, the existence—of the pond. These two paths intersect, and ascend a brushy hillside to an overlook, which offers views of the park and surrounding mountains.

■ ARROYO SEQUIT
Arroyo Sequit Loop Trail
2-mile loop with 200-foot elevation gain

Wildflowers, waterfalls and weekend walk to remember are the attractions of Arroyo Sequit Park, a gem of a little preserve located just off Mulholland Highway in the Santa Monica Mountains.

Hikers can experience the park's considerable charms via a winding loop trail system that travels through open meadows and dips in and out of the gorge cut by the headwaters of the east fork of Arroyo Sequit. Along the way are grand views of Boney Mountain, western sentinel of the Santa Monicas.

Despite a treasure trove of flowering plants, this 155-acre mountain hideaway, now under the stewardship of the National Park Service, receives few visitors. In fact, ever since this former private ranch was purchased by the Santa Monica Mountains Conservancy and a park created in the mid-1980s, Arroyo Sequit has received little attention.

For many years, the park had a weekend-only visitation policy, further discouraging hikers.

Another reason for Arroyo Sequit's anonymity is its isolation from other parks. Long-planned trails intended to link the park with nearby National Park Service properties such as Malibu Springs and Circle X Ranch have not got off the drawing board and onto the ground. Should the park ever get connected by trail to surrounding destinations, Arroyo Sequit will emerge as a compelling destination or superb trailhead for long rambles through the wild west end of the Santa Monica Mountains.

For now at least, Arroyo Sequit is a family-friendly destination for a nature walk and a picnic. Visit in winter after a rainstorm to view the park's small waterfalls or take a hike in spring to marvel at the many wildflowers.

"The loop around Arroyo Sequit is one of my favorite wildflower hikes," declares Milt McAuley, author of the definitive *Wildflowers of the Santa Monica Mountains.* Some 50 to 75 species of flowers bloom during the spring, the author-naturalist reports.

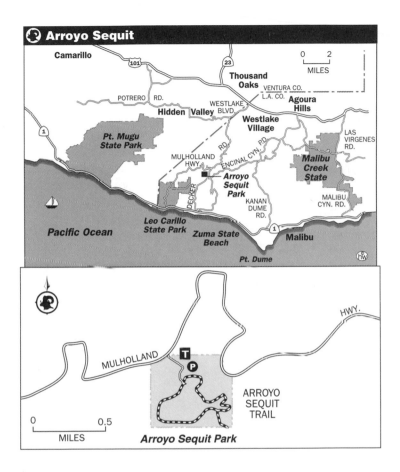

Spring celebrants include lupine, large-flowered phacelia, monkeyflower, owl's clover and thickets of California roses. Look for white star lily and bleeding heart along the trail heading out of Arroyo Sequit gorge. Hardy inhabitants of the park's nutrient-poor volcanic-rock region include blue larkspur, shooting star, fuchsia and ferns.

DIRECTIONS TO TRAILHEAD From Pacific Coast Highway, just up-coast from Leo Carrillo State Park on the Los Angeles-Ventura county line, drive north and then west on Mulholland Highway 5.6 miles. Turn right (south) at the Arroyo Sequit entry gate and park in the lot. Those journeying from the San Fernando Valley side of the mountains can exit the Ventura Freeway on West-lake Boulevard (23) in Westlake Village, and head south to Mulholland Highway, continuing south, then west on Mulholland to the park.

THE HIKE Follow the paved road 0.25 mile to the ranch house (now a care-taker's residence) and old barn. You'll pass a Santa Monica College astronomical observation site; star-gazing is excellent here, far from the lights of the big city. Join the signed path (which boasts a couple of plant identification plaques) that soon crosses a meadow and leads to the rim of the canyon. Savor the particularly dramatic view of Boney Mountain.

The trail descends rather steeply, with the help of some switchbacks, to the bottom of Arroyo Sequit. The trail crosses and re-crosses the creek a couple times as it follows the canyon bottom. Just as it seems as if this hike is about to dead-end in a box canyon, the path crosses the creek a final time and begins climbing the wall of the gorge.

The moderately steep but well-graded trail returns you to the top of the gorge then heads west to the park's picnic area. Continue on the trail back to the paved road and then on to the parking area.

■ SOLSTICE CANYON
Solstice Canyon Trail
3 miles round trip

Solstice Canyon Trail leads visitors along a year-around creek and introduces them to the flora and history of the Santa Monica Mountains.

The path is a narrow country road—suitable for strollers and wheelchairs—which offers an easy family hike in the shade of grand old oaks and towering sycamores.

Solstice Canyon in the Santa Monica Mountains is enjoyable year-round, but autumn and winter are particularly fine times to ramble through the quiet canyon. In autumn, enjoy the color display of the sycamores and in winter, from the park's upper slopes, look for gray whales migrating past Point Dume.

Solstice Canyon opened on summer solstice, 1988. The Santa Monica Mountains Conservancy purchased the land from the Roberts family and transformed the 550-acre Roberts Ranch into a park. Ranch roads became foot trails. Milk thistle, castor bean and other assorted nonnative plants were almost eliminated (although they have since returned); picnic areas and a visitor contact station were built. Today, National Park Service rangers are the stewards of Solstice Canyon.

Solstice Canyon's strangest structure resembles a futurist farm house with a silo attached, and really defies architectural categorization. Bauhaus, maybe. Or perhaps Grain Elevator Modern. From 1961 to 1973 Space Tech Labs, a subsidiary of TRW, used the building to conduct tests to determine the magnetic sensitivity of satellite instrumentation. The Santa Monica Mountains Conservancy was headquartered here for many years.

DIRECTIONS TO TRAILHEAD From Pacific Coast Highway, about 17 miles up-coast from Santa Monica and 3.5 miles up-coast from Malibu Canyon Road, turn inland on Corral Canyon Road. At the first bend in the road, you'll leave the road and proceed straight to the very small Solstice Canyon parking lot.

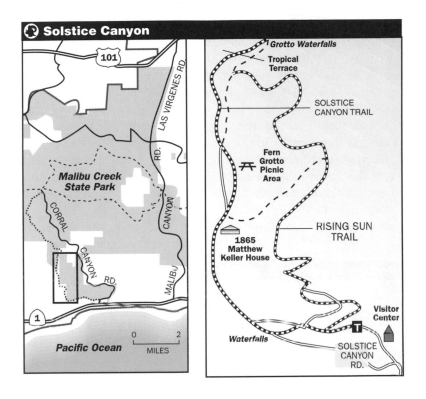

THE HIKE Stop at the bulletin board and pick up a trail brochure.

About halfway along, you'll pass the 1865 Mathew Keller House and in a few more minutes—Fern Grotto. The road travels under the shade of oak and sycamore to its end at the remains of the old Roberts Ranch House. The architecturally-noted house burned to the ground in a 1982 wildfire. Palms, agave, bamboo and bird of paradise and many more tropical plants thrive in the Roberts' family garden gone wild. A waterfall, a fountain and an old dam are some of the other special features found in this paradisiacal setting known as Tropical Terrace.

Across the creek from Tropical Terrace is signed Rising Sun Trail, which climbs a ridge for rewarding canyon and ocean views. The 2-mile trail offers an excellent but more difficult return route.

■ CHEESEBORO CANYON

Cheeseboro Canyon, Sulphur Springs Trails

To Picnic Area is 3.2 miles round trip; to Sulphur Springs is 6.6 miles round trip with 100-foot elevation gain; to Sheep Corral is 9.5 miles round trip with 200-foot gain

I t's the old California of the ranchos: Oak-studded potreros, rolling foothills that glow amber in the dry months, emerald green in springtime. It's easy to imagine vaqueros rounding up tough Mexican range cattle.

For years this last vestige of old California faced an uncertain future, but thanks to the efforts of conservationists it was saved from golf course and suburban development in 1991.

In times past, the Chumash occupied this land, and came to the canyon to gather acorns, a staple of their diet. A family required about 500 pounds of acorns a year, anthropologists estimate. It was quite an operation to gather, dry, and grind the acorns into meal, then leach the meal to remove the tannic acid.

From the days of the ranchos to 1985, Cheeseboro Canyon was heavily grazed by cattle. Grazing altered canyon ecology by displacing native flora and allowing opportunistic plants such as mustard and thistle to invade. As you walk through the canyon, you'll see signs indicating research areas. The National Park Service is attempting to re-colonize native flora and eradicate nonnatives.

Old ranch roads and trails explore the canyon, which offers both family walks and longer loops.

DIRECTIONS TO TRAILHEAD

From the Ventura Freeway (101) in Agoura, exit on Chesebro Road. Loop inland very briefly on Palo Comado Canyon Road, then turn right on Chesebro Road, which leads to the National Park Service's parking lot.

THE HIKE Note your return route, Modelo Trail, snaking north up the wall of the canyon, but follow the fire road (Cheeseboro Canyon Trail) east into Cheeseboro Canyon. The fire road soon swings north and dips into the canyon. You'll pass a signed intersection with Canyon View Trail, a less-than-thrilling side trail that leads to a knoll overlooking the Calabasas landfill.

After this junction, the main canyon trail, now known as Sulphur Springs Trail, winds through valley-oak-dotted grassland and the coast live oak-lined canyon. Watch for mule deer browsing in the meadows and a multitude of squirrels scurrying amongst the oaks. The picnic area, located 1.6 miles from the trailhead, is a pleasant rest stop and could be a good turnaround point for a family walk.

The old road crisscrosses an (usually) all-but-dry streambed. A bit more than 3 miles from the trailhead, your nose will tell you that you've arrived at Sulphur Springs. You can turn around here or continue another 1.75 miles up a narrowing trail and narrowing canyon to an old sheep corral.

You can continue a bit farther on the trail to a junction with Palo Comado Canyon Trail and head south on this path back toward the trailhead. Ranch Center Trail, a 1.1-mile long path, connects Palo Comado and Cheeseboro canyons, as does the 1.5 mile Palo Comado Connector Trail. The latter path leads to a junction with Modelo Trail 0.7 mile from the trailhead. Modelo Trail ascends a ridgetop for a good view of Cheeseboro Canyon and one of the finest remaining oak woodlands in Southern California.

At a signed junction, stay with Modelo Trail, which loops around the head of a ravine, then descends to the trailhead.

■ SANDSTONE PEAK
Mishe Mokwa Trail
From Circle X Ranch to Sandstone Peak
is 3 miles round trip with 1,100-foot elevation gain

Sandstone Peak, highest peak in the Santa Monica Mountains, is one of the highlights of a visit to Circle X Ranch, 1,655 acres of National Park Service land on the border of Los Angeles and Ventura counties. The park boasts more than 15 miles of trail plus a much-needed public campground.

Half a century ago the land belonged to a number of gentlemen ranchers, including movie actor Donald Crisp, who starred in *How Green Was My Valley*. Members of the Exchange Club purchased the nucleus of the park in 1949 for $25,000 and gave it to the Boy Scouts. The emblem for the Exchange Club was a circled X—hence the name of the ranch.

During the 1960s, in an attempt to honor Circle X benefactor Herbert Allen, the Scouts petitioned the United States Department of the Interior to

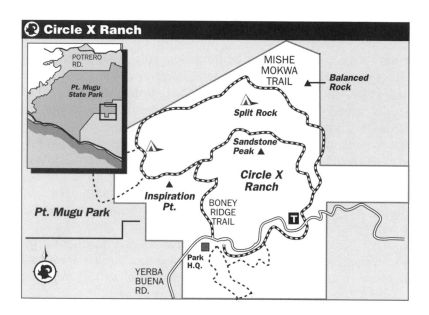

rename Sandstone Peak. The request for "Mt. Allen" was denied because of a long-standing policy that prohibited naming geographical features after living persons. Nevertheless, the Scouts held an "unofficial" dedication ceremony in 1969 to honor their leader.

Sandstone Peak—or Mt. Allen if you prefer—offers outstanding views from its 3,111-foot summit. If the 3-mile up-and-back hike to the peak isn't sufficiently taxing, park rangers can suggest some terrific extensions.

DIRECTIONS TO TRAILHEAD   Drive up-coast on Pacific Coast Highway past the outer reaches of Malibu, a mile past the Los Angeles County line. Turn inland on Yerba Buena Road and proceed 5.5 miles to Circle X Ranch. You'll pass the park's tiny contact station and continue 1 more mile to the signed trailhead on your left. There's plenty of parking.

THE HIKE   From the signed trailhead, walk up the fire road. A short quarter-mile of travel brings you to a signed junction with Mishe Mokwa Trail. Leave the fire road here and join the trail, which climbs and contours over the brushy slopes of Boney Mountain.

Breaks in the brush offer good views to the right of historic Triunfo Pass, which was used by the Chumash to travel to coastal areas. Mishe Mokwa Trail levels for a time and tunnels beneath some handsome red shanks.

The trail then descends into Carlisle Canyon. Across the canyon are some striking red volcanic formations, among them well-named Balanced Rock. The path, shaded by oak and laurel, drops into the canyon at another aptly named rock formation—Split Rock.

Split Rock is the locale of an old trail camp, shaded by oak and sycamore. An all-year creek and a spring add to the camp's charm.

From Split Rock continue on the trail and begin your ascent out of Carlisle Canyon. From the trail's high point, look straight ahead up at a pyramid-like volcanic rock formation the Boy Scouts call Egyptian Rock. To the northwest is Point Mugu State Park. You are now walking on the Backbone Trail.

The fire road turns south and you'll pass an old trail camp located amidst some cottonwoods. Past the camp, the fire road angles east. Look sharply to the right for a short, unsigned trail that leads to Inspiration Point. Mt. Baldy and Catalina are among the inspiring sights pointed out by a geographical locator monument.

Continue ascending on the fire road. After a few switchbacks look for a steep trail on the right. Follow this trail to the top of Sandstone Peak. "Sandstone" is certainly a misnomer; the peak is one of the largest masses of volcanic rock in the Santa Monica Mountains. Sign the summit register and enjoy commanding, clear-day views: the Topatopa Mountains, haunt of the condors, the Oxnard Plain, the Channel Islands, and the wide blue Pacific. After you've enjoyed the view, you'll descend a bit more than a mile on the fire road back to the trailhead.

■ CIRCLE X RANCH: THE GROTTO
Grotto Trail
To Grotto is 3 miles round trip with 600-foot elevation gain

B eloved by generations of Boy Scouts, The Grotto is a stream-cut gorge surrounded by impressive rock walls. It's one of the most pleasant hideaways in the Santa Monica Mountains.

Scouts trekked to The Grotto when it was part of their Circle X Ranch and continue to hike there today now that the site is part of Santa Monica Mountains National Recreation Area.

Circle X is divided into two parts by Yerba Buena Road, North of the road is famed Sandstone Peak (3,111 feet), highest summit in the Santa Monica Mountains.

Hikers can head straight for The Grotto or explore the park on 15 miles of trail. Note that the trek to The Grotto is an upside-down hike; the elevation gain occurs on the return leg of the trip.

DIRECTIONS TO TRAILHEAD Drive up-coast on Pacific Coast Highway past the outer reaches of Malibu, a mile past the Los Angeles/Ventura County line. Turn inland on Yerba Buena Road and proceed 5.5 miles to Circle X Ranch. You can leave your car near the small park headquarters building.

THE HIKE From Circle X contact station, join the dirt road descending toward Happy Hollow Campground. After 100 yards or so, look left for the entrance to a group campground area and hike through the campground.

At the edge of the camp, pick up signed Grotto Trail, which follows a shaded, seasonal creek on a southerly course. The path emerges from the creekbed into an open meadow, and you're treated to a striking, over-the-shoulder view to the northwest of Boney Mountain towering above nearby Pt. Mugu State Park.

Grotto Trail continues descending to an old dirt road that leads to Happy Hollow Picnic Area. Turn left. Grotto Trail angles left through a handsome oak grove, then meanders along with a sprightly creek to The Grotto. Boulder-hop along the creek, noting the impressive rock formations. The creek itself is partly subterranean; in places, you can hear it but can't see it.

Return by trail the same way, or hike up the dirt road leading from the picnic area. The road offers an easier ascent but isn't half as scenic as the trail.

■ RANCHO SIERRA VISTA/SATWIWA
Satwiwa Loop Trail
1.5 miles round trip with 200-foot elevation gain; to Waterfall is 5.6 miles round trip (from parking area, add 0.5 mile round trip to all hikes)

Satwiwa Native American Natural Area offers a chance to explore a place where Chumash walked for thousands of years before Europeans arrived on the scene. A Visitor Center and guest speakers help moderns learn the habits of birds and animals, note the changes the seasons bring, and gain insight into the ceremonies that kept—and still keep—the Chumash bonded to the earth.

For hunter-gatherers, as anthropologists call them, this land on the wild west end of the Santa Monica Mountains was truly bountiful: seeds, roots, bulbs, berries, acorns and black walnuts. Birds, deer and squirrel were plentiful, as were fish and shellfish from nearby Mugu Lagoon. It was this abundant food supply that helped the Chumash become the largest tribal group in California at the time of Cabrillo's arrival in 1542.

Chumash territory ranged from Topanga Canyon near the east end of the Santa Monica Mountains all the way up the coast to San Luis Obispo and out to the Channel Islands. Satwiwa "The Bluffs," was the name of a Chumash settlement located at this end of the Santa Monica Mountains.

The name of this park site, Rancho Sierra Vista/Satwiwa reflects its history as both a longtime (1870s–1970s) horse and cattle ranch and ancestral land of the Chumash. Many visitors are surprised to learn of the extent of Chumash settlement and even more surprised to be greeted by a living Chumash and discover that these proud people still maintain may of their historic traditions.

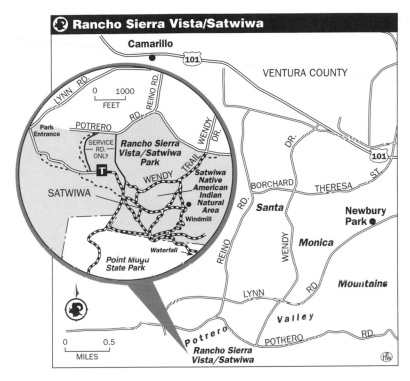

The National Park Service prefers to call Satwiwa a culture center rather than a museum, in order to keep the emphasis on living Native Americans. Satwiwa Native American Indian Culture Center, operated by Friends of Satwiwa in association with the National Park Service, is open Saturday and Sunday. The Park Service decided not to interpret the loop trail through Satwiwa with plant ID plaques and brochures; instead of the usual natural history lessons, it's hoped that hikers will come away with a more spiritual experience of the land.

The National Park Service opened a new park entry lane off Lynn Road as well as a large day-use parking lot and a new trailhead. These improvements make accessing the trail systems of Rancho Sierra Vista/Satwiwa and adjacent Pt. Mugu State Park a bit easier.

DIRECTIONS TO TRAILHEAD From Highway 101 in Newbury Park, exit on Wendy Drive and head south a short mile to Borchard Road. Turn right and travel 0.5 mile to Reino Road. Turn left and proceed 1.2 miles to Lynn Road, turn right and continue another 1.2 miles to the park entrance road (Via Goleta) on the south side of the road opposite the Dos Vientos housing development.

The paved park road passes an equestrian parking area on the right and a small day-use parking lot on the left before dead-ending at a large, brand-new parking lot 0.7 miles from Lynn Road.

THE HIKE From the parking lot, follow the signed footpath a short quarter-mile to the Satwiwa Native American Indian Culture Center. Signed Satwiwa Loop Trail begins its clockwise journey by leading past an old cattle pond, now a haven for waterfowl and wildlife.

The path then crosses a landscape in transition-from grazing land back to native grasses and wildflowers. You'll pass a junction with Wendy Trail, a pathway that connects the Satwiwa area with Wendy Drive.

Next the trail traverses a narrow, oak-filled ravine, then ascends to an old windmill. From the trail's high point near the windmill, the hiker gains excellent vistas to the north of Conejo Valley and scattered suburbs. To the west lies a landmark, cone-shaped prominence, 1,814-foot Conejo Mountain.

Dominating the view to the south are Boney Mountain, a series of sheer cliffs and some of the highest peaks in the Santa Monica Mountains. Shamans gathered some of their power from Boney Mountain, long considered, and still considered, by the Chumash to be a sanctuary.

Satwiwa Loop Trail descends to a junction with Hidden Valley Connector Trail (an opportunity to extend your hike to a waterfall or other destinations in Pt. Mugu State Park). The loop trail descends back to the culture center.

CHAPTER TWENTY

20

CABRILLO NATIONAL MONUMENT

■ CABRILLO NATIONAL MONUMENT
Bayside Trail
From Old Point Loma Lighthouse to National Monument
boundary is 2 miles round trip

Cabrillo National Monument, located on the tip of Point Loma, marks the point where Portuguese navigator Juan Rodríguez Cabrillo became the first European to set foot on California soil. He landed near Ballast Point in 1542 and claimed San Diego Bay for Spain. Cabrillo liked this "closed and very good port" and said so in his report to the King of Spain.

One highlight of a visit to the national monument is the Old Point Loma Lighthouse. This lighthouse, built by the federal government, first shined its beacon in 1855. Because fog often obscured the light, the station was abandoned in 1891 and a new one was built on lower ground at the tip of Point Loma. The 1891 lighthouse is still in service today, operated by the U.S. Coast Guard. The lighthouse has been wonderfully restored to the way it looked when Captain Israel and his family lived there in the 1880s.

Bayside Trail begins at the old lighthouse and winds past yucca and prickly pear, sage and buckwheat. The monument protects one of the last patches of native flora in southernmost California, a hint at how San Diego Bay may have looked when Cabrillo's two small ships anchored here.

Explorer Juan Rodríguez Cabrillo

DIRECTIONS TO THE TRAILHEAD Exit Interstate 5 on Rosecrans Street (Highway 209 south) and follow the signs to Cabrillo National Monument. Obtain a trail guide at the Visitor Center.

THE HIKE The first part of the Bayside Trail winding down from the old lighthouse is a paved road. At a barrier, you bear left on a gravel road, once a military patrol road. During World War II, the Navy hid bunkers and searchlights along these coastal bluffs.

Bayside Trail provides fine views of the San Diego Harbor shipping lanes. Sometimes when ships pass, park rangers broadcast descriptions of the vessels. Also along the trail is one of Southern California's most popular panoramic views: miles of seashore, 6,000-foot mountains to the east and Mexico to the south. The trail dead-ends at the park boundary.

The Old Point Loma Lighthouse looks particularly lonely in this 19th-century view.

The lighthouse today.

CHAPTER TWENTY-ONE

RIVERS, TRAILS AND CONSERVATION ASSISTANCE PROGRAM

When curious citizens discover National Park Service staff walking alongside irrigation canals, abandoned rail lines and across other tracts of land that time forgot, they may wonder, "What's a nice park ranger like you doing in a place like this?"

From a greenbelt down the middle of Exposition Boulevard in the shadow of the Los Angeles Coliseum to a pathway alongside the ailing, but recovering, Alhambra Creek in downtown Martinez, some unusual California landscapes are benefiting from a little-known Park Service program. This assistance to close-to-home environments comes from the Rivers, Trails and Conservation Assistance Program, founded to create trails and greenways, and to preserve and restore creeks and rivers.

Up and down California from Santa Ana to Santa Cruz to Santa Rosa, RTCA works with community organizations and local governments to master-plan watershed and walkway improvements. RTCA staff works by invitation only; that is to say, they're summoned from their San Francisco offices to the scene by local parties wishing to tap the environmental and planning expertise of the nation's premiere conservation agency.

RTCA's Mission Statement is simple, bold and direct: "Our vision for the 21st century is a network of rivers, trails and greenways that link people where they live and work to the countryside."

The National Park Service typically works with natural corridors such as creeks, rivers and ridgelines, as well as human-created transportation corridors such as railways, roadways and canals. RTCA also works on greenways, which provide much-needed open space and recreational opportunities bordering housing developments.

In any given year, the RTCA's west coast office provides assistance to some two dozen projects in California, Hawaii and Nevada. The National Park Service name—and reputation—often serve to boost a project's status, as well as its potential for success.

Some river efforts, such as Merced River Trail on the doorstep of Yosemite National Park, seem like naturals for RTCA, while other projects, such as the restoration of the Los Angeles River, seem like downright unusual undertakings for the National Park Service. RTCA projects include the much-promoted Bay Area Ridge Trail and De Anza National Historic Trail, as well as the virtually unknown Mokelumne Coast to Crest Trail and Santa Ana River Trail.

The Santa Ana River Trail traces the Southland's longest river from the San Bernardino Mountains to the sea.

RTCA's primary role is an advisory one: program staff help reconcile the often conflicting interests of environmentalists, developers, and diverse user-groups, as well as various regional state and federal government agencies. When plans are complete, community organizations then coordinate the necessary labor—digging, dredging, pruning, planting and whatever it takes to rehabilitate a river or fashion a footpath.

A riverbank restored or a walkway established inevitably leads to a resurgence of community pride as well as smiles on the faces of hikers, cyclists, visitor bureaus and chambers of commerce. Often when a new trail is established, nearby historic buildings are restored, nature centers are built and environmental education and cultural events increase.

RTCA project trails, like their wilder, more pristine national parkland counterparts, link us to our natural environment; in addition, they often link us to our history, cultural heritage and local economy as well. Such connections are crucial both to the human spirit and to the environment that surrounds us. As John Muir put it, "When we try to pick out anything by itself, we find it hitched to everything else in the universe."

With the help of RTCA staff, I've selected and profiled some trails worth a walk for their natural and historic interest. These five trails are meant to be a representative sampling of projects the National Park Service has completed/is undertaking in California. For a complete listing of projects, contact RTCA staff in San Francisco.

Santa Ana River Trail follows Southern California's longest river for 112 miles from its headwaters high in the San Bernardino Mountains to its end at the Pacific Ocean in Orange County. The trail tours some natural parts of the river, as well as long lengths of a thoroughly domesticated watercourse leading through the metropolis.

Los Angeles River Trail Back in the 1980s RTCA helped lead efforts to restore and revitalize this important river and transform it from metropolitan eyesore to community asset. The recently completed River Walk, a pathway located in the Los Feliz Boulevard area, shows off successful efforts at creating a riverside greenway and points out the potential of the entire river.

Circle Trail leads hikers from downtown Santa Cruz along the San Lorenzo River to the beauty of nearby redwood groves. Encircling the city, the path explores park and greenbelt lands, as well as the magnificent shoreline of Monterey Bay. My favorite of the completed sections is through Pogonip, a city park with many miles of trail.

Alhambra Creek Trail explores a mile of contrasts on the edge of the city of Martinez: a handsome arched bridge and an ugly industrial area, a duck pond and the antique stores of a revitalized Main Street. Interpretive panels tell the story of the natural and commercial history of the Carquinez Strait.

Juan Bautista de Anza National Historic Trail Just about the time American colonists began battling British soldiers at Bunker Hill, Concord and other East Coast locales, the Spanish sought to establish control over the Pacific Coast of what is today's United States. The viceroy of New Spain assigned Captain Juan Bautista de Anza to press Spain's claim to the New World.

The De Anza Trail was the route of the Juan Bautista de Anza Expedition of 1775-6, which brought 200 colonists from Mexico across the Colorado Desert and up the coast to found the city of San Francisco. In 1990 Congress established the Juan Bautista de Anza National Historic Trail and assigned the National Park Service to preserve, develop and sign the path.

For the most part, the historic trail, today followed closely by paved highways will be an auto route with many interpretive displays along the way. In addition, there are numerous hiking opportunities along the trail in Mexico, Arizona and California.

Historically, the Anza Trail is much better documented than the Lewis and Clark or other trails that opened up the West. This is due to the meticulous diary-keeping of Anza and the expedition's chaplain, Father Font.

In California, the Anza Trail travels through cities and along pristine coastline, through bird sanctuaries and shopping malls. For example, Anza's route through what is now metropolitan Los Angeles followed the Los Angeles River into the San Fernando Valley, then along present-day Highway 101 to the coast.

■ NAPA VALLEY
Napa River Trail
From Trancas Street to Lincoln Avenue is 2.5 miles round trip; through Kennedy Park is 2 miles round trip.

The site for the city of Napa was chosen for good reason: it was as far up-river as boats could navigate in 1848. Location is everything for a riverfront town and Napa had a great one in this era of river transportation.

Napa Valley farmers and ranchers shipped wheat, fruit and cattle to San Francisco. As many as 50 ships a day crowded alongside Napa's seven wharves. Scow schooners, specialized watercraft that carried heavy loads in shallow waters, moved agricultural products down-river to the big city and returned with machinery, tools and other manufactured goods.

Napa prospered for more than a half-century, then declined precipitously in the 1920s when cars, better roads and bridges made commercial river transport less important. Decades of environmental abuse followed. Sewer lines and industrial waste emptied into the river, creating a toxic stew that killed fish and peeled paint from waterfront buildings. Not until the 1950s were sanitation- and river-restoration measures implemented.

After more than 50 years of prosperity, 50 years of abuse and some 50 years of restoration, at least some of the river resembles that watercourse of old. Conservationists, city planners and residents have teamed with the National Park Service's Rivers, Trails & Conservation Assistance Program to develop the Napa River Trail. After years of effort, it's still a work-in-progress, but eventually the trail will extend 6 miles.

The river route offers a little bit of everything: bird-watching, panoramic views of Napa Valley, even proximity to city life in the form of old downtown Napa and its revitalized Main Street. Along the way, hikers can look at historic homes, industrial buildings and boat docks—reminders of an era when the river was a vital commercial strip.

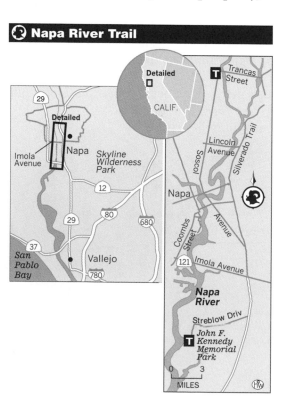

You can get a good sampling of the trail from two segments—one suburban section and one through the city's Kennedy Park.

DIRECTIONS TO THE TRAILHEAD Reach the river trail's laid-back suburbia section by following Highway 29 to Trancas Street, then driving 1.5 miles east to the river.

The Napa River Trail connects parkland and historic downtown Napa.

Watch for the trail-access sign on the west side of the water.

THE HIKE The path begins as a wide trail of crushed granite. It meanders riverbanks cloaked in oak and bay and choked with ivy and blackberry. The easy walk ends when the trail meets loud, busy Lincoln Avenue.

The second segment is in John F. Kennedy Memorial Park, Napa's largest park, popular with bird-watchers, anglers and boaters.

Start near the boat launch area, reached by following Highway 29 to Napa and taking Imola Avenue east. Turn right on Soscol Avenue and follow it past Napa Valley College, then turn right on Streblow Drive and follow it past a golf course to the boat-launch area. The walk along an earthen levee provides great views of mallards, geese and many species of resident and migratory waterfowl.

CALIFORNIA NATIONAL PARKS OFFICES

Cabrillo National Monument
1800 Cabrillo Memorial Drive
San Diego, CA 92106
(619) 557-5450

Channel Islands National Park
1901 Spinnaker Dr.
Ventura, CA 93001
(805) 658-5730

Death Valley National Park
Death Valley, CA 92328
(760) 786-3200

Devils Postpile National Monument
P.O. Box 3999
Mammoth Lakes, CA 93546
(760) 934-2289

Eugene O'Neill National Historic Site
P.O. Box 280
Danville, CA 94526
(925) 838-0249

Golden Gate National Recreation Area
Fort Mason, Bldg. 201
San Francisco, CA 94123
(415) 561-4700

John Muir National Historic Site
4202 Alhambra Ave.
Martinez, CA 94553
(925) 228-8860

Joshua Tree National Park
74485 National Park Drive
Twentynine Palms, CA 92277
(760) 367-5500

Lassen Volcanic National Park
P.O. Box 100
Mineral, CA 96063
(530) 595-4444

Lava Beds National Monument
1 Indian Well Headquarters
Tulelake, CA 96134
(530) 667-8100

Manzanar National Historic Site
P.O. Box 426
Independence, CA 93526
(760) 878-2932

Mojave National Preserve
2701 Barstow Road
Barstow, CA 92311
(760) 252-6100

Muir Woods National Monument
Mill Valley, CA 94941
(415) 388-2595

Pinnacles National Monument
5000 Highway 146
Paicines, CA 95043
(831) 389-4485

Point Reyes National Seashore
Point Reyes Station, CA 94956
(415) 464-5100

Redwood National Park
1111 Second Street
Crescent City, CA 95531
(707) 464-6101

**Santa Monica Mountains
National Recreation Area**
401 Hillcrest Dr.
Thousand Oaks, CA 91360
(805) 370-2301

**Sequoia and Kings Canyon
National Parks**
Three Rivers, CA 93271
(209) 565-3341

Whiskeytown National Recreation Area
P.O. Box 188
Whiskeytown, CA 96095
(530) 246-1225

Yosemite National Park
P.O. Box 577
Yosemite National Park, CA 95389
(209) 372-0200

THE HIKER'S INDEX: CALIFORNIA'S NATIONAL PARKS

Celebrating the Scenic, the Sublime and Sensational
Points of Interest in California's National Parks

STATE WITH THE MOST NATIONAL PARKS
California with 8 (tie with Alaska)

LARGEST NATIONAL PARK IN THE CONTINENTAL U.S.
Death Valley with 3.3 million acres

THIRD LARGEST NATIONAL PARK IN THE CONTINENTAL U.S.
Mojave National Preserve with 1.6 million acres

FOGGIEST PLACE ON THE WEST COAST
Point Reyes Lighthouse, Point Reyes National Seashore

WORLD'S TALLEST TREE
367-foot high Coast Redwood in Tall Trees Grove, Redwood National Park

WORLD'S LARGEST TREE
General Sherman Tree, 275 feet tall, with a base circumference of 102 feet, believed to be about 2,500 years old, growing in Giant Forest area of Sequoia National Park.

WORLD'S LARGEST-IN-DIAMETER TREE
General Grant Tree, more than 40 feet in diameter at its base. Dubbed "the nation's Christmas tree," this 2,000-year old giant growing in Kings Canyon National Park is the third-largest tree in the world.

Largest tree: General Sherman

LARGEST JOSHUA TREE FOREST
Mojave National Preserve

HONORING JOHN MUIR
Muir Grove (Sequoia National Park)
Muir Woods (Muir Woods National Monument)
John Muir National Historic Site
John Muir Trail in Yosemite and Sequoia-Kings Canyon national parks

LOST IN THE OZONE
Scientists have discovered that trees in Sequoia and Kings Canyon national parks endure the worst ozone levels of all national parks, in part because of their proximity to farm-belt air pollution in the San Joaquin Valley.

LARGEST ELEPHANT SEAL POPULATION ON EARTH
San Miguel Island, Channel Islands National Park

MOST INAPPROPRIATE PLACE NAME
Sandstone Peak—it's granite—in Santa Monica Mountains National Recreation Area

HIGHEST POINT IN CONTINENTAL U.S.
Mt. Whitney (14,495 feet in elevation) on the far eastern boundary of Sequoia National Park

LOWEST POINT IN WESTERN HEMISPHERE
Badwater (282 feet below sea level) in Death Valley National Park

DEVIL OF A TIME
Devils Postpile (Devils Postpile National Monument)
Bumpass Hell and Devils Kitchen (Lassen Volcanic National Park)
Dantes View, Hell's Gate (Death Valley National Park)

SPIRITUAL JOURNEYS
Cathedral Lakes (Yosemite National Park)
Godwood Creek (Redwood National and State Parks)
Paradise Creek (Sequoia National Park),
Moses Spring (Pinnacles National Monument)

LEAST-INSPIRATIONAL NAME (FOUR-WAY TIE)
Inspiration Point (Lassen National Park)
Inspiration Point (Santa Monica Mountains National Recreation Area)
Inspiration Point (Yosemite National Park)
Inspiration Point (Channel Island National Park)

CALIFORNIA'S LARGEST ISLAND
Santa Cruz Island (Channel Islands National Park)

ONLY MAJOR METROPOLIS BISECTED BY A MOUNTAIN RANGE
Los Angeles by the Santa Monica Mountains (Santa Monica Mountains National Recreation Area)

LARGEST HIGH SIERRA MEADOW
Tuolumne Meadows in Yosemite National Park

HIGHEST WATERFALL IN NORTH AMERICA
Yosemite Falls, at 2,425 feet, in Yosemite National Park

CALIFORNIA'S HIGHEST SAND DUNES
Eureka Dunes (nearly 700 feet high) in Death Valley National Park

Highest waterfall: Yosemite Falls

INDEX